A SMALL COUNTRY

SCOTLAND 1700–1830

A SMALL COUNTRY

SCOTLAND 1700–1830

Neil McCallum

1983

JAMES THIN
The Mercat Press, Edinburgh

JAMES THIN
The Mercat Press
53–59 South Bridge
Edinburgh

First published 1983

© Neil McCallum

ISBN 0 901834 70 4

Printed in Great Britain by: Billing & Sons Ltd, Worcester

CONTENTS

PREFACE

THIS IS the story of a country. It happened between 1700 and 1830. Many things were contained in the Scotland of that period. There was witch-burning, torture, slavery, dictatorship, martyrdom, the cruel indignities that men suffer at the hands of their fellows, some battles, some foolish pageantry, and a great deal of abysmal poverty and squalor.

The achievements of the Scots were considerable. There was the discovery of a number of new sciences, the advancement of medicine, the creation of steam power, a great deal of building and engineering, a vast amount of writing and philosophising, and important advances in numerous technologies. It was a hugely creative age. There emerged from it the people we recognise today as the scientist, the sceptic, and the romantic.

David Hume was perhaps the most important of a number of remarkable men who lived and worked in eighteenth-century Scotland. Hume, the genial bachelor who loved to play with children ('An innocent good soul,' said Carlyle), has his place in the pattern of the story, along with James Watt and his engine, Allan Ramsay and his poetry, Henry Raeburn and his painting, James Hutton who 'invented' geology, the Adam family and their buildings, Thomas Telford and his roads, docks, and bridges, 'Ossian' MacPherson and his strange poems, Janet Horne who was burned as a witch, Robert Fergusson who died in a madhouse, Thomas Muir who was transported, John Porteous who was hanged, Robert Burns, Walter Scott, and scores of others.

Much of the story took place in Edinburgh which, during the first part of the period, seemed to exist on its past, crumbling, scruffy, a city rotting on its foundations so that its tottering high-pinnacled tenement houses occasionally collapsed upon themselves in the spent futility of existence, sometimes were burned down by accident and sometimes were blown up by conscientous magistrates, with sappers using gunpowder and fuses.

Yet that ancient city of Edinburgh, stripped of its privileges, its king, its parliament, and its power, knew a rejuvenation of all the qualities and attitudes of which it seemed most bereft. There is difficulty in drawing the fine line of distinction between the barbarism of the early part of the century and the easy confidence of the well-bred intellects that decorated the later part of the period.

Out of the old city of Edinburgh, its maladorous mediaeval origins very obvious, there sprang the New Town, elegant, spacious, a fit setting for the emerging merchant classes and their professional colleagues. The poor remained in the old city.

The change was happening, hardly noticed, while Edinburgh heard that the Old Pretender and then the Young Pretender had come, with dreams of kingship, to claim a throne that was forever lost to them. Those Pretenders were an echo that was not recognised as such. They had no place in the future that was then being born. The bravery of their warriors, the gallantry of their ensigns, bore no relation to the emerging world of steam and science, of engineering and road-buildings, of new poetry and new prose, of astronomy and geology, physics and metaphysics, of philosophies of the absolute and conjugations of the infinite.

During the century Glasgow grew from a country town into a mercantile city. Its ultimate fate of becoming an industrial slum still lay in the future. Between them, Edinburgh and Glasgow made an intellectual and entre-preneurial city-state. They were the hub of Scottish endeavour.

Periods of achievement are not clear-cut; their virtues do not necessarily stand out sharply against the backwardness, ignorance, and misery of the masses of people who play no heroic role in the narrative, except the heroism of suffering and endurance. Scotland, at the beginning of the eighteenth century, was bitterly poor, swept bare by a century of religious and political fighting. The city streets were filthy with a mess of excreta and offal; the countryside was full of beggars; multitudes were in penury and hunger. In the salt-pans and the coal-mines there were thousands of slaves, bonded to their masters.

Much as been written about what is called the Golden Age of eighteenth-century Scotland, the time of David Hume and Adam Smith, the intellectual peak. What has been neglected is an account of the vast totality of accomplishment in nearly every aspect of human endeavour. The sciences and the arts held a condominium for a hundred years that has not been seen elsewhere, before or since.

Today the poet does not rub willing shoulders with the biologist, nor the mechanic with the academic. That is their mutual loss. In the relatively recent age with which this book is concerned there was a social and cultural relationship between the *savants*, the engineers, the builders, the writers, the philosophers, the scientists and the craftsmen.

In attempting to put this story together I have been conscious that I tread in many specialist fields, and this is an impertinence that specialists do not always care for. But this book is not scholastic or academic. It is a kind of extended journalism in which, it is hoped, the facts are correct, whatever the conclusions and interpretations may be.

Finally, I owe thanks to many institutions and individuals, to the librarians at the National Library of Scotland and the Edinburgh Central Library, and to the librarians at the Widener Library, Harvard, where I first read Hutton's *Theory of the Earth*.

I am grateful for the early encouragement given by Professor R. B. Lucas, whose comments on the chapter dealing with medicine were most invigorating, and to the late Helen B. Cruickshank for the painstaking care with which she read some early chapters.

I am grateful for the meticulous work done on the index by Andrew Beale.

Lastly, but by no means least, I am indebted to David Fletcher, editor extraordinary, whose help and expert assistance at a critical period finally brought this manuscript to a fit state for the printer.

EDINBURGH, 1982

To

WANDA BRYDON McCALLUM

1950 – 1972

The discoveries of men of genius are all so simple that everyone thinks he could have found them out.

BALZAC

That garret of the earth – that knuckle-end of England – that land of Calvin, oat-cakes, and sulphur.

SIDNEY SMITH

We are an obscure poor people, though formerly of better account.

BELHAVEN

The Eighteenth century – a wonderful time in the scientific and literary history of Scotland.

PROFESSOR JOHN REID

I

THE THREE ESTATES AND
A GENTLEMAN VISITOR

A fire.   Parliament Hall.   An English barrister on his
travels.   Brandy at Berwick.   'The most bar'brous
country in the world.'   The Town's College.   Overture
for cleansing the streets.   Washing clothes.   A state
cavalcade.   Propositions for a union of parliaments.

IN THE YEAR 1700, on Saturday 3rd February, flames were seen at eleven at
night in the north-east corner of the Edinburgh meat market. The fire spread to
Parliament Close, destroyed the Kirk-heugh and continued to the High Street.
Between three and four hundred families lost their homes.

> 'The pryde of Edinburgh is sunk; from the Cowgate to the High
> Street all is burnt, and hardly one stone lift upon another . . . the
> Parliament House very hardly escapt; all Registers confounded; Clerks'
> Chambers, and processes, in such a confusion, that the Lords and
> Officers of State are just now mett at Rosse's Taverne, in order to
> adjourneing of the Sessione by reason of the dissorder. Few people are
> lost, if any at all; but ther was neither heart nor hand left amongst them
> for saveing from the fyre, nor a drop of water in the cisternes; twenty
> thousand hands flitting ther trash they know not wher, and hardly
> twenty at work. These babells of ten and fourteen story high, are down
> to the ground, such as Corserig [a Lord of Session] naked, with a child
> under his oxter, hopping for his lyffe . . . the Exchange, vaults, and coal
> cellars under the Parliament Close are still burneing' – letter from
> Duncan Forbes of Culloden.

Fire was not the only disaster that threatened the Scottish Parliament.
Edinburgh was a stirring and busy city. The country round about – Scotland as
a whole – was poor, almost poverty-stricken, but the capital contained an
intense, intriguing, aristocratic life.

The King of Scotland had departed a century before to live in England.
Edinburgh had diminished since then, but at the beginning of the eighteenth
century the city still possessed a tough and strong vitality. The brilliance, the
wit, the elegance of the older age had vanished. Scotland was no longer an

important European nation. It had suffered in the wars of Charles and Cromwell; its fortunes had declined; it had been devastated by plagues, especially by the greatest plague of all – that of religious strife. The country had lost grip of its destiny, though in Edinburgh there was still an atmosphere of importance, of power, of affairs.

The city was a warren of masonry and wood, huddled tightly on a spine of rock. The narrow streets and wynds were thronged by exquisite ladies in fashionable dresses of hooped brocade, unmanageable adornments in the tortuous stairways and alleys. In the broad High Street and the wealthy Cowgate there were resplendent coaches and equipages, attended by uniformed servants more arrogant than their masters. And there were hordes of beggars.

Parliament House was the centre of the capital's life. It stood beside the church of St. Giles, the Mercat Cross, and the Tolbooth. It was surrounded by a complexity of alleys each with its entrances to many-storied buildings containing houses, shops and ale-houses. Parliament House had been built in the middle of the previous century on 'holy ground', part prebendary buildings and part graveyard. The ground had been forfeited from the owners because of religious ill-will.

Parliament House was reputedly designed by Inigo Jones. In 1680 the Duke of York (afterwards James VII) was feasted there. It was not to be visited again by British Royalty for one hundred and forty years when King George IV, his fleshy limbs grotesque in tartan trews, was entertained during the visit to Edinburgh that Walter Scott stage-managed as a piece of monumental pageantry. The success of the visit earned Scott his knighthood.

At the time of the fire which saw Lord Corserig naked in the streets, Parliament House was the meeting-place of the Scottish Three Estates, as the Scottish Parliament was called. There the lords and commons deliberated their affairs. It had been a parliament of free debate for little more than ten years. From 1690 until its dissolution in 1707 it existed as a body enjoying its full rights, passing laws that might or might not please the court in London. For this brief period Parliament was 'the voice by which the country spoke with England on equal terms'.

In the magnificent building, the interior of which is unchanged to this day, the members of the Three Estates played their game of power. In fact, only the nobles and the commons were then involved in Parliament. The third estate, the clergy, no longer took part and had not done so since the abolition of episcopacy in 1689. The clergy had many other opportunities, mostly self-created, of imposing their will and so adding to the general mischief. Even though the throne was detached from the country, the game of politics was full of zest and of destiny, and Parliament had its share of those practitioners of the craft of politics whose personal interests were strangely parallel with what they claimed to be the needs of their country. Under the hammerbeams of the ancient roof, the human story of endeavour and deceit was writ continuously by the one hundred and forty-five nobles, and the one hundred and sixty commoners who assembled there.

The small low-ceilinged rooms of Edinburgh's many-storied buildings were thronged with patriots, royalists, covenanters, republicans, zealots, traitors, men of commerce, power-seekers, fanatics, with their friends and enemies, their adherents, supplicants, servants and camp-followers, their wives, children, relatives and mistresses. Edinburgh was a crowded city. As Defoe said: 'Though many cities have more people in them, yet I believe that in no city in the world so many people live in so little room.' – *Tour through the Whole Island of Great Britain.*

In the streets were pedlars, beggars, water-carriers, and an army of waifs and strays of all ages who existed as well as they could and slept in cellars. The multifarious needs of the citizens and visitors were dealt with by a semi-organised contingent of ragged youths, impudent and worldly wise, who knew every nook and cranny of the city. They had a street-sparrow's knowledge of affairs and were not abashed by rank, dignity, or wealth. They were essential employees for strangers trying to find a way among the honeycomb buildings that stretched down each side of the High Street and the Canongate. Principally they were guides, messengers, and porters; they were called 'caddies' and the word is now known throughout the world because of the game of golf.

Though most of the commoners in Parliament were Lowland Scots, many of the Lords were Highland chiefs, petty princes in their own right, with power of 'pit and gallows' over their fellows. This power they were to lose nearly half a century later, after the Highlanders had been beaten at Culloden. When these powerful petty princes came to Edinburgh, they brought a retinue of clansmen who were haughty and insolent towards the Lowlanders. Another type of Highlander, men from broken clans or independent adventurers, had become permanent denizens of the city and had a monopoly in the business of carrying sedan chairs.

Defoe described the Highlanders in Edinburgh at that time:
'They are formidable fellows and I only wish Her Majesty had
25,000 of them in Spain, as a nation equally proud and barbarous like
themselves. They are all gentlemen, will take affront from no man, and
insolent to the last degree. But certainly the absurdity is ridiculous to
see a man in his mountain habit, armed with a broadsword, target
[shield], at his girdle a dagger, and staff, walking down the High Street
as upright and haughty as if he were a lord, and withal driving a cow.'

Down at the foot of the High Street was Holyrood Palace, 'the empty nest whence Scotland's Kings had flown'. At the head of the street, above the city on the historic rock of the castle, was the garrison – a small force of Queen Anne's soldiers who could not possibly uphold royal authority against the great Scottish nobles, if those nobles had ever been in sufficient agreement amongst themselves to put their combined followers in the field. 'The idle soldiers looked down upon the reek and roof of Edinburgh, in perpetual wonder at what was brewing below in the most turbulent spot in Britain, and what riot – religious, political, or economic – it would be their next duty to quell.' It is possible they looked forward to the burning of a witch.

The turbulence was there, and the times were about to change. The Lord Treasurer of England said in a letter to the Scottish Chancellor: 'We are now in so critical a conjuncture with respect to other nations that all Europe must in some measure be affected by the good or ill ending of the Parliament of Scotland.'

In 1705 an English barrister, Joseph Taylor, travelled to Scotland with a friend. He wrote a journal of his experiences. He was more familiar with the comfortable conventions of the Inner Temple than the rigours of travel. 'Everyone reckoned our journey extremely dangerous, and told us 'twould be difficult to escape with our lives, much less without the Distemper of the country, yet notwithstanding all these sad representations, we resolv'd to proceed, and stand by one another to the last.' These excitable forebodings were not unusual. Scotland, to the English, was an unknown country, reputedly inhabited by under-civilised tribes.

Taylor and his companion reached the fortified city of Berwick on 30th August 1705. They were carrying firearms, in the manner of the day, and there was a small misunderstanding when the raw soldiers of a newly raised English regiment allowed them to pass into the city without relieving them of their weapons. The Governor of Berwick heard of this lapse on the part of his guard and expressed his displeasure. The travellers were closely questioned about their intentions, and the incident was hospitably forgotten over two bowls of punch. That evening they ate a meal of badly dressed salmon which reminded Taylor of the proverb that God sends meat but the devil sends cooks.

The officers of the garrison took Taylor with them on their evening rounds. Attended by a file of musketeers he toured the posts and listened to the sentries demanding the password of the day. He enquired about the state of the defences of the city, and was told that in the event of trouble with the Scots it was intended 'to let in the Sea all round the Town, and levell an adjacent hill, to make the place defensible'.

The remainder of the evening was spent drinking brandy with the officers. Next morning Taylor left early, and the town gate was specially opened to allow his departure into the north. He and his companion were accompanied by a post-boy. Taylor noted that Berwick with its free land, was two miles in length and six in width, 'and every freeman has four acres of ground allow'd him for his own use'.

(Berwick was an anomaly. The strongest army kept it. It had been one of the first four royal burghs of Scotland. The English took it in 1174, 1272, and 1295. Bruce captured it in 1318. The English took it in 1333, the Scots in 1353, and the English once more in the following year. The Scots took it again in 1377; in 1406 the English took it back, using cannon for the first time. This appears to have been about six all, and for mutual convenience Berwick was declared neutral territory in 1551. When Taylor went there, Berwick was still a free town and neutral, its neutrality being 'protected' by the English troops.)

Taylor's account of Berwick gives an impression of two countries, one at least in a state of wary preparation for trouble. Though the two countries shared one loyalty to one Queen, they were still separate states. Only a few miles away from Berwick, young James Thomson was growing up in a Scottish country manse. In due course Thomson (1700–1748) would underline the union of the countries by writing *Rule Britannia*, and by that time the garrison of Berwick would have disappeared.

Taylor was travelling on the coastal road running north and he was a trifle excited and apprehensive.

'About a mile distance we came to a small Dike, which is the Boundary between England and Scotland: Upon our first Entrance into Scotland we embrac'd one another with all the friendship imaginable: We were now got into a very desolate Country, and could see nothing about us but barren mountaines and black Northern Seas: we often cast our Eys back at dear England, and were pleased so long as we could but see the top of the mountain Cheviot, but at length that also withdrew from our Eys; We had a great deal of cause to leave our Country with regret, upon account of the discouragements we receiv'd from every body, even upon the borders of Scotland, and by what I could gather from the discourse of all persons I convers'd with, I concluded I was going into the most barb'rous Country in the world.'

Barbarity was stayed for a moment when the travellers halted at Cockburnspath, some miles north of Berwick. They asked at the inn for canary, 'instead of which the Landlord brought us some excellent French white wine and brandy'. With regret Taylor noted the 'nastiness and ill-manners of the inhabitants' who gathered to stare at the Englishmen. The post-boy was sent back to Berwick.

The exhausting ride to Edinburgh was accomplished by evening 'finding the road very good, all the way, which may easily be accounted for in a Country of little trade, and where instead of Carts with wheeles, the Countrymen use a sort of Sledge, in imitation of a Cart, which is generally drawn by one horse, and carryes but a small weight'.

This cavilling at the 'little trade' was reasonable enough. Scottish trade had been brought almost to a standstill through the refusal of the English Government to allow the Scots to trade with the colonies. London's Navigation Act, by which goods had to be carried in 'English bottoms', and the failure of the over-optimistic Darien Scheme, bringing impoverishment to the Scots, were exacerbating the bitterness between the countries.

Earlier negotiations between the countries had broken down over the refusal to grant equal trading privileges to the Scots. The year previous to Taylor's visit had been full of alarms. Troop movements in Scotland, exaggerated by rumour, had persuaded England to quarter its own troops on the Borders. This explained the new garrison of raw soldiers at Berwick. Godolphin had decided that peace in Britain could only be made secure by a military occupation of the north, or by granting the Scots, in an Act of Union, the trading rights they demanded. Taylor had every reason, therefore, to feel

that he was entering an unsettled and perhaps hostile land. Earlier in the year of
his visit there had been a horrible affair in Edinburgh when some English
seamen, accused of murder, had been put through a travesty of a trial and then
hanged, to the howling of the Edinburgh mob lusting for English blood. Time
proved the Englishmen innocent.

When Taylor reached Edinburgh he showed a reluctance to be impressed
and a desire to be fair. It was difficult not to be the sophisticated Londoner, not
to patronise the barbarians. Conscientiously he reminded himself that he and
the Scots shared a common loyalty to Queen Anne.

'When first I came in sight of Edenborough, I thought the loftiness
of the houses, and the prospect of the Castle made a fine show, but I
was soon of the same opinion with the English Captain, who having
been well entertain'd by the Scotch, was ask't how he liked the
Country, he answered not at all, upon which enquiring into the reason
he told them, he thought they had not so much Religion as other
Nations. At that they were amazed, knowing their religion even carry'd
them to Superstition, so they requir'd why he thought soe, because
sayes the English Captain, you have but 8 commandments, they told
him they had 10, as well as he. No says the Captain, you have but 8, for
you have nothing to covet, nor nothing to steale.'

The Palace of Holyroodhouse, Taylor found, 'was not so noble as might be
expected'. The gardens, too, 'were all out of Order'. He was anxious to compare
the intellectual and legislative amenities of Edinburgh and London, and made a
most selective and interesting entry in his journal. He went to:

'The Colledge of King James the 6th, founded Anno Domini 1580,
in which is a good Library, with Variety of books neatly kept, Over
which are plac't the pictures of diverse Princes, and memorable
persons, There is also the Skull of Buchanan, so thinn, that one may see
thro it, kept for a great rarity, to which a principal of the Colledge,
having stole the head by bribing the Sexton, has annex't an ingenious
copy of verses; there is also a Letter of Cardinal Richleu's to the
French Embassador at Rome, concerning a Benedictine Fryar, wrote in
a double fac't manner in two Columns, which being both read together
is in praise of the Bearer, but the first column read by itself is quite
contrary, and according to the Cardinal's meaning gives a most
detestable character of him; there is also the Bohemian Protest,
concerning the Burning of Huss and Prague, with severall other
Rarityes, and under the Library is the publick printing house: tho' this
Colledge is endow'd with the Priviledges of a University, yet the worst
of our Inns of Court at London have as good Lodgings: There is a
Colledge of Phisitians, founded by King Charles the 2nd, and a
Colledge of Justice, with a Library well furnish'd with books of Law
and Divinity, There's nothing else worth notice, Except the excellent
Chimes in every steeple, which play a Quarter of an hour together, and
the fine Monuments in the Churchyards, built after the manner of

Mausoleums, of the best marble, under which are convenient Vaults'.

Taylor thought the countryside around Glasgow, then a small town, was very pleasant. The land near Edinburgh was less perfect.

''Tis all open, and abounds with Oats; near the City are severall Noblemen's houses, particularly along the Shore of the Frith: the meadow ground hereabouts, is very inconsiderable, it's generally enclos'd with a mud or stone wall, and goes by the name of a park, but is rather a pasture for catle, and according to the Reputation of these parks, they set a price upon the Catle which come from them.'

In Edinburgh he shared the amazement of all strangers at the height of the houses 'which are perhaps the highest houses in the world, for we counted one 14 story high'. He noted that one stairway might be the entrance to the separate abodes of twenty-eight families (two on each 'landing' of fourteen stories), and he likened this to his beloved Inns of Court.

If Edinburgh's buildings amazed him, and its chimes delighted his ears, he found his nose dreadfully affronted by the stench of the town. He made the complaint of every traveller, a complaint that was to be reiterated for the remainder of the century and after, phrased most illustriously when Dr Johnson said of Boswell that in Edinburgh he could 'smell him in the dark'.

The smell of Edinburgh was more than unpleasant. It was the persistent smell of rotting human ordure lying in the streets. Taylor thought that this might be one of the reasons why Scotland was so much despised by the English.

'Every street shows the nastiness of the Inhabitants, the excrements lye in heaps, and there is not above one house of Office in the Town, which may not improperly be call'd a house of Office itself. In a Morning the scent was so offensive, that we were forc't to hold our Noses as we past the streets, and take care where we trod for fear of disobliging our shoes, and to walk in the middle at night, for fear of an accident on our heads'. (The reference was to the custom of emptying the household slops from the windows of the high buildings, with a preliminary shout of "Gardyloo" – *Gardez-l'eau*).

'The Lodgings,' he wrote, 'are as nasty as the streets, and wash't so seldom that the dirt is thick eno' to be par'd off with a Shovell; Every room is well scented with a close stoole, and the Master, Mistress, and Servents lye all on a floor, like so many Swine in a Hogsty, this with the rest of their Sluttishness, is no doubt the occasion of the Itch, which is so common amongst them'.

Taylor was entertained by Sir Alexander Brand, a man who was concerned about the state of Edinburgh's streets. Brand was a wealthy citizen, an importer of Spanish leather, the gilt leather hanging that was used to decorate the interior of the better houses. He had a 'civill and genteale expression of his respect for the English Nation . . . his home as well as his entertainment seem'd to us the most like the English fashion of any we saw in Scotland'.

Brand was the author of a broadside entitled *Overture for cleansing the streets*, in which he offered to see to the cleaning of the city every day 'so that no nastiness or glar [filth] shall be seen anywhere'. The fee that he asked from the magistrates he intended to distribute to the needy, to show that his interest in cleanliness was civic pride and not commercial gain. His proposal was not accepted.

The scrupulous Taylor deplored the way in which clothes were washed in public. 'They put their cloaths with a little cows dung into a large tubb of water, and then plucking their pettycoats up to their bellyes, get into the Tubb, and dance about it to tread the cloaths, instead of washing them with their hands, and this the women doe in the open streets, without any manner of shame or modesty.' That this should happen in a city where the fierce Kirk sat on perpetual guard against any breath of immorality suggests a charming duplicity. Taylor found that behaviour in general was most unmannered, either immodest or self-righteous, and though he came with prejudice there is no reason to doubt the fairness of his opinion.

'As the Scotch are nasty, so I found them as prophane, and vitious, as other people, notwithstanding all the pretended sanctity of their Kirk. There is indeed a high Kirk Treasurer, who punishes offenders, but we were inform'd that a present of 3 Guineas at first coming to Town will be a good indemnity against all Complaints of that nature, unless in cases of adultery, which is certain death.'

Taylor saw the pageantry surrounding the Queen's Lord High Commissioner. Argyle had the appointment and he lived at Holyrood, 'attended with as Much State as a Prince'.

'We saw him go to the Parliament house in this manner, First a Coach and six horses for his Gentlemen, then a Trumpet, then his own Coach with six white horses, which were very fine, being those presented by King William to the Duke of Queensbury, and by him sold to the Duke of Argyle, as we were inform'd for 300 l.: next goes a Troop of Horse guards, cloath'd like my Lord of Oxfords Regiment, but the horses are of severall colours, and the Lord Chancellor, and the Secretary of State, and the Lord cheif Justice Clerk, and other Officers of State close the Cavalcade in Coaches and six horses. Thus the Commissioner goes and returns every day, and also goes in the same manner to Church.'

Taylor attended Parliament when it debated the proposed Act of Union.

'The grand debate this day, being about the Act for a Treaty with England, many learned speeches were made on the occasion. Some were for passing no act till England had given the satisfaction for the affront they pretended was put upon them, by the act pass'd last session in England, which not only declar'd them Aliens, but prohibited their goods, and thereby touch't them in the most sensible part, Fletcher said, that England could not make them aliens, since they were naturall born subjects to the Queen, For, says he, to whome should we seek for protection but to our Queen . . . After his debate, others were for making the English Aliens in Scotland, as a Retaliation for our making them soe in England: Belhaven said it did not consist with the honour of an ancient independent Nation to treat with England, till satisfaction was given by the English for their blunder, for he could call the English Act no other.'

The question of the day was to consider how the commissioners from each country should be appointed. These gentlemen were to draw up the clauses of the proposed Treaty of Union. Should the Scots commissioners be nominated by the Queen or by Parliament? Fletcher (a brilliant republican, far in advance of his age) opposed the Queen. 'You had as good leave it to my lord Godolphin, and we know that our Queen is in England, under the Influences of an English Ministry, and 'tis not to be expected that the Interest of Scotland should be so much considered by her, as the inclinations of an English Parliament'.

The Duke of Hamilton, to the surprise of Parliament and his own party, favoured the Queen because she, 'who was free from partiality, might doubtless make a good choice, but added he, if she should make a bad one wee will be safe, for all must return to them again, and they might send the Act back to the place from whence it came'.

In the end the Queen was carried by four votes. That evening 'severall Lords and parliament men' went to Taylor's lodgings and 'embrac'd us with all the outward marks of love and kindness, and seem'd mightily pleas'd at what was done; and told us we should now be no more English and Scotch, but Brittons'. On the following day Taylor went to see a dogfight and a cockfight.

2

GOD, DAMNATION AND
THE QUEEN'S COMMISSIONERS

The elect of Calvin.   Guilty lumps.   The story of
Robinson Crusoe.   Claret and gloom in Edinburgh.
The Squadrone Volante.   Belhaven speaks in Parliament.
'Mother Caledonia.'   A day of fasting.   The Duke of
Hamilton's toothache.   The end of an auld sang.

THE OUTLOOK of Scottish Calvinists was the pride and arrogance of God's elect. In the previous century Calvinism in Scotland had turned into a harsh, dour dictatorship of intolerance. This was not the original teaching of Calvin but a northern development of it, in which much of his teaching was misrepresented owing to environment and circumstance.

During the vacillation of Charles First, the revolution of Cromwell, the weakness and folly of Charles Second, Calvinism in Scotland became an implacable enemy not only of the south but also of the well-being of the Scottish People. The creed became hardened, though not tempered, in the fires of opposition and persecution. The descendants of the martyrs of the Covenant were dour bigots. When Calvinism and the Scottish Kirk won the day they proved a hard master, lacking the virtues of charity, love, kindness, tolerance, and forgiveness.

Calvinist theology produced, to justify its persecutions, a ramification of tortuous arguments. It smote, it suppressed, it punished, it showed no mercy. Its ministers worshipped a jeering demoniac god, a divinity whom they saw made in their own image, vengeful, choleric, swift to strike the weak, and pitiless.

According to the teaching of Calvin his followers were the elect of God. Those outside the church were damned from the start. But within the church even the elect were not assured of salvation. God made his choice quite capriciously. The Confession of Faith of the Scottish Church stated bluntly that God would save a minority of people to show that He was merciful, and would damn the rest to show that He was just.

In striving and wrestling for the souls of their congregations, the puritan ministers were forced by tactics – even if they were not committed by nature – to use language conveying the strongest and most fearful emotions, to threaten with promises of eternal agony. They turned words into whips and lashed their listeners, promising that God would continue when they desisted; this they did in the name of a church that was in a death-struggle with the vivid pagan superstitions that still lived in the country, especially in the countryside. God was made real and personal in the imagination; He was a revelation of malevolence before which the ordinary man could only quail. To be gay, to make love, to cultivate in any way the pleasures of a civilised life, brought the immediate censure of the church. Witchcraft had been one primitive way of opposing this, and many had been hanged or burned for no other cause than that they had been accused of witchcraft by a pious enemy.

The peak of fanaticism, exercised through a scrupulous but perverted logic, was reached by Thomas Boston (1676-1732), a minister in Ettrick in the Borders. In his *Fourfold State* he announced some of the most curious opinions that were ever fathered on Calvin. It was he who was the originator of the Marrowmen, a group of clergymen who carried dogma to conclusions of callous absurdity.

A burden of fear and guilt and neurotic frustration twisted the minds of the fanatical preachers, distorting every sentence they uttered. Good and evil actions, the responsible personal choice of right and wrong, were outside their teachings. All that man did was vile. He was to be saved by divine grace alone, and that was visited upon him not by the merit of his example, but by the whim of God. In any event, God would not visit grace upon anyone outside the Calvinist church.

Men were 'guilty lumps of hell'. That virtuous behaviour might save a man was a heresy. 'We putrified in Adam as our root.' Without grace they remained in their natural state of putrefaction. 'Art thou yet in thy natural state? Truly then thy duties are sins.' Virtue was almost irrelevant to this scheme of things. It was said 'to be desirable no doubt, but helped in no degree towards salvation'.

Here was the perversion of the teaching. No man could be saved by what he did. A virtuous life was a life of sin if a man was in his natural state. If an infant or child died before it had come to understand the revelations of Calvinism, then it was condemned for all eternity. Why, it was said, should God think any more of destroying a newborn babe than a man of destroying vermin?

'No wonder the grave opens its devouring mouth for us, as soon as the womb has cast us forth; and that the cradle be turned into a coffin, to receive the corrupt lump: For we are all, in a spiritual sense, dead born, yea, and filthy, Psalm xiv, 3, noisome, rank, and stinking, as a corrupt thing, as the word imports'.

Foulness, stench, corruption, torture, death, destruction, filth, depravity – those were the day-to-day concepts in which religion presented itself as a metaphysical mirror to man. The smallest, most ridiculous peccadilloes were rewarded with public punishment, though as Taylor pointed out money might mitigate the offence. Sexual offences were regarded with a clamorous horror, and offenders were often dealt with in public.

(In an indirect way, the severity of the Scottish Kirk was responsible for the creation of Robinson Crusoe. Alexander Selkirk, the hero whose adventures Defoe wrote and embellished, was a 'scape-grace lad' in the Fife fishing village of Largo. The Session Records of the local church show that he misconducted himself and was summoned to appear before the Session. The kirk-officer went to look for the boy, who had not arrived before his self-appointed judges. He had run off to sea. Six years later he returned and, in a fit of furious temper, he shot his half-wit brother. For this he was rebuked and made to do penance, an interesting comment on the scale of punishments. A witch would be burned; a murderer rebuked. Alexander Selkirk vanished again, and there followed his four years alone as a castaway on Juan Fernandez. Defoe came across him after his rescue and safe return to Bristol.)

The men of God and the men of the state had done their worst. In the capital of Edinburgh there was little obvious gaiety in the beginning of the century. Politics and religion had exhausted the country, and even aristocratic pageantry was no more than a gloss over a dreariness of spirit. Religion had done more than exhaust, it had suppressed. The theatre, music, the arts were forbidden or debased.

All the muses had been sent packing. They had served the Catholic church until the reformation in music, liturgy, decoration, painting, and sculpture. They were therefore tainted and immoral, whores of the Pope. They fled Scotland, and some of them have but recently returned. The Scottish episcopalian church survived the harsher extremes, and the 'Piskies' were for long the guardians of civilised abilities. They maintained a love of literature and the arts, they had cultural intercourse with England and the Continent during the long age when the Presbyterians were using the whip and the lash on all things worldly. They were strong in the north-east, and elsewhere were numerous enough to resist absorption. They carried as it were the torch of culture when the Presbyterians plunged into the abyss that they believed to be the way to paradise.

In the early years of the century a lethargic clotting of the wits was the overtone of Edinburgh. Claret was the strongest weapon in warding off dull oppression. Cheaply and copiously, and of excellent quality, it was supplied in the multitude of taverns and eating houses, the 'howffs' of Edinburgh. Some were no more than dirty ill-lit cellars, which were entered through the dark closes and wynds that separated one towering 'land' from another.

Claret on the one hand, gloom on the other, fought for man's humour. Before the Union, there was the fear that it would happen; afterwards, there was fatalistic resignation. But the most ponderous burden laid upon the citizens of Edinburgh was that of the church.

Meanwhile, in 1705, the Union was fast becoming fact. A new board of commissioners was appointed by Queen Anne, representing Scotland and England. The Scots won their point about trading privileges (though there were plenty to say it was a trap and England had no intention of keeping its word). A full set of Articles of Union was drawn up, and in the autumn of 1706 the Scottish Estates began to debate the articles. Though the idea of union ravaged the sentiments of many Scots, the need for union was imposed by the imperative of political and economic necessity. The issue could not be dodged any more.

> 'We see how, step by step, they were driven to the conclusion that the only way to ensure the Hanoverian succession, the Presbyterian form of worship, and equal trading rights with England was by an absolute union with her; they had no love for union in itself, seeing clearly what it entailed; but it seemed to them to be the least of the many evils hovering over Scotland.'

That was the attitude of the 'Squadrone volante', a new and small party of determined and powerful politicians who did much to negotiate the Union.

The Estates began to debate separately each of the twenty-five articles. The failure of one to be accepted meant that the treaty, as it stood, could not be ratified. But amendments were permissible with the approval of the commissioners.

The anti-Unionists were clamorous. One faction of them, the Jacobites who rested their hopes in a Stuart returning to the throne and who were anti-Presbyterian as well as anti-Union, found that recent events in England's Continental wars had weakened their position. In April the Battle of Ramillies had been won by Marlborough, and since then the Continental enemies of England (many of whom were partisans of the Jacobites and shared their dreams of revolution in Britain) had been on the defensive. It was hopeless for Highland Jacobites to look for armed help from the French, and thus make war with England an alternative to union.

The mob of Edinburgh found the parliamentary debate a stimulant to its activities. It cheered the Duke of Hamilton, who was one of the major figures against the Union. It hurled abuse – as well as stones and filth – on the supporters of the Union, especially on Queensberry, who still acted as Queen Anne's commissioner. (A State appointment distinct from the board of commissioners which was called into existence for the purpose of the treaty alone.)

Occasionally the mob got out of hand and did what mischief it could. University professors were instructed by the Privy Council to see to the behaviour of the students; master tradesmen were warned not to allow their apprentices to become unruly; military forces were called in to reinforce the small town guard. In this state of semi-martial protection the Scottish Parliament proceeded to perform the act of self-immolation.

Fletcher of Saltoun, the wise eccentric ('poisoned with democracy and deism,' said the historian Struthers), along with Hamilton and Lord Belhaven, made the chief speeches against the Union. Proceedings began with one of the commissioners stating, without passion, the case for union. He extrolled the virtues of incorporation. In Scotland's deplorable situation it was a union, he explained, not of utility but of necessity.

Belhaven was young, passionate, and haughty. He made a speech which the historian Burton described as 'an event in the history of Scotland', adding that 'in spite of Scotticisms, Gallicisms, over-stretched classicality, and monstrous affectation, it would stand beside any efforts of later English oratory'. The pity is that no Scottish *Hansard* recorded the pungent Scots oratory that rumbled in fierce dialect through Parliament House. Belhaven's phrases were powerful and moving, but no words could prevail against utility.

'None can destroy Scotland save Scotland's self – hold your hands from the pen and you are secure,' he said. Belhaven's long and enthralling speech was a superb piece of speculative pessimism, and even its unbelievable triteness vanished under its passion, its yearning, and its prophecy. It has been anglicised in the various versions that survive.

> 'I think I see a free and independent kingdom, delivering up that which all the world hath been fighting for since the days of Nimrod; yea, that for which most of all the empires, kingdoms, states, principalities, and dukedoms of Europe, are at this very time engaged in the most bloody and cruel wars that ever were, to wit, a power to manage their own affairs by themselves, without the assistance and counsel of any other.'

Belhaven took each section of Scottish life and held it to the mournful mirror of the future.

> 'I think I see the present peers of Scotland, whose noble ancestors conquered provinces, over-ran countries . . . walking in the court of requests, like so many English attorneys; laying aside their walking swords when in company with English peers, lest their self-defence should be found murder. I think I see the honourable estate of barons, the bold assertors of the nation's rights and liberties in the worst of times, now setting a watch upon their lips, lest they be found guilty of *scandalum magnatum*.'

He reviewed the royal burghs, and the lawyers, the tradesmen and the mariners.

> 'I think I see the laborious ploughman, with his corn spilling on his hands for want of sale, cursing the day of his birth, dreading the expense of his burial, and uncertain whether to marry or do worse. I think I see the landed men, fettered under the golden chair of equivalents, their pretty daughters petitioning for want of husbands, and their sons for want of employment. But above all, my lord, I think I see our ancient mother Caledonia, like Caesar, sitting in the midst of our Senate, ruefully looking round about her, covering herself with her royal garment, attending the fatal blow, and breathing out her last with a *et tu quoque me fili*.'

He contrasted the growing wealth and prosperity of the English nation with the condition of Scotland. 'We are an obscure poor people though formerly of better account, removed to a remote corner of the world, without name, and without alliances.' Why should the Scots not lay aside their internal differences and unite in defiance of the proposed union!

'Our all is at stake. Hannibal, my lord, is at our gates! Hannibal is come within our gates! Hannibal is come the length of this table! He is at the foot of this throne! He will demolish this throne! If we take not notice, he'll seize upon these regalia, he'll take them as our *spolia opima*, and whip us out of this house never to return again.'

The house was deeply moved. The proud Belhaven was on his knees, in tears. Then a point of order was made about the subsequent speaker, and patriotic emotion cooled in an argument over procedure. The Earl of Marchmont rose to reply. 'We have heard a very long speech, but it requires only a very short answer. Behold he dreamed, but lo! when he awoke, he found it was a dream.'

The house was convulsed. In great humour the debate was adjourned. To delay was to postpone the Union. But on Monday, 4th November the first article was carried. Forty-seven lords, thirty-seven barons, thirty-three burgesses voted in its favour. Twenty-one lords, thirty-three barons and twenty-nine burgesses voted against.

After the approval of the first article there came the debate on the second. Fervour and the rhodomontade of patriotism cut no ice with the practical men who favoured the Union. Days and weeks passed, and passionate hours of debate marked the slow contest. But each successive article was approved. The Scots Parliament was destroying itself, by democratic majority.

The opposition continued its work, in and out of the House. Political stunts were considered. A national day of fasting was appointed to expiate the 'sins of the land', but the pretended religious solemnity was so obviously political that Parliament refused to sanction it legislatively. The Church of Scotland, meeting in assembly, agreed with some astuteness to appoint a similar day of fasting. It then took the pith out of the day by making it more religious and Presbyterian than political and Jacobite. In this the church helped to cement its own power in the country and obtain, in due course, the Westminster Act of Security in which its religious authority is still vested. (This Act was subscribed by Queen Elizabeth on 8th February 1952.)

Outside Edinburgh the fires of discontent were burning. The Catholic Jacobites, drawing strength from the Highlands, were planning and plotting, but their teeth had been drawn by Marlborough. There were overtures between them and their sworn enemies, the fierce 'hill-men', the ultra-Presbyterian Cameronians who were too extreme for the Church of Scotland. The Cameronians issued a proclamation with the title *Protestation and Testimony of the United Societies of the Witnessing Remnant of the anti-Popish, anti-Prelatic, anti-Sectarian, true Presbyterian Church of Christ in Scotland, against the Sinful Incorporating Union.* Some of the elect of Calvin were in opposition.

In Glasgow the mob rose – on the day after the day of fasting and humiliation appointed by the church – and gutted the provost's house. This unfortunate gentleman had earned their wrath by being too prudent. His city lay at the meeting place of north and south, of Catholic Jacobites and Calvinist

Cameronians. He had refused a suggestion that his town council should send a protest to Parliament in the name of both factions. Such alliances were taking place. At one stage of the disturbances a band of Presbyterians, led by a Catholic, set off from the west in search of an enemy, travelling generally in the direction of Edinburgh. After a short time they found no enemy, and wisely agreed to disperse. In Dumfries the Articles of Union were publicly burned in the market-place.

Scotland was divided against itself. The most united people were those pressing for union, steering it forcefully through Parliament. The opposition was split into a dozen fragments, and, though it might claim the majority of the Scottish people for its adherants, there was never any formidable coherence in its ranks.

In Edinburgh the New Year came and went. Article after article was tediously debated and then accepted by majority. For the opposition in the House the situation was desperate. Even the longest debate could not forever stall the Union. The opposition tried to gather its forces, sink its differences, and by a bold move so embarrass Parliament that the Act would not be ratified. They intended to make a formal protest and, when it was refused, to withdraw in a body, leaving the House to its own devices. This would be dramatic, confusing, explicit, and forceful, and there was a chance that it might succeed. The formal argument was 'that a body of legislators are not the owners or masters of a people. They are not entitled to bargain away the nation they represent, or make it cease to exist.' The opposition intended to claim that the debate on the Union was, in fact, *ultra vires*, a practical answer to the rhetorical question *quis custodiet ipsos custodes?*

The popular Duke of Hamilton agreed to lead this move. He exhorted the different factions of the opposition to a last united effort on behalf of their dying country. Success could only come if they buried their quarrels and united their strength. The protestation was drawn up, presenting all the arguments against the Union. The Duke of Atholl could not agree with its terms and refused to sign, but he agreed to quit Parliament with the rest.

The day of protest arrived, and the Duke of Hamilton, appointed leader of his country's independence, refused to leave his lodgings. He said he had toothache. His presence was peremptorily demanded, and he wisely complied. In the House he stated with disarming innocence that, while he would certainly support the protest, he had no intention of tabling it.

This unbelievable betrayal spiked the opposition. In the middle of January 1707 the last article was carried, and the Earl of Seafield, the Lord Chancellor, put his signature to the treaty and handed the papers to the clerk. He then made the utterance that has come down the years: 'There's the end of an auld sang' – a sentence that has remained an enigma, a curious obituary to a country's demise.

'When on May 1st 1707, the Act of Union came into force, the bells of St. Giles began the day with the tune *Why should I be sad on my wedding day?* Indeed, as it turned out, Scotland had reason to be sad for

many years, as carefully nursed manufactures were sent south under
the pressure of English competition and a system of free trade between
the countries, and new as well as more strictly exacted excise-duties
afflicted some basic industries.' – Sir John Clerk, *Memoirs.*

Part of the bargain of union was that Scotland should be paid a sum of
money. To the people of Edinburgh this suggested that their country's
independence had been sold in a commercial bargain, and there were rowdy
scenes when the carriages containing the money arrived in town.

The calculation of this monetary 'equivalent' was made by Professor David
Gregory and William Paterson. Sir John Clerk of Penicuik was one of those
appointed to review and approve the equivalent. A sum of £398,085 10s was
agreed on. It was partly to cover increased taxation and partly compensation for
the disaster of the Darien Scheme. The Bank of England paid the money.
There was some ingenious humour in this as William Paterson, the Scot who
helped to calculate the sum, had founded the Bank of England and had also
been a promoter of the Darien Scheme.

Sir John Clerk, a Baron of the Exchequer, was a man of great ability. He was
solidly for the Union, and was moved more by commonsense patriotism than
self-advancement. In his *Memoirs* he left an unusual description of Queen
Anne.

> 'One day I had occasion to observe the calamities which attend
> human nature even in the greatest dignities of life. Her majesty was
> labouring under a fit of gout, and in extreme pain and agony, and on
> this occasion every thing about her was much in the same disorder as
> about the meanest of her subjects. Her face, which was red and spotted,
> was rendered something frightful by her negligent dress, and the foot
> affected was tied up with a poultice and some nasty bandages. I was
> much affected at this sight, and the more when she had occasion to
> mention her people of Scotland, which she did frequently to the duke
> [Queensbury]. What are you, poor mean like mortal, I thought, who
> talks in the style of a sovereign?'

Sir John was one of the Scots who went to London to the new Parliament.
There were only sixteen peers to represent the Scottish nobility (there had been
145 in Parliament House), and sixty commoners (there had been 160). On
horseback, in carriages of slow ponderous discomfort, the Scottish Members of
Parliament hacked and lurched the four hundred miles to the city of London,
where they were received with disdain and lodged at prices they could not
afford. All for what?

> 'To find themselves obscure and unhonoured in the crowd of
> English society and the unfamiliar intrigues of English politics, where
> they were despised for their poverty, ridiculed for their speech, sneered
> at for their manners, and ignored in spite of their votes by the Ministers
> and Government.'

3

TOWN AND COUNTRY

Grass grows in the High Street.　　The countryside.　　'I
hate tyranny'.　　Pigeons and cattle.　　School-books.
How to say grace.　　The folk-lore of the people.　　The
mob of Edinburgh.　　A man of independent air.

AFTER THE UNION grass grew in the High Street of Edinburgh, sprouting
between the cobblestones like mould on a tombstone. What had this moribund
country to offer its citizens? What more could happen except its total
annihilation as the years passed and the story of Scotland became forgotten in
unread history books? There was no king, no parliament, no industry, little
trade. Scotland was a backwater in Europe: the life that had once moved busily
in it had gone elsewhere.

Scotland was very poor. The Union did not help matters. It brought no
succour, but a plague of tax-gatherers. Scotland's greatest enterprise, the
Darien Scheme, had failed some years before and was the major cause of the
lack of wealth in the country. Fortunes, to which all classes had contributed,
vanished in the disaster. The scheme had been promoted to found a Scottish
colony on the isthmus between the Americas, and had been defeated by English
politics, Spanish weapons, tropical diseases, and bad management.

In the countryside agriculture was backward, almost primitive. But it was
the land and the sea that provided such small exports as Scotland had. Salmon,
of which there was an abundance, and small tough cattle were sent to England;
Holland received coal and salmon; Norway took salt and lead; and the prudent
Scottish Presbyterians exported cured herring to Catholic Spain. Scotland's
greatest export was its own men. They emigrated. They went abroad to fight
other men's wars in the mercenary tradition. In France, where since the
Middle Ages Scottish archers had provided the royal guard, there were
Scottish regiments fighting for Marlborough against Louis XIV, whose own
army contained other Scots.

On the land money was scarce and goods were exchanged for services and
rent. Malt, meal, fish went to the laird as rent for his earth-floored cottages.
The laird himself probably had earth floors in some of his rooms. Rent was also
paid in part with so many 'dargues' – a day's work. (The word darg is still
current Scots to express hard work.)

Defoe believed that the misery of the Scottish peasantry was the result of the mediaeval system of land tenure. By the end of the first quarter of the century things were improving, and one of the land improvers – John Cockburn of Ormiston – gave the point of view of the new enlightened landlord: 'I hate tyranny in every shape, and shall always have greater pleasure in seeing my tenants making something under me which they can call their own than in getting a little more myself by squeezing a hundred poor families till their necessities make them my slaves!' This was more than agricultural enlightenment. 'I hate tyranny in every shape' expressed a principle that was then growing throughout Britain. But the bulk of the Scottish people on the land had to wait until the peaceful days of mid-century allowed new ideas to be put into practice.

At the beginning of the century the countryside was a place of misery for man and beast, landlord and tenant. Cockburn described it:

'The upper lands were heath-clad moor, perpetually grazed by half-starved cattle; the hollows by the river-side undrained marsh, from which in dry seasons some poor hay was secured as the only winter fodder available. Ten crofters near the village held patches of arable infield in run-dale or long narrow strips, on which crops of bere, oats, or pease were raised in succession till a year in the natural dress of weeds gave repose.'

Even the castles of the nobility were bare and without comfort. Such refinements as carpets were almost unknown. (Halfway through the century only two carpets existed in the town of Jedburgh. At the beginning of the century the royal dwelling-place of Cawdor House had a carpet only in the 'king's room'.) There were no pictures on the walls, and the 'Spanish leather' that Sir Alexander Brand made was the most usual kind of hanging decoration for those who could afford it.

'Though the land was generally barren of woods, without hedge or tree as far as the eye could reach, round many of the country houses in the lowlands, especially in the Lothians, clumps of trees planted for shelter – ash, elm, sycamore – clustered so close to the walls that they blocked out light and air from the small narrow windows, with their tiny three-cornered panes of glass.'

Most lairds' houses had a 'doocot' from which murmurings of pigeons descended on the tenants' crops, and so grew fat for the laird's table.

Though methods of using the land became more enlightened during the century, the habits of the peasants did not change greatly. Their houses were hovels. Their cattle were so starved by lack of winter feeding, so weakened by being shut in dark sheds throughout the winter months without exercise, that they often had to be carried out to the fields in springtime. Food and drink were of the simplest, and not always very ample.

In *Scottish Men of Letters of the Eighteenth Century*, Gray Graham gives a vivid description of life in the country:

'Farmers and workers were much about the same rank; and indeed, in the holdings or "mailings", most of the work was done by the

tenant's family, with the aid of two or three men and women who lived
with them. They all met at the same board, sat together by the fireside
at night, when the women spun the flax and men shod their brogues;
and partook of the same food out of the same dish, which was rarely
cleaned. Each man had his horn spoon, which he kept by his side or
fastened in his bonnet, to "sup" the kail, porridge, or sowans; while his
fingers and teeth did duty for knife and fork on the rare occasions when
they were called into requisition by the death of "crock ewe" – the meat
being cut off by the farmer with his clasp knife. The houses inside and
outside were filthy, though the dirt of their homes, of their food, and of
their persons did not distress them, except in the familiar disease which
too often came over their bodies.

'They loved this state; it kept them warm; it saved them trouble;
and they enshrined their tastes in their sayings – "The mair dirt the less
hurt", "the clartier [dirtier] the cosier". The exposure to all weathers
outside and to peat reek within, which filled the room with smoke and
feathered the rafters with soot, made their skin hard, brown, and
withered, and old-looking before their time.'

The lairds kept small gardens, but not for beauty. They grew plants and
herbs for the kitchen and 'physick'. Turnips were unknown at the beginning of
the century, as were onions. Only a few rich and enterprising gentlemen grew
potatoes. The social background of the age was grim in its lack of material
comfort, and dismal in its apparent lack of civilised accomplishment.

Gray Graham emphasises the inadequacy of life:

'There was the depressing poverty of the land (which it was hoped
the Union would rectify) whose nobles, merchants, and farmers were
alike in sore straits for money, the people lived humbly, spent
sparingly, travelled seldom, and read little. It was enough that in a
laird's bookshelves was his ragged array of old school-books – a well-
thumbed Caesar or Horace, or Buchanan's *Latin Psalms* – reminiscent
of a flagellated boyhood. There side by side lay a dilapidated *Ovid*,
Samuel Rutherford's Letters, Despauter's *Grammar*, and a *Confession of
Faith* – telling of years when he had been drilled in Latinity at school
and harrowed with piety at home.

'In several old country mansions, and in a few Edinburgh flats,
there were, however, libraries which showed that their owners or their
ancestors had some taste for polite letters. Gentlemen who had finished
their college course by study at Paris or Leyden or Gröningen very
often had collections of classics of no mean size or worth. These men,
when they went into winter quarters in Edinburgh, consorted with
lawyers and "physicals" who had learned their law or their physic and
improved their Latinity at Utrecht or Leyden, and in maturer years
had not forgotten their classics in devotion to drink.'

Most of the men of that early part of the century who had any taste for
letters were Episcopalians and Jacobites, whose sentiments were more

cultivated than was permitted by the Kirk. But the differences were often very small. The Episcopalians stood to say grace; the Presbyterians sat on their thrawn black-clad bottoms. 'Their differences were as foolish and whimsical as when the aristocratic Ghibellines cut their fruit cross-ways at table, and the democratic Guelphs sliced theirs long-ways.'

The general picture was of unrelieved confusion and despair, and it is that picture which impressed the journalists of the time, and was later emphasised by historians. But many of the contemporary recorders of the scene were inaccurate or partisan. Defoe, who was acting as a political spy for the south, was often a babbler. Taylor, generally an accurate observer, had his partisan blind spots.

The enduring quality of a people cannot be forgotten, nor their capacity to pass on traditional amusements, folklore, and small accomplishments, in spite of political unrest and religious persecution. The Scottish peasants were not entirely boorish and churlish, nor were they as like animals as made no difference; they were poor and often hungry, they were dirty, but they were not always illiterate. They were naturally suspicious of foreigners – such as Defoe and Taylor – as peasants still are.

Gray Graham was a Scotsman of the Victorian age, describing the past from the comfort and security of a time of imperial greatness. He looked back to the early eighteenth century with an indulgent sympathy, but he could not resist the contrast, in all aspects of life, between his own age of plenty and the earlier age of poverty. Writing of Edinburgh immediately after the Union, Graham said:

'No wonder the Union was specially unpopular in Edinburgh, for it deprived the city of national dignity, carried from citizens their fashions, and spoiled their trade. A gloom fell over the Scots capital: society was dull, business was duller still, the lodgings once filled with persons of quality were left empty – many decayed from want of tenants, some fell almost into ruin. For many a year there was little social life, scanty intellectual culture, and few traces of business enterprise. Gaiety and amusement were indulged in only under the censure of the Church and the depressing air of that gloomy piety which held undisputed and fuller away when the influence of rank and fashion no longer existed to counteract it.'

That is entirely true, yet something was left unsaid by Graham. People were vital and vigorous in their lives, however inadequate the peasant may have been as an agriculturalist, or the town-dweller as an industrious merchant. (Lacking agricultural method, lacking industry and trade, they worked as well as they might.) But they were not a vitiated lack-lustre people. Their mothers and grandmothers had tilted their caps at the devil, and often been burned because of it. They were a strong, enduring, tough people who survived mightily under the penury of their occupations, the moral flail of their church, and the indifference of their landlords. The countrymen frequently wore no shoes and were dressed in rough homespun, but they were the solid foundation of their country and from their loins sprang men of greatness. There was, in town and country, a heritage of songs and ballads that, even then, was being acquired by educated men who saw, dimly and without understanding, the cultural roots that must exist to feed the foliage of literacy.

In the schools and universities, in the houses of the lairds, and the flats of the town-dwellers, there were many people who continued, not at all uneasily, traditions of scholarship and the arts, who gathered the riches of the past and staked a claim to the future.

Though Calvinism pushed its unreasonable logic with brutal authority, its vindictiveness was on the wane. In the name of God it cursed and punished, but the slaughter was diminishing, even as theology became more absurdly intellectual with the Marrowmen. The last witch in Edinburgh was burned in 1703. Edinburgh was large. Its notorious mob was responsible to no authority when it took the law into its own hands. There were also a number of 'corrupt lumps' whose minds warmed to different values. They emerged to defy the Kirk, to tear its fantastic structure of cruelty to pieces, to topple the pedlars of misery and their infamous god.

These persons who defied the powers of their day were not innovators. They drew their values from an earlier Scotland. Most of them are now forgotten, and those whose names are known have been neglected, their quiet importance ignored in the tumultuous confusion of their age.

Dr Archibald Pitcairn, a man of medical science, was outstanding among them. Before the end of the previous century he had helped in the establishment of the Edinburgh medical school. In the drinking taverns of Edinburgh, he lashed the fierce puritanism of the church. He was a bon viveur and a rebel. It was whispered that he was also a free-thinker, a man who scorned God and the gospels. The bitter churchman, Robert Wodrow, accused Pitcairn of lampooning the scriptures among his friends and of getting drunk twice a day. There is a story that at an auction sale a large Bible failed to secure an offer. Pitcairn suggested it was little wonder that the Bible stayed in their hands since it was thought that the word of the Lord abideth forever. For this pleasantry he was rebuked.

He wrote Latin verses that were much admired in his day and published posthumously. Dryden and Prior translated a few into English. He wrote a play called *The Assembly, or Scottish Reformation* which was not published till after his death, when printing and publishing were rapidly recovering from the blight of the godly. In all that he did he showed the independence of the new scholarship. He fought Calvinism because it was credulous and cruel. He was aware that they ordered things better in the south, as far as tolerance was concerned.

But if the south was tolerant, it did not possess the sense of dedicated purpose that was found in Scotland, both in the fanaticism of the religious zealots and in the new teaching of men like Pitcairn. The English universities were wastes of indolence and shabby learning, with no vitality among the professors nor much interest in the pupils. Pitcairn did more than dream of a new outlook and a new conception of the arts. He set about accomplishing these things.

He and his friends, in the dawn of the century, gathered in the pubs and clubs of Edinburgh. These drinking clubs were the meeting-places, formal and informal, of all citizens. They provided much of the social life of the city, with cheap claret to ease tongues that were never backward in encompassing an argument, in discussing the mysteries of the universe or the anatomy of the human body.

When Archibald Pitcairn died in 1713, Allan Ramsay had been married a year and had produced his earliest traceable poem, concerning one of the drinking clubs – 'To the Most Happy Members of the Easy Club'. In the Borders, James Thomson was a young lad, the same age as the century, wandering the countryside around his father's manse. Pitcairn himself had been responsible in 1699 for bringing to Edinburgh a Thomas Ruddiman, whom he had found one evening in the village inn at Laurencekirk in Kincardineshire. Ruddiman was a young schoolmaster who had been produced so that Pitcairn might have an educated companion to dine and talk with. At Pitcairn's encouragement the young dominie, who was a Jacobite, gave up his annual salary of £5 (mostly paid in meal) to become, at a salary of £8, sub-librarian in the Advocates' Library in Edinburgh. In time he became one of the major figures of the city.

Already the pattern was being set of science and the arts cultivating each other. Pitcairn was the first distinct and vivid personality of this marriage.

4

HACKS AND POETS

'The lass with the gowden hair'. Rhymes to suit all occasions. The beginning of journalism. Heaven is a merchant's warehouse. Pirate printers. Pitcairn again.

IN THE FIRST YEARS of the century there were other signs that cultural life was not dead. Henry Playford published the earliest collection of Scottish songs, for violin and flute. In 1706 a collection of traditional Scottish verse was published in Edinburgh by James Watson, a patriot, an anti-Union man, and reputedly a Jacobite. There was a preface which stated:

'As the frequency of Publishing Collections of Miscellaneous Poems in our Neighbouring Kingdoms and States may, in a great measure, justify an Undertaking of this kind with us; so 'tis hoped that this being the first of its Nature which has been publish'd in our own Native *Scots* Dialect, the Candid Reader may be the more easily induced, through the Consideration thereof, to give some Charitable Grains of Allowance, if the Performance come not up to such a point of Exactness as may please an over nice palate . . .'

The 1706 volume was followed by others in 1709 and 1711. These books were an indication of the way that the pressure of England was turning some Scots back to their own language and traditions. But it was with a sense of half-shame and of inferiority that the collections were offered. A nicely turned apology was needed to introduce the verses of rough unpolished dialect. 'Give some charitable grains of allowance. . . .'

What kind of poems were they? Joseph Taylor had come across the tough and bawdy tap-roots of Scottish Balladry. The ballad that captured his imagination appeared in Watson's collection, and Taylor has his own version in his *Journey*.

'And Crampie that married Stainie,
And coft him his breeks to his Arse,
And afterwards hang'd for stealing,
Great mercy it happen'd no worse,
And there will be fairntickl'd Hew,
And Bess with the lillie-white legg,
That gat to the South for breeding,
And bang'd up her Wymb in Mons-Megg

Fy let us All to the Bridal
For there will be lilting there,
For Jock's to be merried to Meggie,
The lass with the Gowden hair.'

It was still a far cry to the romantic revolution in letters, from the lass with
the gowden hair to the lady of the lake. Twenty years later Allan Ramsay took
the same song and printed a more polished version. By that time James
Thomson was a student at Edinburgh University, and was considering a trip to
London to deliver himself of *The Seasons*.

Meanwhile, as the Union took place and Watson busied himself with his
collections, Edinburgh endured its fallow period. Hacks there were in plenty,
failed poets who sold execrable rhymes to bereaved merchants at a few shillings
a stanza. The lords and lordlings themselves had no better taste or wit than to
patronise the rhymesters. On the death of the Marquis of Tullibardine in 1709,
these lines were considered by his family to be a fitting literary tribute:

'What signs, what groans are these I hear always?
What gushing torrents now run down my eyes?
What wofull news, what killing sound is this
That fills all hearts with tears and bitterness?

Ah dolfull news! but they cannot be fled,
The noble Marquis Tullibardin's dead,
That sweet, that noble matchless paragon;
Ah! is he gone? He's gone; alas, he's gone.'

In his *Scottish Men of Letters*, Gray Graham writes:
'Whenever the news passed through the town that a lord of Session,
Merchant, or laird was dead, or had lost his wife, they went to their
garrets, wrote out panegyrics, often in acrostics, and with them neatly
copied out, but abominably spelt, they went up to the door of the house
of mourning and "tirled at the risp". If a composition met with
approval, the poet would receive a few shillings payment, and it was
duly printed as a broadside with an appropriate border of cross-bones,
skulls, spades, and hour-glasses, and sent to the friends of the
bereaved.'

There was no real journalism in Edinburgh till after the Union. In 1705, by
permission of the Privy Council, the *Courant* had appeared as a rival to the
Gazette, also allowed by the Council. Both were official journals inspired by
London, and not dealing with Scottish affairs. When the Privy Council was
abolished, Edinburgh journalism began to develop.

Of the few books that were published many were religious. In 1703 a small
volume appeared with the title: *The Spiritual-Merchant: or the Art of
Merchandizing Spiritualized*. This useful compendium was sub-titled 'How to
be rich towards God, and also how to acquire wordly wealth'. With some
appropriateness it was dedicated to the town council of Glasgow. Its

substantial and solid instruction included such pieces as 'Above all make acquaintance with our Lord Jesus, He hath the Monopoly of Heavens Wares in His Hand, He is the First-hand whole-sale-Merchant, and His Warehouse never runs out'. Long before the Industrial Revolution, Presbyterianism showed how it could adapt itself to the spiritual requirements of money-seekers.

The *Spiritual-Merchant* was blessed by Robert Wodrow, Professor of Divinity at Glasgow, whose book *Analecta* was the production of a well-intentioned tyrant. Wodrow lived as an example of the fury of Calvinism, a hysteria of intellect that presented itself as the path to salvation.

In the dearth of Scottish letters, and the general repudiation by men of education of the 'native Scots dialect', there was ready reception of the works of English writers. After the Union this demand became stronger. Ships to Leith brought the latest works of Addison and Steele. There had been a slow turning to England and English ways. In the previous century Drummond of Hawthornden had written in English. Sir Thomas Urquhart, in the days of King Charles, had translated Rabelais from French into English, but a rich, evolved, and plastic English full of the ripeness of the Scots dialect. The Union meant, and was intended to mean, more and more anglicisation. Hence Watson's apology for publishing in the uncouth Scots tongue.

Scottish printers pirated English books. In Morocco Close in Edinburgh, and in Glasgow's Salt Market, ancient wooden presses housed in the semi-darkness of dingy cellars produced barely readable copies of the *Spectator* and the *Tatler*. Impoverished hacks and a few poor printers – that was almost the total of Scotland's literary life. 'Men of letters there were none; of making of books there seems to have been an end.' Long forgotten were the lusty years of the Scottish Chaucerians, of Dunbar, Henryson, and William Montgomerie.

'The Union of 1707 was the end rather than the beginning of a movement – a movement which had begun in 1568, when Mary Queen of Scots crossed the Solway Firth into England to seek the dubious protection of Queen Elizabeth; a movement which had begun when John Knox recognised that a Protestant Scotland could gain more from association with Protestant England than with Catholic France; which had begun when the rich culture of mediaeval Scotland succumbed to the cold theology of the reforming zealots and the "auld alliance" with France gave place to a series of shifty and evasive overtures to England which certainly did no good either to the Scottish or to the English character.' – Daiches: *Robert Burns*, p. 300.

The 'end of an auld sang' was the end of a period. But as one period ended, another began. Playford's collection of Scottish songs, Watson's collections of Scottish poems, were portents. The Scottish attitude to learning and the arts had been almost lost in the ugly storm of religion and politics. It had been crippled and battered and ejected from the public scene. But it had not vanished.

Today a considerable amount of material is being discovered, in the archives of old houses, to show that under the gloom of the early eighteenth century there was among cultivated people a constant devotion to the arts, especially the oral arts of song and story. As these old manuscripts, music scores, and so on become available, they throw a softer light on the period, and indicate that much of an older tradition was maintained through the bloody years of persecution and the barren poverty of the Union.

A man of ability like Pitcairn blew life into this tradition; it was the essence of his reaction to Calvinism; it fired his imagination to build a medical school; it warmed his humanism. The same spirit that produced the great renaissance age of the Scottish Chaucerians (while England was mute between Chaucer himself and Shakespeare) was again to blow generously throughout the land.

The capital of Scotland appeared to be inhabited by two classes: the apparently illiterate, who spoke nothing but the broadest native Scots but who possessed a tradition of story, song and ballad; and the educated, who could converse in Latin but whose gloss of learning did not hide an aridity of spirit. These were the main divisions, but the leaven was with the Episcopalians and with men like Pitcairn. The songs of the people and the new enquiring scholasticism brought the new age to birth. The offspring, in the days of its maturity, was to resemble neither parent.

Out of Pitcairn – if one uses him as a symbol of the man of reason – there grew not only the medical schools of Glasgow and Edinburgh, but a coherent development of scientific and technical discovery. Out of Watson – using him as a symbol for those who uncovered the foundations of their national literary tradition – there grew the poet Robert Burns.

There was another influence, that of the Union itself. As Gray Graham put it:

'Certainly the Union had a great effect in stimulating Scottish intellectual interest and widening literary tastes. Scots gentry who went as members of parliament to Westminster – some giving their self-sacrificing services to their country for a comfortable salary from their constituency – would bring back books from London, and in various ways literature penetrated to remote rural mansions as well as to city life, conveyed in cadgers' creels.'

Scotland's old contact with France had vanished. The English influence was important. It anglicised the literary language of the Scots who, in turn and in time, contributed to the mainstream of English literature. Two of the major literary figures had been born. They could hardly have been less similar. James Thomson, still a child, was in his father's manse in the Borders. Allan Ramsay was old enough to look with the eager appetite of a sensitive youth at the drama and intrigue in Edinburgh when the Scots dissolved their Parliament.

5

THE RISE OF MEDICINE

From Leyden to the Chirurgeon Apothecaries.   The beginning of medical Edinburgh. A family of Monros.   The
Edinburgh Pharmacopoeia. Concerning inventors.   The
Iatro-mechanicalist playwright..   Toads, dung, spiders'
webs..   The Royal Infirmary of Edinburgh..   Other
medical schools..   A galaxy of names.

DURING THE SEVENTEENTH CENTURY the town of Leyden, in
Holland, became the major centre of European medicine. It had received its
university as a gift from William of Orange, who in 1575 offered the citizens a
choice of being untaxed for a decade or having a university established. This
was a royal offering of thanks for the town's role in the war against Spain. The
university was chosen, and in the subsequent century it became the foremost
teaching centre in Europe, busy with the conflicting theories of the mathematical and chemical explanations of the human body. To Leyden and
its famous teachers there travelled pupils from all Europe, and from America.
Among the Scots who went there were Robert Sibbald and John Monro. It was
there that Archibald Pitcairn taught for a year. Those three doctors shared the
ambition of forming an Edinburgh school of medicine.

Sibbald was the oldest. About 1670 he and Dr. Andrew Balfour decided to
plant a physical garden in Edinburgh as part of the improvement of medicine.
Botany and anatomy were the groundwork of medical knowledge. In spite of
opposition from the Chirurgeon Apothecaries, the project went through with
the blessing of the town council. In 1681 the Edinburgh College of Physicians
came into existence by royal charter. Pitcairn, who had graduated M.D. at
Rheims only the year before, was the youngest original fellow.

Until then the Chirurgeon Apothecaries had been able to resist the
advancement of the new learning. They, the barber-surgeons of Edinburgh,
retained an ancient monopoly of surgery and blood-letting. As far back as 1505
they had been formed into the Incorporation of Barber-Surgeons under a Seal
of Cause confirmed by James IV. The guild had sole rights of medical practice
within the city, and its fellows were authorised to conduct examinations of
those who were anxious to profess its mysteries, including astrological
learning. The guild was also entitled each year to 'ane condamnit man efter he
be deid to mak anatomea of quhairthrow we may heif experience'. This
powerful guild also had the unusual but precious privilege of controlling the

distilling and selling of whisky in Edinburgh. Its authority was exerted against the new scholars who were returning to Edinburgh with outlandish ideas about medical teaching and practice. The founding of the College of Physicians, in opposition to the Surgeons, was a hard-won victory. Proposals had first been mooted in the time of Charles I, and renewed under the Parliament, against the opposition of the town council, the bishops, the universities, and the barber-surgeons.

The establishment of the College of Physicians was a signal that the new teaching was accepted and had official recognition. Four years later in 1685 the town council, which at that time appointed university professors, made its first professor of medicine. Sir Robert Sibbald was chosen. Six months later Dr. Archibald Pitcairn and Dr. James Halket were appointed additional joint professors. No salary was given to the professors and there was no course of lectures. Sibbald and Halket went to discourses at the College of Physicians. Pitcairn organised anatomical demonstrations in the College of Surgeons, which suggests that the barber-surgeons were already adjusting themselves to the new teaching.

At the beginning of the eighteenth century, the Senatus Academicus of the university was composed of the principal, the professors of divinity, of Hebrew, of mathematics, of humanity, and of botany, and four professors of philosophy.

In 1703 Robert Elliott became 'public dissector' and received a salary of £15 per year. In 1708 Adam Drummond was appointed joint 'Professor of anatomy' with Elliott.

The university was still known as the Town's College, and appointments to its staff remained in the hands of the Edinburgh town council. By now the university, the College of Physicians, and the Incorporation of Barber-Surgeons were united in the pursuit of medical knowledge.

The three men most responsible for the transformation of medicine – Sibbald, Pitcairn, and Monro – were a trio who possessed between them the most amazing abilities. John Monro, who died in 1737, was not the most brilliant intellectually, but he was the most curiously indomitable in the way he chose to further his ambition of creating a medical school in Edinburgh on the lines of that at Leyden. His efforts helped towards the appointment of Sibbald, Halket, and Pitcairn as the original professors. He saw botany and chemistry begin to be taught as advanced subjects. He saw the rise of research in anatomy. He was a man of sound learning and had been a surgeon with William of Orange, and so was one of a long succession of medical men who have been stimulated to advance their profession by the carnage of war. Monro's major contribution was unusual. He chose to educate his son to fill the post of professor of anatomy. Elliott and Drummond who held office at the beginning of the century were variously described as 'public dissectors' and 'professors'. It seems that the establishment of a full chair in anatomy, with a defined course of studies, was reserved for John Monro's son. He is certainly credited with being the first professor of anatomy to be appointed in any university.

This man, Alexander Monro, lived from 1697 to 1767. He studied at
Leyden under Boorhaave, the famous anatomist who had been a pupil of
Pitcairn, and in London, under Cheselden, the outstanding English surgeon.
When he was twenty-two his father saw part of his ambition fulfilled.
Alexander became professor of anatomy at Edinburgh, and his first lecture was
attended by the Lord Provost and the council.

John Monro was more successful than he imagined. Not only his son, but
his grandson and then his great-grandson, held the same chair in unbroken
succession, so that Monros were professors of anatomy at Edinburgh from
circa 1718 to 1859.

Robert Sibbald was born in 1641 and lived till 1722. Before he was twenty
he went to Leyden to study for a year and a half. A few years after his success in
promoting the College of Physicians he became a Catholic. Bishop Burnet
wrote that Sir Robert 'had lived in a course of philosophical virtue, but in great
doubt as to revealed religion, and was prevailed on by the Earl of Perth to turn
to the Church of Rome without any previous examination of her principles;
but, when he came to search into them, he was so fully convinced of the errors
of Popery, that he could not be at quiet till he had published his recantation
openly in a church.' It was actually more of a political conversion than Bishop
Burnet admitted, for it took place in 1686. A visit to London and a sense of the
political atmosphere (James II was about to quit the throne) induced him to
recant. The 'most learned antiquary in Scotland' had to trim smartly.

Sibbald compiled the first *Edinburgh Pharmacopoeia*, a volume that was
ready by 1698 but was delayed in publication. It was full of the loathsome
remedies that doctors were not yet ready to discard, but it did to a large extent
systematise drugs and medicines.

Like Pitcairn, Sibbald was a man of many abilities. His major work was an
illustrated natural history of Scotland. He wrote copiously on history and
archaeology, described a number of counties and towns, produced a work on
the Roman ports on the Firth of Forth, and a description of the islands of
Orkney.

But it is Pitcairn who emerges as the greatest medical man of his day.

'To Pitcairn more than anyone else may justly be assigned the credit
not only of originating the Edinburgh medical school, but of doing
much to establish the world-wide reputation it gained, which even in
those days was due largely to its acceptance of the Paduan tradition
which Pitcairn so strenuously upheld.' – Henry Wellcome in his
introduction to Comrie's *History of Scottish Medicine*.

Pitcairn was born in or near Edinburgh on Christmas Day 1652. He was
educated in the classics at Dalkeith and graduated in 1671. The unspecific
studies of theology and philosophy repelled him, and he tackled law. A
breakdown in health was followed by a journey abroad, and in Paris he became
interested in medicine. His father recalled him to Edinburgh, where he studied
mathematics under Dr. David Gregory. He became converted to the
mathematical school of thinking, finding in it a clarity, a reasonableness, and a

precision that he sought in vain elsewhere. Physics appeared to share this precision, and he became convinced that mathematics and physics would be of value in medicine. He saw that the superstitious practices of doctors had little relation to the needs of patients, and human life was often carelessly flung away. In Edinburgh he began to study botany, pharmacy, and *materia medica*, but as there was no medical faculty he again went abroad, and in 1680 graduated M.D. at Rheims. In the following year he became the youngest fellow of the new College of Physicians for which Sibbald had laboured. In due course there followed his appointment as one of the first medical professors at Edinburgh.

Pitcairn's most important work was an essay called *A Solution of the Problem Concerning Inventors*, in which he was concerned with methods of observation and deduction. 'By things demonstrated, I understand then such things whose proofs make it impossible that they should be otherwise than they are; from whence it follows that they are always the same and unalterable.'

This essay was published in 1688. It was a strong defence of Harvey's claim to have discovered the circulation of the blood. Pitcairn is credited with completing Harvey's theory by demonstrating that veins and arteries were linked by capillaries, a discovery he made 'by a kind of mathematical reasoning'.

It was largely this essay, which bore less on the nature of discoveries than on the methods that should be used to make them, that persuaded Leyden to offer him the professorship of medicine in 1691. Pitcairn accepted immediately, partly because of the honour, but also because his politics were impeding his advancement in Scotland. The journey to Leyden was parallel to Sibbald's recantation.

At his inaugural lecture at Leyden, he explained the necessity for exact observation and for the acceptance of what is determined by the senses, irrespective of traditional opinion. He made war on the philosophers whose enquiries about physical causes he called a purposeless wrangle.

> 'Nor ought this to seem strange, since the patrons of sects by attempting the knowledge of the absolute nature, and intimate essences and causes of things, without any regard to the discovery of their properties, were forced to make use of many *Postulata's* and but few *Data's*, by which means they unavoidably fell into great variety of opinions.'

Pitcairn believed in the scientific method. He belaboured unceasingly and in strong language all who busied themselves with fashionable disputation and philosophising. 'That art [medicine] which of all others promises safety and health to mankind, ought not in reason to be involved in the conjectures and dreams of disputants . . . physicians ought to propose the method of astronomers as a pattern for their imitation.' And again: 'It remains then that we cultivate Physic not under the disguise of such fictions as these, but upon the trials of experience.'

Pitcairn knew the gigantic task that faced men of science in correcting the fundamental errors of popular thought. To convince orthodox scholars of the falsity of their thinking was severe enough, but 'to endeavour to bring the vulgar to the right were the undertaking of a mad man.'

As an Iatro-mechanicalist, Pitcairn no doubt believed that in time the truth would out, that the world would be forced to see how the laws of the physical world governed the biology of the body. The more complex story that medicine was to unravel might have disheartened him if he had glimpsed its intricacy. But it was the scrupulously exact methods of investigation which he proposed that made research possible. The University of Leyden was so impressed by the arguments of its new professor that it augmented his salary.

At Leyden Pitcairn taught Boorhaave, the man from whom later generations of European doctors were to learn the new scientific theories of medicine; and among Boorhaave's pupils were many who became famous in the medical schools of Edinburgh and Glasgow.

Personal affairs recalled Pitcairn to Scotland when he had been only a year in office at Leyden. In a tavern near St. Giles, so obscure that it was known as the 'greping' or groping office, Pitcairn sat with his friends, offered medical advice to the sick, turned his Latin epigrams, and discussed the Iatromechanical interpretation of man and the universe. In his sedan chair he was carried from house to house, where he doctored the wealthy for money and the poor for love.

Pitcairn may have been a Jacobite, but he had never any love for the Catholic Church, nor for any church. When Sibbald was 'converted', Pitcairn produced a long poem which began:

'There is lost, there is lost
On the Catholic coast,
A quack of the college's quorum,
Tho' his name be not shown
Yet the man may be known
By his *opus Viginti annorum*.'

The opus was presumably the *Pharmacopoeia* on which Sibbald had laboured so long. Though there was humour in the poem, there were occasions on which Pitcairn appears to have quarrelled with Sibbald. Pitcairn must have held rigidly to his independent views and taken it badly when any comparable intelligence accommodated itself, even temporarily, to the demands of Church or State.

His play, *The Assembly*, was a comedy written in 1692. It is not a work of greatness but bears re-reading, and would have endured better if many of its allusions were not lost in the forgotten religious and political bigotry of the age. But there is an edge to the play, and a later editor, somewhat overpraising it, suggested it helped in modifying the tyrannical attitude of the church. *The Assembly* has none of the grace of Restoration Comedy, though it shares some of the licence.

When Pitcairn died, his library was bought by Peter the Great of Russia. He was buried in Greyfriars Churchyard, in Edinburgh, having seen the new age of medicine come into being.

It is tempting to see men such as Pitcairn and Sibbald as reformers engaged in battle with ignorant opponents defending an age of superstition. Their battle was with the customs and practices that they themselves inherited as part of their education and experience. It was in their own minds, not against their fellows, that they won their greatest victories. They were among the first to use, in a practical craft-science riddled with old wives' remedies, the new broom of objective ascertainable fact. Naturally the broom did not always sweep clean. They established a new technique, and they themselves still accepted as true much that the technique would in time disprove and discard.

One of Pitcairn's remedies for ulcers merits preservation. There was an elaborate ointment and its use was followed by the consumption of specially prepared beer. This was Guiacum Beer, made from Guiacum wood. Two pounds of the wood were put into two hundred pounds of beer that was not 'worked'. It was boiled till a third part was consumed. When it was strained, it was allowed to ferment, and there was hung in it a linen bag containing half a pound of antimony and four ounces of sharp-pointed dock. The beer was then put in a barrel with a little dried rosemary and some rinds of oranges, and to this was added the juice of five or six hundred millipedes. When the beer was clear, the patient was to drink nothing else.

Toads, dung, spiders' webs, and many other traditional specifics were included in the first edition of the *Pharmacopoeia*. In each revised edition more and more were discarded until, by the middle of the century, this 'natural medicine' had gone the way of witches and warlocks.

The new faculty of medicine in Edinburgh had begun to award its own degree of doctor of medicine in 1726. To start with the number of graduates each year was very small, sometimes only two or three, but by mid-century the number rose considerably, though it was still under twenty per year. Students were coming from the colonies in the Americas and the West Indies.

Dr. Thomas Young started Edinburgh's first maternity hospital. It began as little more than a ward in an attic that could hold four women.

In 1778 the old Incorporation of Surgeons became the Royal College of Surgeons, and its members became Fellows. Even so, Monro (secundus) successfully prevented an attempt to have the teaching of surgery made a separate professorship. Dr. Alexander Hamilton, who was then head of the College of Surgeons, detached the maternity ward from the infirmary and set up an independent Lying-In Hospital.

There was a close relationship between the teaching faculties and the Royal Infirmary of Edinburgh, which became a teaching hospital, as it is to this day.

Courses of clinical medicine were offered. Drs. Monro, Cullen, Whytt, and Rutherford (the last-named became the grand-father of Walter Scott) pioneered instruction by clinical lecture, a method that had been favoured earlier in both the Leyden and Paduan schools. Somewhat later similar facilities were provided for lectures on clinical surgery.

Though Edinburgh created and developed its medical school during the eighteenth century, Glasgow had an older tradition, an early study of medicine being forced upon it because of visitation of the plague. Back in 1597 the Glasgow surgeon, Peter Lowe, had published the first edition of his *Chyrgurie*, believed to be the first text-book of surgery written in English.

Peter Lowe's most important work was the creation of the Faculty of Physicians and Surgeons in the west. The charter of what became the Glasgow Medical School drew on ideas that Lowe had learned in the Collège de St. Côme, in Paris, and in 1599 the medico-legal operation of the faculty created what has since been described as 'a very early example of State medicine'. Glasgow University itself did not establish a faculty of medicine until the nineteenth century. The importance of Lowe's Glasgow establishment was that both surgeons and physicians were included in the original charter, and the rivalries that existed between these two skills at other Scottish teaching centres seem to have been avoided.

An apprentice to one of the members of the faculty was Tobias Smollett. In *Roderick Random*, Smollett illustrated the antipathy between the old school of surgeon-apothecaries, who had learned their trade through apprenticeship and practical experience, and the new breed of doctors who began by studying books and attending classes.

King's College, Aberdeen, was the first university in Britain where the teaching of medicine was an integral part of the university's instruction. This was early in the sixteenth century. What was taught was not what is now understood as medicine but a range of studies in botany and 'physic', derived from the monasteries, which was part of the accomplishments of any well-educated man. During the eighteenth century three men of the famous Gregory family followed each other as 'mediciners' at King's College – James Gregory (the elder) in 1725, followed by James Gregory (the younger) in 1732, and John Gregory in 1755.

As Glasgow produced an early surgeon in Peter Lowe, so Aberdeen produced an early physician in Gilbert Skeen. Educated at King's College he examined one of the most important medical matters of his day, and in 1568 he published in Edinburgh *Ane Breve Description of the Pest*. Like the *Chyrgurie* it was written in a modified form of the Scots language.

Scotland's contribution to medical science in the eighteenth century and the early nineteenth was impressive, and out of a galaxy of names it is possible to mention only a few. William Smellie (1697–1763) was 'the master of midwifery' and a leading obstetrician in London. His major work, *Treatise on Midwifery*, which was published in 1752, was revised by his friend Smollett. Another specialist in obstetrics was William Hunter (1718–83), who founded the Windmill Street School of Anatomy in London.

Hunter's brother John (1728–93) devoted his life to research into comparative anatomy and physiology. Sir James Learmonth has said that his 'greatest contribution to surgery was that he changed it from an inexact science to an exact one'. The annual Hunterian Oration of the Royal College of Surgeons of England exists today as a memorial to John Hunter's vast investigations.

One of Hunter's works was *Gunshot Wounds and Inflammation*. It was an age when the poorhouse served the anatomist and the battlefield served the surgeon, and among those who took part in military campaigns were Sir John Pringle (1707–82) and Charles Bell (1774–1842). Pringle was doctor to the Earl of Stair at the Battle of Dettingen (1743) and on his suggestion it was agreed with the French commander that both sides would accept the inviolability of military hospitals. This was the forerunner of what became the Red Cross over a century later. Pringle's works included *Observations on the Diseases of the Army*, and *Experiments upon Septic and Antiseptic Substances* which introduced the new word 'antiseptic'. Charles Bell, who operated on the wounded at Waterloo, produced the first text-book on modern neurology.

James Lind (1716–94) did for the navy what Pringle did for the army. His *Treatise of the Scurvy* advanced the work done by earlier doctors, none of whom knew why lemon or lime was effective against scurvy. When the navy accepted Lind's recommendations, the disease disappeared 'as if by magic'. His *Manual of Tropical Diseases* was the first of its kind.

6

CONTRASTS – RAMSAY AND THOMSON

Country boy becomes wig-maker.   'Tea-Table Miscellany.'
'The Gentle Shepherd.'   Becomes a bookseller.   The first
circulating library.   Lord Grange intervenes.   A theatre
and the goose-pie.   Youth of Thomson. The Border
countryside.   'The Seasons.'   To London, fame and
fortune.   'Rule Britannia.'   Quin's visit to Thomson in
prison.   'O Jemmy Thomson.'

ALLAN RAMSAY, born in 1686, was brought to Edinburgh in 1701 by his step-father. He came from a bare windswept part of Lanarkshire where his father, who had died when the boy was in infancy, had been superintendent of lead-mines in the desolate valleys. His mother had married again but had died in 1700. Allan Ramsay was fourteen when his step-father, a herder of sheep and cattle, performed his duty and apprenticed the boy to a wig-maker in the High Street of Edinburgh, not far from Parliament House.

Young Allan had been educated at a village school, where he had acquired enough Latin to read Horace 'faintly in the original'. With his early years of country solitude behind him, the apprentice was ready to meet what Edinburgh offered. He was vivacious and had a vast curiosity.

Wig-making was a skilled and genteel occupation that hovered somewhere between a trade and a profession. Class distinction was not a profound cleavage in Edinburgh society. There was social rank, but that was another matter. (Class distinction is still of less importance in Scotland than in England. This is perhaps due, to some extent, to the thorough mixing of all ranks in the bustling streets of old Edinburgh, where nobles, tradesmen, servants, and beggars lived almost cheek by jowl, and were of necessity on terms of intimacy with each other.)

As he learned the craft of wig-maker (periwigs, tiewigs, bobwigs, from fourteen shillings to ten pounds), Allan Ramsay mixed with men of education and fashion, with politicians, merchants, soldiers of fortune, scholars, men of independent means and sometimes of independent thought. In the noisy times that surrounded the Union, Ramsay was in the thick of the Edinburgh hubbub. He saw the swift dereliction of the city after the Union – when the streets were deserted and the 'lands' of tenements empty of tenants.

In the year of the Union, Allan Ramsay set up shop on his own. His taste for poetry was already developed. He bought books in the bookshops of Parliament Close. He went to the coffee shops and the taverns. He married in 1712 – a lawyer's daughter – and to that year is traceable his earliest poem, 'To the Most Happy Members of the Easy Club'.

Ramsay knew and admired the London literature – the Queen Anne wits, Defoe, Addison, Swift, Steele. He vastly enjoyed the books and periodicals that came from the south on the erratic coaches, or by ship to the port of Leith. It was to his own language that Ramsay turned when he wrote his poems, and that is an interesting point. Ramsay chose Scots, and paved the way for Fergusson and Burns in the second half of the century. He made his choice, and it was a deliberate choice in an age when all writing that mattered was in English, and yet he was living in Edinburgh, where the English influence was strongest. James Thomson, growing into manhood in the country where the natural influence was Scots, chose to write in English. It is a useful distinction to observe. What Ramsay was in touch with, of course, was the strong current of natural Scots speech in the capital, the country's tradition of song and story. Thomson, isolated in his father's rural manse, rarely meeting a new person, was more fascinated by the tantalising far-off and 'educated' literature of the English tongue.

In 1721 a collection of Ramsay's own poems appeared, subscribed for by four hundred 'advocates and lairds, noblemen and merchants'. Ramsay's local renown became a small fame. In the south, Pope and Gay knew of him and expressed interest. Hogarth inscribed his plates for *Hudibras* to the little wig-maker.

In 1724 came the *Tea-Table Miscellany*, a volume which was a delight in its day. Unfortunately, to suit the increasing circle of genteel readers, Ramsay bowdlerised a great many songs which have since disappeared in their original versions. In the *Miscellany*, the new age of manners made its literary début in the north. Ramsay was assisted in his work by men such as Robert Crauford, best known for his 'Bush Aboon Traquair', and Hamilton of Gilbertfield, the author of 'Willy Was a Wanton Wag'.

Next came *Evergreen*, reputedly a collection of Scots poems written before 1600. It contained the famous *Hardyknute*, of which more will be said later. In *Evergreen* the ballad is seen emerging from the songs and lyrics and light verse that had until then been the preoccupation of collectors, imitators, and original writers.

In 1725 Ramsay sealed his claim to posterity's attention as a writer, with his *Gentle Shepherd*, dedicated to the exquisitely charming Susanna, Countess of Eglinton – a lady whose youthful beauty and then her mature elegance endeared her to many of the great men of the century; she died in the last decade 'a dear old woman of ninety-one'.

It is said that Ramsay received ideas for the plot of *The Gentle Shepherd* from Dr. Alexander Pennecuik, laird of Romanno, whom he used to meet in the company of other leaders of Edinburgh's society. They were 'clubbable' men of hearty appetites, indecorous wit, and considerable abilities. Dr. Pennecuik died at the age of eighty-one, two years after *The Gentle Shepherd* was published. He had been a linguist, and left a number of poems in the broad tradition of Scottish bawdy humour. The importance of this robust tradition – which culminated in *The Merry Muses of Caledonia*, Robert Burns's book of bawdry – cannot be exaggerated. It was the strong home-brew of literature to which the Scots were devoted, and in itself must have been a sturdy defence against polite anglicisation.

Edition upon edition of *The Gentle Shepherd* came from the press. Edinburgh and London were delighted with those hygienic rustics, Patie and Peggy, who were well scrubbed and well mannered and yet quaint enough to speak Scots. Pope in Twickenham had the Scots tongue explained to him by Dr. Arbuthnot, and was pleased. It was the peak of Ramsay's fame, and he quit writing.

He had also quit wig-making and set up shop as a bookseller, a polite and fashionable trade in which he purveyed the latest writing that came from the south, polite and impolite, as well as those collections in which the northern muse had 'improved' the northern folk-songs. His shop was in the Luckenbooths, a row of buildings beside St. Giles, long since swept away. At the door was the bust of Ben Jonson, flanked by that of Jonson's host at Hawthornden, William Drummond. As well as selling books, Ramsay extended his business by hiring them out for a penny a night, and thus started the first circulating library in the kingdom. Congreve, Wycherley, Dryden, Matthew Prior were there for the curious and the interested who could not afford to buy, but were able to read. The men of Calvin were furious at this display of wickedness. The redoubtable Wodrow wailed that 'all the villainous, profane, and obscene books and plays, as printed at London, are got down by Allan Ramsay and lent out, for an easy price, to young boys, servant women of the better sort, and gentlemen.'

The drunken puritan and pious fornicator, Lord Grange, persuaded the magistrates to inspect the bookshop. But Ramsay had been forewarned, and nothing was found by the visitors but the holiest and most reflective volumes.

The godly were not defeated. In the 1730s Ramsay's interests turned to the theatre – or to the idea of the theatre, for none existed. With impetuous optimism he built one, between the Tron Kirk and John Knox's house, in Carrubber's Close. It was quickly closed because of the pressure of Walpole's Licensing Act and the fury of the godly. One of the documents to oppose the theatre was magnificently entitled: 'The Flight of Religious Piety from Scotland upon the Account of Ramsay's Lewd Books, etc. and the Hell-Bred Play-house Comedians who debauch all the Faculties of the Souls of our Rising Generation.'

The years passed. The man of letters had become the chief adornment of Edinburgh, an easy-going gentleman of affairs, a trifle pompous in a lovable way. His famous paunch grew larger and its owner grew lazier. He built a strange house, known as the 'goose-pie', on the lower slopes of the castle hill, above what is now Princess Street gardens. There he lived with his family of daughters and was happy in his local glory and his national fame, while his son, another Allan, climbed to independent fame as an artist.

Gray Graham wrote: 'He went in and out of his shop, adjourned to tavern suppers, trotted up and down the High Street, with his little squat form, his big paunch, his short legs, his head adorned with fair round wig and cocked hat, surmounting a kindly, smirking, self-complacent face – the best-known and vainest man about town. In 1758, January 8, the little poet ended his prosperous career, at the age of seventy-two' – *Scottish Men of Letters of the Eighteenth Century*.

It is too easy to dismiss Ramsay as a quaint character. His height – he was only five feet four inches – and his temperament made him in some ways a comical figure. It was his foresight, his intelligence and his enthusiasm that made him one of the outstanding persons of his age. His energy, and above all his positive faith in his country, gave him a position that time would enhance. To tabulate his many activities is not enough – he wrote a long poem for the practical purpose of developing North Sea fisheries; he was one of a group responsible for the founding of the Academy of St. Luke, now, after many trasformations, the Royal Academy (forty-one years before the founding of the Royal Academy in London). Ramsay, as well as being a considerable minor poet, was the focal point in the capital of Scotland for a new interest and enthusiasm for the arts and crafts of civilised living. He spent his life encouraging this interest, and he has a supreme place in his country's story.

James Thomson was born after Ramsay and died before him. He sought his fortune in the south and, in Saintsbury's words, was 'the first Scotsman after the Union to contribute matter of very great value to English literature'.

He was a son of the manse, born in 1700 at Ednam, near Kelso. When he was a child his father moved to the parish of Southdean, not very far away on the river Jed, a tributary of the Tweed.

Like Ramsay, Thomson was brought up in the countryside, but it was a different kind of country. When Ramsay came to Edinburgh, he immediately forgot the barren austerity of his Lanarkshire hills. But the Border countryside was the inspiration of Thomson's greatest work.

Southdean (which is pronounced 'Sooden') is in the foothills of the Cheviots. To the south are the great bare curves of the mountains, today better clad in parts through the efforts of the Forestry Commission. Around is an astonishing variety of scenery that makes the lower Tweed valley one of the richest regions of Scotland. From the wildness of a high moor to the pleasures of a formal castle garden is a translation of a few miles. From the summits of the modest sweetly curving hills that surround the Jed and the Rule waters there are superb views – vast landscapes and skyscapes that hold all the awe and beauty of the natural world.

A few miles to the north is the River Tweed, entering its last majestic phase, making the final metamorphosis from a babbling hill-brook to a stately river, with water-lilies in the backwaters and swans on its bosom, all in less than a hundred miles.

Here is variety within variety, ploughed fields, sparse uplands, isolated peaks, heights and depths, wooded canyons, lochs, forests, lush pastures, parkland glades. To this can be added a powerful seasoning of history, of Roman roads and gloomy mediaeval dungeons, of fat-pillared abbeys and thick stubborn castles. There is sufficient permutation of weather and climate and natural features to produce, in a sensitive boy, almost every response of which the mind and emotions are capable.

In Thomson's boyhood, recent history was far enough away to have acquired a gloss of glamour, but not so far as to be beyond the memory of older folk who could remember the Marquis of Montrose's forces being surrounded and slaughtered at Philiphaugh.

It is important to dwell on the physical features and the emotional overtones of the land in which Thomson spent his boyhood. It was this countryside that enchained his mind and emerged in *The Seasons* in his late twenties, when he was living in the south.

> 'For me, when I forget the darling theme,
> Whether the blossom blows, the summer ray
> Russets the plain, inspiring autumn gleams,
> Or winter rises in the blackening east –
> Be my tongue mute, my fancy paint no more
> And, dead to joy, forget my heart to beat.'

This was the man who led English writing away from the manner of the Augustan age, the sophistication of Pope, towards an adjustment of taste that was to end in the romantic revolution.

> Johnson wrote of Thomson: 'He thinks in a peculiar train; and he always thinks as a man of genius; he looks round on nature and on life with the eye which nature only bestows on a poet, the eye that distinguishes in everything presented to its view what-ever there is on which imagination can delight to be detained, and with a mind that at once comprehends the vast and attends to the minute. The reader of *The Seasons* wonders that he never saw before what Thomson shows him, and that he never yet felt what Thomson impresses.'

This was high praise from a man who often pretended disgust with the raw countryside, and who professed special abhorrence of this rawness when it was also Scottish.

Thomson, of course, was anything but a child of nature. He was incapable of uttering a wood-note wild. He was classically educated and trained. He admired and digested the elegance of his contemporary English writers. What he did was to contribute sentiment and imagination to the established literature of the day, and so assist in the living change of writing from one fashion to another.

He was equipped with the normal cultural baggage of the early eighteenth century. His own particular genius made him transform a shattered Border peel-tower into a delicately ruined temple. The Doric-speaking men of the Borders, with whom he grew up, had not then been accepted as the men of the border ballads – kinsmen of Jock o' the Side and Kinmont Willie. To Thomson they were swains, and when he made them speak, it was in the faultless iambics of the King's English.

The romantic attitude to the country had not yet properly dawned. But Thomson was aware of it, without defining it. It infused him, like a warm rough pantheism. In his work there are lavish signs of a passionate adoration behind the formal discipline and control of his classical outlook. It was his genius to express this, so that one can relate his achievements quite validly to the countryside in which he grew up. Without his boyhood at Sooden, Thomson might have written poetry, but he would not have written *The Seasons*.

When Thomson was eighteen his father died suddenly. The minister was of the old school of strait-laced Calvinists, and was also deeply influenced by the superstitions that filled the countryside. He was mysteriously struck down at the house of Wolflee, in the Rule valley of the Borders, where he had been summoned to exorcise demons. Young Thomson by this time had become a student at Edinburgh University, where it was intended that he would qualify for the ministry. His father's death brought his mother to the city, with the rest of the young family. She had been co-heiress of a small estate and realised her inheritance for cash, but this was not enough to bring up her children. James took a post as tutor to the Earl of Haddington.

The job did not last. The years were passing, and Thomson fell foul of the academic authorities. It became necessary for him to 'try his fortune', and, as he did not relish the windy turrets of Auld Reekie, he set his eyes southwards. Edinburgh was far inferior to London in its opportunities and its cultural politenesses. The literati were in the south. Two years before Ramsay opened his circulating library, Thomson took a sailing ship for London.

The first part of *The Seasons* was in his pocket, inspired, as he said, 'by some masterly strokes which awakened me' and which had appeared in a poem written by a Border minister called Riccaltoun. This man had been one of the influences of Thomson's youth. He had lived 'in a poor thatched house – a man of learning, of keen thinking, of culture, and fine poetic tastes, who had on his scanty shelves some classics and English literature.'

Unlike Ramsay and the lesser lights of the first quarter of the century, Thomson seems to have felt no deep roots in his own country. His roots had been in the countryside, which was rather different. But the country, Scotland – its people, its affairs – had little appeal for him. Though he spent nine years in Edinburgh, he succumbed neither to its rather recherché literary zeal nor to the vigorous humanity of the city. London promised more to a young man of talent and courage, especially if he had the goad of poverty to urge him.

He was not without recommendation. Lady Grizell Baillie was a distant relative. A cousin was gardener to the Elliots of Minto, near Sooden. He had an introduction to Duncan Forbes of Culloden, the powerful and kindly Lord Advocate.

Millan the publisher (a Scot called MacMillan who had found it helped in London to drop the Scottish Mac) put out *Winter*, the first part of *The Seasons*. Thomson made an appropriate dedication to the Speaker of the House of Commons, which belatedly won him £20, niggardly but probably sufficient, as it was obtained by a conventional assumption of patronage, a delicate kind of blackmail. In due course *Summer*, *Spring*, and *Autumn* appeared, each with its rococo dedication to great men he had not met, but whose favours he prudently sought. These 'dedications' were a necessary artifice of the age, so that a poet might wring a living from society and advance himself in it.

Success came at once. *The Seasons* was accepted and so was Thomson, who cultivated the great, the powerful, and the wealthy. The poet (who had been a boy near Berwick when Taylor drank brandy with the English troops stationed there as a guard against the Scots) wrote *Rule Britannia*, and the verses set a dainty seal on the Union.

> 'When Britain first at Heaven's command
>   Arose from out the azure main,
> This was the charter of the land,
>   And guardian angels sung the strain:
> Rule Britannia, Brittannia rules the waves!
>   Britons never shall be slaves.'

It was an elegant imperial battle-cry. In the lounges of his literary patrons Thomson could easily forget that some of his fellow Lowland Scots were slaves in the coalfields of the Lothians, and that the miners' children were born into the same servitude.

He became the travelling companion of the eldest son of the Lord Advocate. They visited the courts of Europe and dallied in Italy. When the chancellor died, Thomson met the fate of poets from whom patronage was withdrawn. He fell into debt and, now and then, into prison.

In Wilson's *Poets and Poetry of Scotland*, there is an engaging story. During one of his sojourns as a prisoner, Thomson was visited by the actor Quin, who left his green-room to pay his respects to the poet. This grand old man of the theatre was prompted, it appears, by the most amiable motives. He had heard that the author of *The Seasons* was in confinement because of an unpaid debt of about £70. With a charity unusual between one practitioner of the arts and another he hurried to the prison.

'Sir,' he said to Thomson, 'you don't know me I believe; but my name is Quin.'

This delicious formality was continued by Thomson who replied that, though he was unable to boast of a personal acquaintanceship, he was of course no stranger to the honoured name nor to the talents of its bearer. Then he invited Quin to be seated. Quin announced that he had come to sup, but presumed it would be inconvenient to have supper prepared in the place they were in. 'I have taken the liberty of ordering it to be sent from an adjacent tavern.'

Charity could not have been offered more graciously. They ate and drank leisurely and well, and then Quin mentioned that it was time to discuss business. Thomson, assuming that this was a proposition concerning poetry and the drama, offered his ready assistance. 'Sir,' said Quin, 'you mistake my meaning. Soon after I read your *Seasons* I took it into my head that as I had something in the world to leave behind me when I died, I would make my will; and among the rest of my legatees, I set down the author of *The Seasons* for one hundred pounds; and today, hearing that you were in this place, I thought I might as well have the pleasure of paying the money myself as to order my executors to pay it, when perhaps you might have less need of it. And this, Mr. Thomson, is the business I came about.' Thomson saw his host retreat to a dramatic exit, and on the table before him was a note for a hundred pounds.

Soon he was in more comfortable circumstances. He turned to drama. His *Sophonisba* was presented at Drury Lane before Queen Caroline. It was a great success and Thomson hoped he had launched an immortal drama. He never knew how thoroughly and deservedly the play would be forgotten except for the preposterous line 'O Sophonisba, Sophonisba O!', which the author changed after it had been parodied as 'O Jemmy Thomson, Jemmy Thomson O!'

Out of his political poetry and his classical tragedies he made a great name and an adequate fortune. He knew the value of the appropriate sentiment for undoing the purse-strings of his patrons. He persevered with the cultivation of the correct people and the production of the correct verse. But *The Seasons* remained his masterpiece. He had nothing more to say of any significance. London did not serve him as well, poetically, as the Scottish countryside.

A friend in office obtained for him the post of surveyor-general of the Leeward Islands, with a salary of £300 a year. This appointment did not interfere with his poetic and dramatic labours. The duties abroad were performed by a deputy, and Thomson, happy child of an age of patronage, lived at ease in a small house at Richmond, where he entertained and played the accomplished host and man of letters.

He died two weeks before his forty-eighth birthday, through catching a chill after over-heating himself on a walk from London. In the fulness of time a monument was erected in the Poets' Corner of Westminster Abbey.

Burns, who paid careful tribute to his predecessors, wrote that, while the seasons of the year endured, 'So long, sweet poet of the year, Shall bloom that wreath thou well hast won; While Scotia, with exulting tear, Proclaims that Thomson was her son.'

Saintsbury summed up *The Seasons* by saying that 'for their time, and therefore for history, they were of simply paramount importance, but they have a charm not merely of their time.'

7

LADY WARDLAW AND THE ROMANTICS

ALLAN RAMSAY was an example of the Scot turning to the reservoir of his country's native songs and poems. He was a polite 'improver' with an ingenious fancy of his own, a man of modest but engaging talent. James Thomson was the most important of the Scots of his generation who went south and accepted complete anglicisation. He had unusual ability, and in his major work there were flashes of genius. (At the end of the century Thomas Campbell had a poetic career remarkably similar to James Thomson's.)

Ramsay delved into the past (as 'Ossian' Macpherson, Walter Scott, and James Hogg were to do), and was amongst the first to lay bare the historic material which the romantic writers would use. Ramsay, in his own work, retained a somewhat watered but still distinctly Scottish language. Thomson was the first person of his age to adopt the English speech that all the Scots romantics would use. Neither Ramsay nor Thomson were, themselves, part of the romantic movement which they helped to produce. Its strength came long after they had died.

It is necessary now to make a general digression before returning to the early part of the century. Movements, even literary movements, move from one place to another, as well as from one convention to the next. This may mean no more than that a centre of publishing and literary activity is fertilised by writers arriving from other regions, bringing with them their individual contributions to literary change.

The origin of the romantic movement was in the north. Thomson unconsciously pointed the way. Shortly after the middle of the century, James 'Ossian' Macpherson took a strange collection of supposedly legendary poems of Celtic heroes and offered them in English to an astonished audience in the south, where they were received with delighted enthusiasm by some, and with caustic scorn by others who doubted their authenticity. The effect of the Ossian poems was emphatic and far-reaching. Within a few years they were translated into the major European languages. Walpole, Gray, Coleridge, Byron, Burns, Herder, Schiller, Goethe – to mention a very few – were influenced by this revelation of the Celtic north. France rejected Ossian at first; Voltaire was amused by the misty vapourings and the romantic melancholy of the poems. He remarked with irony that 'Rules of taste in all the arts, from epic poems to gardening, came from Scotland.' The taste of France capitulated when Napoleon carried a translation with him on his campaigns.

Long before these events, at a time when Scotland was still divided very strictly into Scottish and Gaelic portions that were barely civil to each other, General Wade was warning His Majesty about the Highlanders 'whose notions of virtue and vice are very different from the more civilised part of mankind.' At that time, shortly before the end of the first quarter of the century, the romantic course of literature had been set in Scotland, but by the Scots speakers and not the Gaelic speakers. It is worth noting that the general inspiration of romanticism should have arisen as a parallel movement to the founding of modern science on firmly inductive lines of reasoning. It was as though the imagination was developing expansively to be complementary to the objective specialisation of the scientists.

This double capacity of intellect and imagination is one of the features of the age. Amongst the outstanding scientists, such as Joseph Black, James Watt, James Hutton, brilliance of intellect and of creative imagination combined to lift science from the drudgery of classification and nomination to a plane where man began to pierce the reality of the universe and understand that he might control it. Conversely, a feeling for the potency of science was part of the imaginative equipment of many of the men of the arts.

In examining such large movements and developments as were then taking place, it is impossible, as it would be incautious and partisan, to indicate a person and a date and say 'here it began'. But, on the literary side alone, it was for a time fashionable to point to one person and one poem and make a statement of origin. There was a signal point in the new literary romanticism of the eighteenth century.

The transformation of tastes, the rise and fall of cultures, the relation between writers and society, are fascinating studies. Did someone write the first book or poem recognisable as having the authentic imprint of the romantic literature that was to follow? If so, was it important, or merely a 'sport'? Did the author in any way 'influence' his successors? These are academic questions, and there can only be very general answers to them.

It is the individual who matters, and not the movement of which he may form a part. The movement itself is a recognisable literary phenomenon. There would have been a romantic revival without 'Ossian' Macpherson, without Scott, or Coleridge, or Wordsworth, just as there would have been an industrial revolution without James Watt. But it is the persons who remain of prime interest. They were the agents of their thoughts; they saw their world and made their individual comments, influenced a great deal by what is called environment.

In history, in its broadest and most human sense, there can be no doubt that the moment creates the man. But when the moment is past, it is the man and his actions that are of interest. The inter-connection between 'society' and the 'individual' is often very obvious. An individual emerges from society in his maturity, having been moulded by it; in turn, if he is strong enough (an original philosopher, a political leader, a poet), he influences it. If he is not an individualist, he fulfils a role during his lifetime within the pattern of his society, which provides him with an occupation such as a banker, a baker, or an atom-bomb maker. But whatever the role of the individual, whether he is a free man or a slave, there is the concept of a 'continuum' in which both society and the individual are seen, during the course of time, as aspects of one continuous process. (The idea of the 'continuum' is ably developed by the Communist critic, Christopher Caudwell. As the argument stems from Marxism, it deserves a place in a chapter on romantics.)

Environment (which society provides for the individual), literary fashions, the march of science, political changes, form only a background to men and women. It is they, behaving as individuals and not as purveyors of a tradition nor as actors in a movement, who make their achievements, and it is they who may, by chance, give a new direction or turn to subsequent events. In current jargon they 'press the trigger', and nothing afterwards is quite the same as it was before. So there emerges in this story the wife of a Fife baronet, Lady Elizabeth Wardlaw.

A poem of 216 lines called *Hardyknute, a Fragment*, appeared in Edinburgh in 1719. It was printed on folio sheets in antique spelling, and appeared to be a piece of old Scottish poetry. It came from the press of the indefatigable James Watson. It was, of course, anonymous. It was accepted as a genuine discovery by those of literary taste.

As the country had no parliament, the highest authority was vested in those who administered the law. By the Treaty of Union, the Scots had retained their own judicature and system of legal administration, as well as their own laws. It was around legal circles that men of taste gathered. They were arbiters of correctness in all walks of life.

(This, to a large extent, explains the role of importance played in the eighteenth century by Scottish judges and advocates. No royal court, no parliament, nor any other natural lay centre of authoritative opinion existed. This role of importance, though nowadays very greatly diminished, can still be observed in Edinburgh, where the man of law plays a societal role greater than in other cities and countries.)

Hardyknute was 'accepted' by Duncan Forbes of Culloden, active a few years before in quelling the rebellion of 1715. He afterwards became Lord Advocate and then Lord President of the Court of Session. One of the Elliots of Minto, Gilbert, later Lord Justice Clerk, also 'accepted' the poem. William Thomson, the musician, believed he had heard part of the ballad when he was a child. There was no real mystery about the appearance of the poem, and the men of law had every reason to believe the story of Sir John Hope Bruce of Kinross that he had found the original manuscript in a Dunfermline vault. Bruce was a soldier, and therefore a man of honour. (He lived till 1766 and died with the rank of Lieutenant-General, unaware that the origin of *Hardyknute* was about to become a matter of public controversy.)

The 216 lines formed an extraordinary ballad. Years later, after the authorship of *Hardyknute* had been established, the ballad exerted a powerful influence on young Walter Scott. When he was a child, sent to the Borders from Edinburgh because of his sickly health, he learned the ballad by heart through hearing it spoken, before he was able to read or write. 'It was the first I ever learnt, and the last I shall ever forget.'

How far *Hardyknute* influenced the malleable mind of the child Scott, in turn to influence European writing, makes one of those absurdly fascinating questions to which there is no final answer.

It began thus:

> 'Stately stept he east the wa',
>   And stately stept he west,
> Full seventy years he now had seen,
>   With scarce seven years of rest,
> He lived when Britons' breach of faith
>   Wrocht Scotland mickle wae;
> And aye his sword tauld to their cost,
>   He was their deadly fae.'

It is not a brilliant ballad, indeed it is not ordinarily good, but it is very powerful, with strange explosive drama. Its importance, if it has any besides that of a literary curiosity, is in its being the first deliberately created ballad, a consciously literary work in a romantic mood.

Hardyknute was reprinted by Allan Ramsay in the 1724 edition of *Evergreen*, the collection that professed to contain Scots poems written before 1600. In the usual manner of the day, the ballad had been amended and 'improved' since its first appearance in 1719. In 1740 *Hardyknute* appeared in London, and the anonymous editor of this edition wrote of 'a grandeur, a majesty of sentiment diffused through the whole, a true sublime which nothing can surpass' – an enthusiasm of abstracts which it would also be difficult to surpass.

Percy included the poem in his *Reliques* in 1765, and it was through this appearance that the poem became well-known and popular. By 1767, after competent critics had constantly accepted for *Hardyknute* the authenticity claimed for it, some doubts were cast by the astute Percy in the second edition of his *Reliques*. These doubts did not arise from the quality of the poem itself (as they might well have done), but from a story that had drifted down the years and had, as it were, come home to roost.

It was said that the ballad *Hardyknute* had been written by a Scottish lady who had died as recently as 1727. Percy learned of this story from Sir David

Dalrymple (Lord Hailes of the Scottish Courts). The law, in its dabbling with literature, had given the poem; now the law was taking it away. The authoress was Elizabeth Halket. She had been born in 1677 to the wife of a Fife baronet. At the age of nineteen she had married another Fifeshire baronet, Sir Henry Wardlaw of Pitreavie.

The reason for her anonymity as a ballad-maker, carefully maintained throughout her life, can only be conjectured. That she may have gone to the extent of deceiving the honest soldier, Sir John Bruce, who was her brother-in-law, is itself interesting. Had *Hardyknute* been brought to Edinburgh as the composition of a middle-aged woman in Fife, there is little doubt it would have been rejected out of hand, and no attention would have been paid to it. In a time of changing values age was one certain criterion, and, though it was not always applied with laboratory exactness, there was no profound deception in publishing *Hardyknute* as an old ballad. The men of law valued antiquity, not novelty. They would have abhorred a feminine novelty in the world of letters. Elizabeth Wardlaw was very astute.

The whole question of so-called 'frauds' in literature is fascinating, and it is interesting to speculate on this talented Fife woman forced by circumstances to be anonymous if her efforts at authorship were to receive attention. The ingenious mind that contrived this romantic composition, quite away from the polite Addisonian tastes of the day, may also have delighted in a deliberate mystery.

She can now be credited with being the first of the romantic school of writers, the first to write deliberately in the manner which later came to be known as romantic – the combination of emotional vividness with an overtone of tragedy, the peculiar blending of reality and fantasy and sentiment. Though *Hardyknute* is not important as literature, its force and drama are undeniable.

Who was Elizabeth Halket or Wardlaw? She can be seen, to all outward appearances, as a typical laird's wife, with friends and acquaintances both above and below her station, a person somewhat static and circumscribed in her way of life, yet able, through friends, to exert a little influence, to command if need be polite attention in the legal hierarchy of Edinburgh.

If Elizabeth Halket's upbringing was typical of her day and age, then her circumstances would have been comfortable enough, though not luxurious. A laird's house would be stone-built, though perhaps with little refinement.

A girl would be taught to read and write, but would be unlikely to receive any extension of these basic accomplishments. Latin was for boys. Greek was the province of the universities, who guarded the teaching of it jealously.

If Elizabeth had received private instruction in the classics some hint of this might have emerged in her writing. In all probability she would be trained in womanly accomplishments – sewing, knitting, spinning, and weaving – with perhaps a lady-like acquaintance with music.

But it has been discovered, and quite recently, that in some respects her up-bringing was not typical of the period. She may have had access to a considerable library. Certainly she was in a book-collecting family.

Sir Charles Halket, Elizabeth's father, and Sir John Halket (his relationship to Charles is not clear), both apparently of Pitferran, amassed a considerable collection of books and papers which had been the property of John Wedderburn, the Scot who had become personal doctor to Charles II. These books may have been bought or inherited. At any rate the books appear to have remained in the family. Sir Charles, father of Elizabeth (and of Charlotte who married Sir John Bruce) had been born a Wedderburn. He had renounced the name on marrying the heiress of Pitferran. He had a baronetcy in his own right and transmitted this to a lineal male descendant.

Elizabeth can be seen growing up in a family of considerable liveliness, with very strong royalist connections. Part of the Halket-Wedderburn library consisted of material presented to John Wedderburn by Colbert, and may have derived from Mazarin.

Though this throws no light on the content of *Hardyknute* itself, it gives Elizabeth a background in which her native imagination and talent would not wither. But still, outwith her civilised family, she might well choose to hide her literary gift. A literary woman would not always be well received in a provincial country society in that century.

Whatever the reason for secrecy, and for that matter for deceit, Elizabeth Wardlaw allowed the manuscript to be 'discovered' and furnished with sufficient credentials to impress persons of taste in Edinburgh and persuade them to accept its antiquity as authentic. (The situation can be compared with the acceptance of *Ossian* some time later in the same city.)

Elizabeth Wardlaw must have taken someone into her confidence, or the story of her authorship would never have emerged. But that she wrote *Hardyknute*, the first composition of the romantic revival, is now beyond doubt.

After her authorship had been established, a school of critics arose who tried to make her responsible for many of the better-known ballads, such as *Sir Patrick Spens, Gilderoy, Edom o' Gordon*. Robert Chambers, one of the two brothers who founded *Chamber's Journal*, was a leader in this misguided attempt to provide an origin for the genuine balls of anonymity.

8

GLASGOW, LONDON, AND SHERIFFMUIR

Growth of Glasgow.   Beginning of trade.   Ponies to Port
Glasgow.   A beautiful town.   The debate in the House
of Lords against the Union.   Queen Anne's dead.   A
thousand pounds reward.   Bobbing John.   The rebellion of '15.   The Old Pretender arrives – and departs.
The Spaniards invade Ross-shire.   The last witch.

THE METROPOLIS OF GLASGOW was once a town of devout quietness.
In 1600 it was the eleventh city of Scotland with a modest population of 5,000.
By 1700 it had about 12,000 people, and ranked the second city of the country.
This advance in status came about during the century of Cromwell and
Calvinism, and was due to a small development of simple manufactures and
trades, especially the weaving of linen and wool. The town remained a place of
almost rural peace.

Glasgow has been called the oldest town in Scotland. The cathedral was
founded in 1136, the university in 1451. Its mediaeval builders sited it well up
the Clyde, and in times to come this gave a great deal of trouble because it
impeded the development of an ocean-going trade.

The ancient monks built their cathedral, the old nub of the city, near the
Stockwell shallows. There was a ford across the river for people travelling
between north and south, and it was far enough distant from the deep water of
the Clyde to be out of range of Norse maurauders. In 1245 a stone bridge was
built across the river on eight piers. It was a lovely bridge of beautiful
proportions. The piers supported a roadway that spanned the river in one long
lithe arch. The Stockwell bridge carried traffic until the nineteenth century,
when the practical men of the industrial revolution considered it was no longer
sufficient for their needs. Neither the beauty nor the history of the bridge could
win a reprieve. It was demolished in 1847, and the masons who did the job said
it was as sound as when it had been built. By that time, rural Glasgow was a
thing of the past.

At the beginning of the eighteenth century, Glasgow lived around its
university and occupied itself with small scale manufacturing and trading. It
lived sparsely, physically and mentally. One of the staple foods was salmon.

The fish was so abundant that it was considered a coarse and inelegant food.

In the university the doctrines of Calvinism were taught by James Wodrow, the professor of divinity and father of the author of the *Analecta*. The new attitude to learning, which was already altering the teaching of medicine and mathematics in Edinburgh, had not reached Glasgow. There was little traffic between the cities, and they had then little influence on each other. The *forte* of Glasgow's university was its teaching of theology. To the town there travelled intending ministers from Scotland and Presbyterian Ulster.

There seemed no reason why Glasgow should expect rapid development and growth. It was not near enough to the sea (owing to the caution of the early monks) to become a large trading port, nor was there any reason to consider expansion in this way. The trade of the country was conducted by east coast ports sending ships to the Continent. Leith, Kirkcaldy, Montrose, and ports to the north – all on the German Ocean – sent their vessels to the Baltic, the Low Countries, France, and further south. Glasgow's simple needs were served by the small fishing ports on the Clyde, one of which was known as Port Glasgow, and whatever came to the town by sea or was taken away from it had to be carried along the banks of the Clyde to Port Glasgow on ponies and pack-horses.

It was the union with England that opened the way for Glasgow's rise to vast prosperity. The articles that were debated in Parliament Hall at Edinburgh included the English laws that prevented the Scots trading westwards with the Indies and the Americas. The Union opened up trade to the Scots, and repealed the enactment that only English 'bottoms' should trade with English colonies.

On the signing of the treaty, it took some time for the merchants and traders of this quiet town to see their opportunity. Between them they did not possess an ocean-going vessel. After some years a few Glasgow citizens chartered their first ship to make the journey across the Atlantic. They had to go south to find it, at Whitehaven in Cumberland. It made the journey to America with a cargo of merchandise and came back with sugar and tobacco, the commodities that were to build a new Glasgow out of the wealth they created.

By 1718 a merchant owned his own vessel for the Atlantic trade. By 1735 there were fifteen ocean-going ships owned by Glaswegians.

'The method in which the early transactions of these trading ventures were conducted was a model of simplicity and self-protecting caution. The prudent shopkeepers (who chartered the ship) bargained with those who supplied the manufactures for sale, that they should not be paid till the vessels returned with their cargoes to Port Glasgow. By this ingenious arrangement, with which weavers and fish-curers were obliged to comply, they who furnished the goods ran most of the risk, while the astute traders got most of the profits, and paced the Trongate with easy minds till the ships they did not own, and the cargoes for which others had paid, returned safely home.' – Gray Graham, *Social Life of Scotland in the Eighteenth Century*.

The Glasgow shop-keepers had profited from their reading of the *Spiritual-Merchant*, in which God was a wholesale-warehouse keeper.

During the greater part of the eighteenth century, when the town expanded from its eight streets into a young metropolis, Glasgow retained much of its ancient attraction and charm. Defoe thought it was 'one of the cleanest, most beautiful, and best built cities in Great Britain.' Smollett (who was a west of Scotland man) found it agreeably pleasant. Edward Burt, writing in the 1720s, said that 'Glasgow is, to outward appearances, the prettiest and most uniform town that I ever saw; and I believe there is nothing like it in Britain.'

Until the city became very busy, after the middle of the century, its citizens continued their regular and methodical life of early rising and frugal living. At six in the morning a gun was fired to announce the arrival of the post from Edinburgh (the mail came on horseback, as there was at that time no wheeled traffic between the two towns). Letters were collected from the postmaster – orders and invoices to the merchants, communications to the professors of the university. Breakfast followed, a meal of porridge, herring, and ale. Shops were open until eleven-thirty in the morning when, as in Edinburgh, the city bells rang out and the men of business left their premises to have a drink – the 'meridian' – in the nearest tavern. Beef, soup, and boiled fowl, again with ale, made the midday meal. In the afternoon shops reopened, and did not shut till eight o'clock, when the key was turned for the day and the shopkeeper had another drink with his friends, discussed the arrival of a ship at Port Glasgow, talked about buying and selling, and was home by nine o'clock to his supper, his prayers, and his bed. In comparison with Edinburgh, Glasgow was a dull backwater. Its burgesses were solemn, modest, and not very ambitious, mostly men of small affairs content with their small world. But there were a few who looked westwards with vision, enterprise, and even greed.

The early trade of Glasgow was long in developing, and much longer in producing the wealth that created the Tobacco Lords, those fantastic men of riches who (after mid-century and before the American War of Independence) handled the bulk of the British tobacco trade, dressed themselves in red cloaks, and walked the cobbled streets of Glasgow with the arrogance of feudal barons.

In the first year after the Union, Glasgow's lethargic dullness was shared by the rest of Scotland. The failure of the country to respond promptly to the tonic of the Union caused great concern and distress. There was famine in 1709. Trade was at a standstill. The sacrifices that had been made to achieve one parliament in London had brought none of the promised relief. There was throughout the country a great deal of support for the house of Stuart, and a greater amount of sympathy that might be stirred to action.

In the House of Lords the representative Scottish peers were nervously uncertain about the Union. In 1713 there was a debate on a motion that the Union should be dissolved, as it had failed to secure its objects. When the House divided, there were equal numbers – fifty-four peers – for and against. The unity of Britain appeared to tremble for a moment, but there had to be taken into account the proxy votes of absent peers. When this was done, the motion was defeated by a majority of four. The man who moved the motion was none other than Seafield who, as Scottish Chancellor, had pronounced his enigmatic requiem eight years before – 'That's the end of an auld sang.'

The status of Scotland and who was to be successor to the British throne were the topics of the day, but before the argument had an opportunity of developing, the occupant of the throne suddenly died. It was a startling moment. The death of dull Anna Augusta increased to even greater pace the whirling convolutions of intrigue.

Who was to be king – James Stuart, the grandson of Charles I, or George of Hanover, the grandson of the sister of Charles I?

Some years later Hume wrote that an 'impartial patriot' might have been puzzled to decide whether Anne should be succeeded by Stuart or Hanoverian. The Stuart cause might be favoured because of a 'succession clear and undisputed'; a Hanoverian succession could claim to end hereditary rights and establish a more responsible relationship between king and people, as well as safeguarding the reformed religion. As every minister in his Geneva gown knew to his bitter horror, the Stuarts in exile were contaminated by the red popery of the Catholic Church.

George of Hanover did not await the decisions of his potential subjects. He took ship from the continent and arrived at Greenwich, was proclaimed king, and prudently made the offer of a thousand pounds for the Stuart Pretender, should that person be captured in any part of Britain.

In London there were rumours of Jacobite readiness to strike at the British throne. James Stuart, the Pretender, the Chevallier, the papist, the dead Queen's only brother, was preparing to take his crown by force. George sent his troops to the areas of danger. It was an uneasy time, but early in 1715 the parliamentary elections seemed to favour the House of Hanover. Scottish Whigs filled the Commons, and in the Lords every Scottish representative peer was chosen from the list prepared by the king's advisers. The king had packed his parliament.

But the Jacobites were not expected to accept defeat. Their 'vanity, insolence, arrogance, and madness' were duly reported to Forbes of Culloden.

John Byrom celebrated the competition for kingship:

> 'God bless the King – I mean the faith's defender!
> God bless (no harm in blessing!) the Pretender!
> But who pretender is, or who is king –
> God bless us all! – that's quite another thing.'

George's promptitude in coming to Britain was accompanied by an act of important decision. At Greenwich, before he was properly in the country, he refused to accept the oath of allegiance from the Earl of Mar, who was Secretary of State for Scotland. The Earl was divested of office. George may have been well advised to get rid of a doubtful man, for Mar had the reputation of being a timid opportunist and a weak patriot, and was quite liable to play Box and Cox with Hanoverians and Stuarts. He had been given the name of Bobbing John.

Like Hamilton at the time of the Union, Mar was one of those equivocal Scots to whom history has frequently given high office and then seen that office misused. Mar had been an advocate of the Union. More recently he had supported the motion of Seafield (now styled Lord Findlater) for the repeal of the Union. Many other Scottish nobles had behaved in the same way, disappointed either patriotically or in a more personal way about the outcome of the Union.

But Mar was persistently lukewarm in an age that liked its men to be hot or cold, or either in succession, but not both at the same time. As Queen Anne's Secretary for Scotland, he had been responsible for distributing money from the royal exchequer to some Highland chiefs. This was straightforward bribery, to sway the men to the Hanoverian cause. But the majority of the chiefs were avowed Jacobites. However, the greatest of all was Argyll, and he was indubitably a Hanoverian. He was the most powerful princeling in Scotland, and of great influence in the south. He accused Mar of using the money to foment a Jacobite rebellion.

If Mar had been playing a double game, he now knew where his interests lay. Since George spurned his loyalty, Mar withdrew the offer of it, and looked to his other master. The Pretender sent word from the continent that Mar was to start the rebellion. He went north to his own country and raised the standard of the Stuarts on his own land, the historic Braes of Mar.

The Jacobites rallied to the standard, and the Hanoverians mustered their troops under Argyll. Bobbing John was a bad soldier. A short blundering campaign led the armies of the two royal dynasties to the field of Sheriffmuir near Stirling. There were Highlanders on both sides. Argyll (the renowned MacCallummore) was the leader of the Hanoverian army and his clansmen were with him. When the armies were drawn up for battle one November day, the chief of the right wing of the Jacobite army is reported to have declaimed: 'Yonder stands MacCallummore for King George – here stands MacLean for King James: God bless MacLean and King James! Charge, gentlemen!' Such a battlefield declamation deserves to be true.

The gentlemen of the two kings charged and provided a curious spectacle. The country was undulating, and neither army could see the full field of battle. The right wing of each was victorious. The left wing of each was defeated. The field of battle revolved anti-clockwise. This comedy of arms was put to verse:

> 'There's some say that we wan,
> Some say that they wan,
> Some say that nane wan at a', man:
> But one thing I'm sure,
> That at Sheriffmuir,
> A battle there was, which I saw, man.'

An account written in Stirling, three days after the battle, said that 'Providence has so ordered that no flesh should boast. On the field near Dublain our right wing beat their left and their right wing beat our left.'

At the time, neither side knew the extent of its own triumph and disaster. The position was equivocal, and Mar was too faint-hearted to snatch triumph, as he might have done, from partial defeat. He retreated towards Perth, and so conceded complete victory to MacCallummore.

There was now little difficulty in containing the rebels in the north. In December the Pretender arrived himself. James Stuart set up court at Scone, and his feeble appearance and listless manner did little to fire the Highlanders with new enthusiasm. Under an inspiring personal leadership they might have followed James to the south. With Stuart optimism, James arranged to be crowned on the 23rd January 1716, but Argyll did not permit this coronation to take place. His troops constantly harried the Jacobites. James had little staying power. At the beginning of February, James, the man who came to be king, left the port of Montrose, a fugitive from Scotland and a deserter from his own army. Mar went with him. A letter written on 8th Feburary described the departure. 'The Pretender is now ship'd for France. Mar his friend is along and my Lord Penmuir with the atendants and French officers came over with him ... he gave his army the slipe and his friends are left to shift for themselves.'

Argyll, whose resolution had been so much responsible for the failure of the revolt, returned to London to be acclaimed by George, but for a time he lost favour by pleading for mercy towards the Jacobite prisoners.

There were other men of power interested in removing George from his throne, and this brought about the last invasion of Scotland (to date) by foreign troops.

Charles XII of Sweden formed a confederacy with Count Alberoni, the Spanish Prime Minister, to restore the Stuarts as kings of Britain. Though Charles died in 1718, before much was accomplished, Alberoni mounted a powerful invasion fleet which sailed for Scotland. Had it arrived, George might in turn have been a fugitive. But the fleet was scattered by a storm in the Bay of Biscay, and most of the ships were destroyed. Two vessels reached Scotland with around two hundred Spanish soldiers. They landed in the far north-west, and Highlanders increased the force to about a thousand. There were plans to march to Inverness and there raise the country in rebellion, but there was also delay and indecision. By the time the Jacobites were halfway to Inverness, they were met at Glenshiel by an equal force of Hanoverians under General Wightman, who had marched out of Inverness. There was a small engagement of troops, and the Spaniards were captured and the Highlanders dispersed. The plans of Sweden and of Spain crumbled to nothing at a skirmish whose name is hardly remembered.

That was in 1719, and for the time being it was the end of the Jacobite dream. While these matters of royal moment were being decided, Edinburgh was changing its drinking habits and, to some extent, its way of life. Tea, not yet inexpensive, was becoming a fashionable drink with ladies. The church was moderating its vehemence, though the zealous, gathered in pockets of power throughout the country, still administered their harsh and holy justice.

In 1720 Bonnie Prince Charlie was born. His father, James Stuart, was never to set foot again in Britain. In that year David Hume was at school in the Borders, and suffering the inhumanity of the Scottish Sabbath when pregnant lasses, who lacked husbands, were solemnly censured before the congregation as 'lewd fornicators'. Pitcairn had been dead for some time, but the school of medicine was growing under the new professor of anatomy and his colleagues. William Smellie, a doctor from Lanark, was a young man about to set out for London to become the leading obstetrician in the country. William Cullen, due to found the Glasgow school of medicine, was a lad of ten. James Syme, 'the Napoleon of surgery', was twenty-one. Lind, the naval surgeon, was a toddler of four. In 1720 Allan Ramsay was gathering more songs and dreaming of his Gentle Shepherd. His son, to become court painter to George III, was a youngster of seven. Dr. Arbuthnot, the first St. Andrews medical graduate, was in the thick of London's literary life – the Augustan age that Scotland never knew.

In 1720 it was sixteen years before the birth of James Watt, three years before the birth of Adam Smith, two before that of 'Jupiter' Carlyle, the garrulous, gregarious, and slightly snobbish clergyman who was to chronicle much of the century, and only one before the birth of Tobias Smollett in Dumbartonshire.

In 1720 a woman, Janet Horne, led a quiet decent life in the north of Scotland. In 1727 she achieved her place in history by being burned in a barrel of tar, the last Scottish witch to be legally despatched from the mortal Presbyterian world.

9

A TIME OF CHANGE

IN THE 1720s AND '30s, SCOTLAND EMERGED from its years of
dereliction and cruel piety. It was a time of change, of the continued struggle to
improve the life of town and country. The problem of the Jacobite Highlands
was not solved, and awaited the drastic treatment of Culloden. The debased life
of serfs in collieries and salt-pans was not made any easier. Wages were low;
there was unemployment and famine.

In the more privileged sections of society, the surface of life began to show a
glitter and polish. The warm winds of Augustan England blew northwards to
aerate the mustiness of Edinburgh and Glasgow, and help to liberate the Scot
from the shackles of his theology. To Edinburgh there came music and the
dance, as a public instead of a private enjoyment. To Glasgow's academy of
learning there came the teaching of a tolerant philosophy. To the Highlands –
less tractable to early Georgian influences – there came relays of redcoat
battalions.

In the tavern of the Crosskeys in Edinburgh there was music from the violin
of the host, Patrick Steel (who ran the hostelry and also made the violins). In
this howff, off the Canongate, Steel was joined by Forbes of Newhall who
played the viola da gamba, by Lord Colville on the harpsichord, and Sir Gilbert
Elliot of Minto on the instrument he had introduced to Scotland, the German
flute. A polite company met in the afternoon to listen to 'the best Italian
sonatas'. 'Artistic noblemen and lairds who had travelled the melodious south
brought the pieces which they (aided by professional musicians) performed to
an enthusiastic throng of beauties, who went into raptures as my Lords Colville
and Haddington sat down to the harpsichord or the cello,' wrote Gray Graham.

A short way up the High Street, near John Knox's House, an Italian lady,
Signora Violante, gave exhibitions of dancing and tumbling on week-days, and
doubtless concerned herself with the souls of the Presbyterian heretics on the
Sabbath.

Dancing, both in classes and at gatherings, was cautious and modest,

though the church censured it as vicious sensuality. As early as 1710 there had
been public balls, and even in Glasgow there had still earlier been a dancing
master. As the years passed, the fashionable assemblies in Edinburgh attracted
more and more of the aristoctacy and gentry, who were beginning to make a
winter season in the capital. Minuets were danced in 'maiden sets', 'married
sets', and 'beauty sets', which may have been modest but must have been
invidious. Men whose family names had resounded in their country's history,
the Dukes of Hamilton, of Douglas, Lord Annandale, Lord Dundonald, trod
their measures to the sound of the virginal. Silk hose and powdered wig set to
crinoline and beauty patch. London was far off. Travel was nerve-racking and
lengthy. It was more convenient, and infinitely cheaper, to create one's
amusements in Edinburgh.

By 1737 young men intended for the ministry were permitted to acquire the
art of dancing. 'Jupiter' Carlyle was allowed to take lessons (which he eagerly
sought) when his father had persuaded himself, from reading the *Spectator*,
that 'dancing would make me a more accomplished preacher'. Carlyle attended
Signora Violante's academy. 'I became a favourite of this dancing-mistress,
and attended her very faithfully with two or three of my companions, and had
my choice of partners on all occasions, insomuch that I became a great
proficient in this branch at little or no expense.' (Alexander Carlyle was the
minister-diarist of Inveresk, near Edinburgh. He was known as 'Jupiter'
because of his imposing and handsome bearing, and he should not be confused
with Thomas Carlyle of Ecclefechan, known as the Sage of Chelsea. 'Jupiter'
Carlyle was a very partial diarist: he recorded polite society and ignored
everything else.)

New diversions spread through society from the upper classes downwards.
Meanwhile, Allan Ramsay was pillaging the folk-song and balladry that was
truly vulgar – of the people – to turn it into a daintier thing for more refined
taste. In Edinburgh there emerged an altered set of values, of manners, and
appreciations.

Much of this was possible because the Old Pretender was sulking across the
sea. There was a breathing space for civilities to flourish. Jacobitism, the
forbidden loyalty, was too popular to be denied, and its social glamour was
enhanced when its political threat was dulled. It gave a romantic leaven to
daily life, and it was spiced with danger. In addition the Jacobite, Episcopal,
and Tory families had in general been more cultured than Presbyterian and
Whiggish families.

For the first time in centuries – during the 1720s and '30s – Scotland was not
faced with a king coming to claim his own, or an English army coming to claim
Scotland. There was peace, and the expansiveness that came with it. People
were still aware of the dismal jeremiads of Wodrow and his sour colleagues, but
they cared less about it. Men might be 'guilty lumps': they were learning to be
merry ones.

This was more a superficial change than a change of nature. In much earlier
times the city Scot had been a merry fellow. In the years of the most repressive

Calvinism, and in the gloom that surrounded the Union, there had remained a vivid undercurrent of hearty living. It was this independent hedonism – both devil-may-care and maturely responsible – that Pitcairn had advocated by his example.

The modification of public behaviour in the city was encouraged by the travelled aristocracy. But that alone would not have been enough to sanction the change. There was also a shift in the stern teaching of the church. A moderate party was arising, whose God was benevolent rather than malevolent. The civilising theology came from Glasgow. The moderates gained in power and social authority because they expressed the more expansive feeling of the bulk of the people. This happened to the horror of the continuing fanatics, especially the Marrowmen.

Thomas Boston, the minister of Ettrick, author of the *Fourfold Estate*, was one who believed that 'we putrify in Adam as our root'. He came upon a copy of a forgotten publication, the *Marrow of Modern Divinity*, originally written about 1644 by Edward Fisher, who was said to have been a barber in London before becoming an independent minister. The *Marrow* was republished in 1718, and a number of Scottish clergy subscribed to its teaching.

The Marrowmen were 'believers'; they said that a believer could not commit sin, and in any case the Lord would pardon him. This useful paradox was summed up by John McKerrow: 'A believer hath no cause either to confess his sins, or to crave pardon at the hand of God for them, either to fast or mourn, or humble himself before the Lord for them.' Though the Marrowmen believed their teaching was 'a bundle of sweet and pleasant gospel truths', the assembly of the Church of Scotland sniffed the heresy of antinomianism. Long, tedious arguments followed, uncomplimentary to the intelligence of both parties.

In points of meticulous dogma the Marrowmen excelled even their forebears. They believed, for example, that Adam achieved salvation by accepting Christ at precisely three o'clock in the afternoon. The general assembly of the church, under the influence of the moderates – and possibly realising the difficulty of establishing the exact time in the Garden of Eden with neither mechanical clock nor sun-dial – declared the teaching of the Marrowmen to be unsound and dangerous. In this way a break was made with the remorseless doctrine of 'the elect'.

While the church was conducting such intellectual exercises, the social graces continued to be cultivated. In 1720 Adam Petrie published his *Rules of Good Deportment* to teach his readers how to polish their manners. 'A gentleman ought not to run or walk too fast in the streets, lest he be suspected to be going on a message.' 'Do not smell at what you eat or drink, and it is most rude to do it to what another eats or drinks.'

The result in Edinburgh of new influences on old traditions was very simple. It helped to create the eighteenth century middle classes. The merchants grew in wealth and social importance as they took part in increasing trade and enjoyed their new freedoms. Their daughters acquired fashionable accomplishments. Their sons were more liberally educated and entered the professions. Their wives took tea in cosy groups. It was possible to be religious without being puritanical, to be joyful without being licentious.

Through the complexity of human nature there emerged a partly genteel, partly robust society, educated, civilised, appreciative rather than creative, but with many vigorous traits and personalities. There was still a resident aristocracy exerting its cultural influence (a function it has since discarded). Social life became quite rich and confident in the tightly packed city, where everyone of note knew everyone else, where a loquacious caddy was on terms of friendliness, and even of friendship, with a justice of the bench.

The rise of the genuine middle classes opened this varied society to all the smug faults of excessive gentility. This was staved off for a hundred years, by which time the aristocracy had vanished from Edinburgh, the lower classes had become proletarianised, and the Industrial Revolution provided the opportunity for the middle classes to become dull dogs of commerce.

In 1741 David Hume commented on what would now be called the 'class structure' of Scotland. 'There are only two ranks of men among us; gentlemen who have some fortune and education, and the meanest slaving poor; without any considerable number of that middling rank of men, which abound more in England, both in cities and in the country, than in any other part of the world.' This was true for Scotland as a whole, but certainly not for Edinburgh and Glasgow. In his comparison Hume minimised the importance of the rising middle class in the capital city, seeing it as an appendage to the city-dwelling gentry with which it shared much of its social and intellectual pleasures and outlook. He did not realise that the tail would soon wag the dog.

In the '20s and '30s the new influences were at work in other ways. Thomas Ruddiman, who had been brought to Edinburgh as a young man by Pitcairn, was for many years in charge of the Advocates' Library (the origin of the present National Library of Scotland). He was an assiduous scholar and grammarian, not without wit. His famous grammar, a text-book for a hundred and fifty years, was impishly called *Latin Rudiments*. He bought books, sold them, ran a newspaper, set up a printing press, wrote treatises and pamphlets, and worked constantly behind the scenes during the early growth of letters, philosophy, and science. When in the 1750s – an old man going blind – he demitted office as librarian, he was succeeded by David Hume. Ruddiman's life and work was a bridge between the outlook of the seventeenth century and the period of Edinburgh's greatest achievements.

Allan Ramsay's cronies were part of the changing scene, eager to taste their own more or less polite literature, but also redolent of the older and more forthright way of life. There was Sir John Clerk of Penicuik (whose descendant was to decorate the walls of his mansion, a few miles from Edinburgh, with huge murals depicting scenes from Ossianic legend). There was old Dr. Alexander Pennicuik, with a Restoration licence in his conversation and a rapscallion nephew who wrote an amusing history of Peeblesshire and consorted with gypsies. There was Forbes of Newhall, the musician of the viola da gamba in the Crosskeys. These men were lairds, or gentry, as was their companion William Aikman, who painted their congenial portraits and was the artist of the well-known picture of Ramsay in his stocking cap.

There were others, less noted for their manner of life than for their manners. There were the imitative beaus. John Law, who went to France and became disastrously involved as a financier, was known in his youth as Jessamy John because of his love of oil of jessamine. Another gentleman, who wrote a book called *The Polite Philosophere*, used to display himself on his balcony in the High Street. He was powdered by his valet while he showed himself in a chintz negligé to the passers-by.

The old world of four-bottle men, making robust jokes in Latin or Scots as they drank in their taverns, became blended with the new world of tea-making and party manners. There was a growing devotion to letters, and a number of minor writers made their brief gestures to fame.

Willy Hamilton of Bangour, a laird's son, attended the dancing assemblies and occupied himself with a succession of rather faint-hearted love affairs. In 1724 he wrote the song *The Braes o' Yarrow*, a piece of fashionable melancholy that won immediate renown.

'Wash, oh, wash his wounds in tears,
　　His wounds in tears o' dule and sorrow
And wrap his limbs in mourning weids,
　　And lay him in the banks of Yarrow.

Busk ye, busk ye, my bonnie, bonnie bride!
　　Busk ye, busk ye, my winsome marrow!
Busk ye, busk ye, my bonnie, bonnie bride,
　　And think nae mair of the braes of Yarrow.'

This song, and many others that were more mortal, suited the mood of the times when romantic elegance, tinged with pathos, was a polite escape from the home-spun life of a city made even homelier by a Britain at peace with itself. In this type of song, of which the century was to produce an abundance of excellent examples, it is possible to discern both a melancholy preoccupation with death and dissolution (which is essentially religious and comes out of Calvinism), and a softer pathos that is Jacobite and feminine.

Willy Hamilton wrote tolerably well in English – an accomplishment that appears to have been neglected since the days of Drummond of Hawthornden and Thomas Urquhart. Hamilton was credited with being the first Scotsman of his century to write poetry in good English, a distinction rather different from writing good poetry in English. (James Thomson, writing better poetry than Hamilton, and in better English, had not then made his reputation, and in any case appears to have forfeited his Scottishness in the eyes of his countrymen when he went to London).

Willy Hamilton bestowed his English verses on a succession of young ladies whom he courted in public at dances and assemblies. His rhymes praised their charms – their lips, their faces, their shapes, and that most singular attribute, their 'snowy breast'. Like many of his age he deplored the increasing 'tea-faced generation', and he used to disappear into the deeper howffs 'as to the bowels of the earth with unequal steps to drink claret from tin cans.' It was Hamilton who wrote the dedication of *The Gentle Shepherd* to the Countess of Eglinton.

Though a cautious Whig by nature, he was too romantic to resist a friendly clap on the shoulder that he received one day when he was visiting Rome. 'How now, Mr. Hamilton,' said the Young Pretender, and Willy Hamilton's fate was sealed. He escaped from Culloden, and spent the rest of his life with the Scots fugitives in France. His songs came back in his stead. His *Ode to the Battle of Gladsmuir* celebrated Prince Charlie's victory at Prestonpans. In 1748, eight years before he died at Lyons, his poems were published in Glasgow under the editorship of Adam Smith.

Another man to be broken on the Jacobite wheel of fortune was William Meston, who wrote verses in Latin and Scots. He had once been professor of Latin at Aberdeen. He was of the old breed of scholarly topers, and he gradually succumbed to the bottle, ill-fortune, and the humiliation of living on charity.

Not only Jacobites found solace in the pen. Robert Blair, grandson of his namesake who had treated between Charles I and Cromwell, was a Presbyterian minister in East Lothian. He inherited a full measure of the melancholy of his creed. He was a sober and industrious man with a facility for funereal poetry, and he distrusted the levity of the younger generation growing up in an age of moderation and music.

'Jupiter' Carlyle said of Blair (whom he knew little more than by gossip) that he was 'so austere and void of urbanity as to make him quite disagreeable to young people.' Blair's wife was the entire opposite of her husband, 'frank and open, and uncommonly handsome', and it was probably she who attracted the attention of the susceptible young Carlyle.

Blair's poem, *The Grave*, at first found no publisher. It was a long poem about death and kirk-yards, and London publishers felt that their public would not relish the charnel house as a dwelling place of the Muse. Blair returned to his study, itself known as the 'grave', to amend his dank iambics until they were fit as he said, 'to go down with a licentious age which cares for none of these things.' Though his alterations can hardly have affected the melancholy of the poem, publication was achieved, and *The Grave* had an unexpected success. It countered temporal wit and Augustan humour with a bitter metaphysical draught.

The poem provided Blake with one of his most macabre inspirations. It reeks of death and old bones, the corruption of the flesh and mouldering mortality. Its author is the finest example of the Scots Calvinist turning poet. Blair accepted the manner of writing of the Augustans (there is nothing in Scots in *The Grave*), but was quite unmodified by either English felicity or Scottish pathos.

'What is this world?
What but a spacious burial-field unwalled
Strewed with death's spoils, the spoils of animals
Savage and tame, and full of dead men's bones.
The very turf on which we tread once lived,
And we that live must lend our carcases
To cover our own off-spring.'

In those years leading up to mid-century, the new love of letters in Scotland grew strongly. The *literati* of the capital city and the country manse were not writing for a living, but were mostly professional men or lairds enjoying the new freedom of mind and manners. Writers who lived entirely by the pen were arising in the south in London. They were still unknown in Scotland.

Ramsay, Blair, Hamilton, and a host of minor writers were laying the foundation of a new national self-expression from which others, in later generations, would draw nourishment. England moved powerfully in its strong uninterrupted tradition of literature, producing a succession of writers of outstanding ability. Scotland was at a new beginning after the years of the dictatorship of the church. In the first half of the century it produced no outstanding person whatsoever. Both Thomson and Ramsay were secondary figures. In prose there was Smollett (*Roderick Random* was published in 1748), but he developed in the south and he was part of the new movement that wrote in prose fiction.

It was at this time that David Hume was bitterly disappointed at not being accepted as a man of letters, rather than as a philosopher. His ambitions were literary. But Scotland's old literary tradition had been destroyed, and a new one had still to be created. There was little chance of a genius of letters flourishing, since writing is a social art and requires a developed social and literary background.

The question of whether to write in Scots or English was beginning to preoccupy people. Those who wrote in English, like Hume, were conscious of a disadvantage. Rightly or wrongly they were sensible of an inferiority in their own Scots language, but they were unfamiliar with the niceties of English usage. The apology for the 'native Scots dialect' that Watson had made was early evidence of this lack of confidence. English was 'refined', and many people strained to acquire English and erase Scotticisms.

It was an awkward age for Scottish writers. Scots was accepted as good enough for ballads and songs, the entertainment of the drawing-room. English had to be used for major works in philosophy and other learned subjects. When a poet wrote in English, he was almost invariably second-rate. It was not accidental that the next two writers of importance were both poets who wrote in their own Scots tongue – Robert Fergusson and Robert Burns.

Meanwhile – as Edinburgh danced and trifled with verse – Glasgow was experiencing the sweetness of philosophy. From the beginning of the century Gersholm Carmichael taught philosophy at the university there. He was the son of a covenanting minister. An early colleague and fellow professor, James Wodrow of the chair of divinity, appeared to approve of Carmichael, who made safe intellectual journeys into realms of thought that the church might properly imagine to be a shade dangerous. Carmichael must have been singularly dull and unspeculative. He taught for the first thirty years of the century, and, during his period of office, there developed in his younger contemporaries the gradual shift of attitude that gave rise to the moderate party in the church.

Glasgow was the centre of theological teaching. In 1702 it had about 400 students in philosophy and divinity. A large number were from the lower classes, since it was the ambition of many mothers to have a son improve his station in life by entering the ministry.

Carmichael, dealing with students both couth and uncouth, used Puffendorf as his master. He ignored, because he did not understand, the line of thought from Descartes, through Locke, to his own conctemporary, Berkeley. While he held sternly to outmoded tediousness, his pupils acquired an appetite for more polished fare.

Glasgow University, in clutching the dying past so strongly, made a strange contrast with Edinburgh. In the capital city, the modern outlook of the teachers of medicine had become firmly established.

In Edinburgh there had been the brilliant mathematician, Professor David Gregory, son of the man who had discovered the principle of the reflecting telescope. Gregory introduced the Newtonian philosophy to Edinburgh. His teaching and his text-books made a deep impression. In 1692 he accepted a call to Oxford to be Savilian Professor of Astronomy. He was succeeded in the Edinburgh chair by his brother James.

In 1725, on the recommendation of Sir Isaac Newton, who wrote specially to the magistrates of Edinburgh, Colin McLaurin was elected joint professor with James Gregory. He came from Aberdeen University to his new post, but his career in Edinburgh was cut short by his death at forty-eight in 1746. 'Jupiter' Carlyle, who sat under him, described McLaurin as 'the clearest and most agreeable lecturer on that abstract science that ever I heard. He made mathematics a fashionable study, which was felt afterwards in the war that followed in 1743, when nine-tenths of the engineers of the army were Scottish officers. The Academy at Woolwich was not then established.' McLaurin also taught astronomy, mechanics, and natural philosophy.

Glasgow at that time had a very able mathematician on its staff, but the emphasis of its teaching was in dogmatic theology. The new attitude that was developing in Scotland was not to be denied. The rise of religious moderation required a philosophic attitude that did not work hand-in-glove with dogma, as Carmichael had worked hand-in-glove with Wodrow.

In 1730 Francis Hutcheson succeeded Gersholm Carmichael in the chair of philosophy. Puffendorf was cast away, and nine years later Hume published his *Treatise of Human Nature*. It was an astonishing nine years in which the intellectual overthrow of the essentially superstitious argument of the Calvinists was completed. Very few, besides Hume, were able to understand how complete the overthrow was. It is correct to see Hume as the counterblast to Calvinism. Hutcheson did not agree with Hume, but he helped to prepare a generation that was more able to appreciate – though still not to accept – Hume's clarity of reason.

When Hutcheson took over the chair of philosophy, he was a young man of thirty-six. He matched his hour. He was temperamentally equipped with the attributes that were most needed to bring philosophy – and theology – back to the human scene. He had charity, tolerance, and kindliness. He had been brought up in Ireland, the son of a Presbyterian minister in County Down, the grandson of a minister from Ayrshire. He was 'intended' for the ministry, and was sent to study at Glasgow. As a young man of twenty, he preached his first sermon in his father's church, on a day that his father was unable through infirmity to attend the pulpit. The congregation, accustomed to having hell fire and damnation hurled at them from the pulpit, did not take well to the charitable discourse that young Hutcheson gave them. An elder of the kirk reported to Hutcheson's father: 'He has been babbling an hour about a good benevolent God, and that the souls of the heathen themselves will go to heaven if they follow the light of their conscience. Not a word did the daft fellow say about the good old comfortable doctrine of election, reprobration, original sin, and faith.'

When Hutcheson took over the chair of moral philosophy, the modest classes that Carmichael used to teach began to swell. Dissenting students came from England and Ireland to hear the lively, enthusiastic man who added to the attraction of his classroom by being the first professor to stop lecturing in Latin.

He revived the topic of virtue as a fit subject for young divines and philosophers to discuss. Virtue, benevolence, and optimism were the challenge he flung at the 'high-flying' Calvinists and Marrowmen. Hutcheson's God was served by morality instead of the unyielding faith of the elect to whom virtue was a matter of irrelevance. Hutcheson was not a profound philosopher, but he was an inspiring teacher. The west of Scotland was then the home of the most bigoted clergy, and their power in Glasgow was considerable. Hutcheson influenced young men who, in reaction to their elders, were looking for a more tender and hopeful system of thought than had been hitherto offered them.

The successor of Wodrow was Dr. Leechman, who later became principal of the university. Leechman shared the spirit of moderation. He dismissed theological doctrine as of secondary importance to morality, and Hutcheson said that 'this man would put a new face on the theology of Scotland'.

Hutcheson, as a moral philosopher, was able to discourse on subjects outside Leechman's stricter province. Natural religion, the law, politics, ethics, were dealt with by his sane and kindly wisdom. In place of the vengeful tyrant that the Calvinists called God, he substituted a creator 'whose world shows happiness, whose chastisements are tender admonitions'. Adam Smith, who sat under him, called him 'the never to be forgotten Hutcheson'. In his essay *Inquiry Concerning Moral Good and Evil*, Hutcheson used the phrase that Jeremy Bentham developed, 'that that action is best which procured the greatest happiness of the greatest numbers.' Hutcheson was a man of practical Christian virtue, and many of his ideas were taken from the teaching of the New Testament.

David Hume, whose thought went beyond the moral kindliness of Hutcheson, was in friendly correspondence with him for some years. It was Hutcheson who was responsible for showing Hume's first works to young Adam Smith, and later he arranged the meeting of the two men who were to become warm friends.

But the tolerant generosity of Hutcheson had its limitations. He did not approve of Hume's almost total scepticism. When in 1744 Hume was proposed for the Edinburgh chair of ethics, both Hutcheson and Leechman, whose opinions were asked, were against the appointment. Hutcheson's greatness was in his influence on the younger generation. If he had been intellectually equipped to understand and accept the arguments of Hume, he would not have been the sentimental optimist who irrigated the desert of orthodox Calvinism with a love of his fellow men.

He died on a visit to Ireland in 1746, the year that also saw the death of Colin Maclaurin, and the defeat of Prince Charlie at Culloden.

Four new influences were now at work in Scotland. The first of them was the scientific method introduced through the Edinburgh medical school. The second was the influence of England and its Augustan age, to which can be coupled the very strong influence of the Continent. The third was the change in Calvinism and the re-enthronement of moral virtue. The fourth was the investigation of the folk-literature of the country by Watson and Ramsay.

IO

TO CULLODEN MOOR

English Whiggery.   Enclosing the land.   Crimes and
punishments.   Description of a Scottish estate.   Potatoes
and turnips.   The Porteous riot.   Good claret and
bad lodgings.   Prince Charlie comes to Scotland and pays
his own passage.   From Prestonpans to Falkirk.
How the Highlander fought   Defeat in the north.
Butcher Cumberland and peace.

UNDER WALPOLE England enjoyed a steadily growing prosperity. Trade
increased, agricultural reform altered the appearance as well as the produce
of the countryside, and modest social reforms were accepted. Scottish
members of parliament partook of the corrupt sweets of office as readily as their
English colleagues. One Scottish M.P. of the period said that 'I have heard
many arguments which convinced my judgment, but never one which
influenced my vote.' The broad and fairly placid stream of English Whiggery
did not totally engulf the Jacobites, who continued to nurse their dreams –
dreams which, as the years passed, became more romantic and chivalrous,
already part of legend instead of reality.

In the Highlands, still a nest of vipers to the eyes of London, the zealous and
not unkindly General Wade pursued his duty of introducing southern
civilisation. In his preliminary report in 1724 he estimated the state of loyalty of
the Highlanders:

'The number of men able to carry arms in the Highlands (including
the inhabitants of the isles) is by the nearest computation about 22,000
men, of which number about 10,000 are vassals to the superiors well
affected to your majesty's government; most of the remaining 12,000
have been engaged in rebellion against your majesty, and are ready,
whenever encouraged by their superiors or chiefs of clans, to create new
troubles and rise in arms in favour of the pretender.'

Wade proposed that regular companies of Highland troops should be
established, drawn from men of known loyalty. He thought of building a
military ship on Loch Ness. He suggested another act of parliament to punish
Highlanders in 'the most uncivilized parts of the country' who were foolish
enough to carry or conceal arms. He advised that the crime of carrying arms be
a felony with the possibility of transportation for a first offence. And he wanted
local taxation to be raised for 'defraying the charges of apprehending,

prosecuting, and maintaining of criminals while in goal.'

The new Disarming Act was passed. It was not the first, but it was intended to apply it strictly. The result was that the Highlander hid his weapons – which might be new muskets brought by the Spaniards in 1719 – and carried a stick.

The roads that Wade built opened up the Highlands as far as the Great Glen. Forty-two bridges and 250 miles of roadway were constructed in about eleven years in a mountainous country that had hitherto known little more than bridle paths. Wade carried northwards the work of civil engineering from where the Romans had left off sixteen hundred years before.

The country in the south of Scotland, though peaceful and fairly populous, still endured the poverty that had hardly been mitigated since the beginning of the century. Travellers were full of protests about the inns where they lodged.

Edward Burt, an English officer of the engineers, who spent many years in Scotland in the '20s and '30s, was dismayed at the inn he went to near Kelso when he first arrived in the country. Though the claret was good the food was appalling, and the state of the room so squalid that he left it to ride in search of better accommodation. Nightfall found him at a small house on a moor.

> 'At my first entrance I perceived some things like shadows moving about before the fire, which was made with peats; and going nearer to them, I could just discern, and that was all, two small children in motion, stark naked, and a very old man sitting by the fire-side. . . .
>
> Here I was told I might have a breast of mutton done upon the *brander* (or gridiron): but when it was brought me, it appeared to have been smoked and dried in the chimney corner; and it looked like the glue that hangs up in an ironmonger's shop.'

Burt was able to make a meal of fresh eggs, and then he found to his surprise that his bed-linen was excellent. 'Here I must take notice of what I have since found almost everywhere, but chiefly in the low-country, that is, good linen.'

Of Edinburgh he said that:

> 'When I first came into the high-street of that city, I thought I had not seen anything of the kind more magnificent: the extreme height of the houses, which are, for the most part, built of stone, and well sashed, the breadth and length of the street, and (it being dry weather) a cleanness made by the high winds, I was extremely pleased to note every thing to be so unlike that description of that town which had been given me by some of my countrymen.
>
> 'Being a stranger, I was invited to sup at a tavern. The cook was too filthy to be described; another English gentleman whispered to me and said, he believed, if the fellow was to be thrown against the wall, he would stick to it. . . . We supped very plentifully and drank good French claret, and were very merry until the clock struck ten, the hour when everybody is at liberty, by the beat of the city drum, to throw their filth out at the windows. Then the company began to light pieces of paper, and throw them upon the table to smoke the room, and, as I thought, to mix one bad smell with another.

'Being in my retreat to pass through a long narrow *wynde* or alley, to
go to my new lodgings, a guide was assigned to me, who went before
me to prevent my disgrace, crying out all the way, with a loud voice,
"Hud your haunds". The throwing up of a sash, or otherwise opening a
window, made me tremble, while behind and before me, at some little
distance, fell the terrible shower.'

Important changes were taking place in the countryside. Famine and
distress brought about by primitive methods of cultivation were forcing the
pace towards new methods of farming. But before this was possible – and
Scotland lagged behind England – there was a reshifting of populations and a
redistribution of lands.

A large landowner, with feudalism vanishing, no longer measured his
wealth in his 'tail of tenantry'. The land itself was becoming more important.
The enclosing of ground, the building up of large farms and estates, was for the
eventual good of agriculture, but it brought immediate distress and caused
many small farms and villages to vanish completely. Many years of famine and
near-famine impelled the better type of farmer and landowner to improve his
methods of cultivation. Much of this improvement, such as enclosing,
inevitably meant the end of old methods to which the peasants were
accustomed.

Legislation passed by the old Scottish parliament was invoked by some
landowners to claim further lands to which they had no real title. There was
trouble between lords and burghs over the ownership of 'common ground'. A
vast amount of upland territory was held as 'common ground'. In previous
centuries it had been of little use for agriculture, which concentrated on the
fertile tilth of river valleys and coastal regions. It had therefore not been seized
by church or barons.

Burghs and villages possessed ground, sometimes of vast extent, which was
used for common grazing. It was held by very ancient usage, and in different
parts of Scotland was a heritage of Celtic, Saxon, or Norse customs. Though
this ground had belonged to the people from time immemorial, it was now
filched from them to create new private estates.

'The inland, the upland, the moor, the mountain, were really not
occupied at all for agricultural purposes, or served only to keep the poor
and their cattle from starving. They were not thought of when charters
were made and lands feudalised. Now, as cultivation increased, the
tendency in the agricultural mind was to occupy these wide commons,
and our lawyers lent themselves to appropriate the poor man's grazing
ground to the neighbouring baron. They pointed to his charter with its
clause of parts and pertinents, with its general clauses of mosses and
moors – clauses taken from the style book, not with any reference to the
territory conveyed in that charter; and although the charter was
hundreds of years old, and the lord had never possessed any of the
common, when it came to be divided the lord got the whole that was
allocated to the estates, and the poor cottar had none. The poor had no

lawyers' – Cosmo Innes.

A great deal of what is decorously called social unrest was caused by this readjustment of land and people. The countryside had its bands of 'randy sorners' or wild beggars. Courts were busy dealing their punishments of death, flogging or transportation. Yet serious crime was rare and prisons were strangely empty. The death penalty was exacted far less frequently than in England, where it was the statutory punishment for a vast catalogue of offences and where, after an assize, prisoners were sometimes despatched in batches. In Scotland hanging was rare, partly because of the low incidence of major crime, and partly because judges had discretionary powers to award lesser punishment.

Of common brutality there was plenty. Petty crime and the sins of the flesh still earned punishments of physical sadism. A man would be nailed by his ear to a door until he summoned courage to tear away 'the lug with the gristle'. An entry in the records of the Tolbooth prison of Edinburgh reads: '1728, Oct 25 – John Gibson; forging a declaration, 18th January, 1727. His lug nailed to the Tron, and dismissed.' If a man were more fortunate, his ear would be cut off neatly by the hangman while the public watched. Women were stripped to the waist and scourged publicly.

In the north the barons still had their power of 'pit and gallows', which gave them entire jurisdiction over any who appeared before them. Of one it was said: 'He'd hang them up just of his own word: none of your law!' There was a considerable amount of kidnapping, especially on the east coast, for impressed service at sea.

While the poor lived in their houses of thatch and mud floors, a new kind of enlightened landowner was emerging. Cockburn of Ormiston was a cultivator. Sir John Clerk of Penicuik was a planter of trees who did an immense amount in making bare upland country do a useful job. He left one of the finest descriptions of eighteenth-century Scottish countryside. In a letter written in Latin to his old friend Boorhaave, Sir John described his house and his estates:

'On the west stretches a plain for some miles, varied with hills, valleys, streams, springs, and shrubberies. Parts are uncultivated and marshy, but this gives work for my tenants and servants, who are daily improving it. Meanwhile there is no part, however swampy, which has not its use, for the moors are suited for sport. There is an abundance of hares. The birds thrive in the heather, wild geese, partridge, quails, etc. abundantly provide for the conviviality of guests. . . . On the east lies the most fertile, and, as I believe, most cultivated region of all Scotland – the greater part, that is, of the counties of Edinburgh and Haddington, where some noble estates render the prospect varied and agreeable. . . . This country domain of mine is distinguished by many enclosures and preserves, and is everywhere fed with springs and rivulets. Some 500 acres give employment to my servants. Part is destined for pasturage, part for hay, and part for grain. Here, too, the variety greatly pleases the eye – plantations of timber, forest trees, hills and rocks interspersed, covered with shrubs and thickets. Nor are there wanting rugged and contorted boulders, those relics of an ancient world which, if not terrible of aspect, adorn the face of nature. . . .'

Of his house Sir John said it was 'ample rather than magnificent'. 'Throughout the hall, supper-room, dining-room, etc., are seen certain pictures, most elegant of their kind. Not indeed, those painted by the hands of the Greeks, of Apelles, Parrhasius, Zenides, or Protogenes, but such as others, I hardly believe of less note, have produced, such as Raphael of Urbino, the Rhenish Guido, Rubens, Vandyck, Paul Veronese, and Francis Imperialis.'

Around the house were the gardens, preserves, fish-ponds, and the apiary.

'Among other gardens there is one, or rather an aviary, near the windows of my chamber, where sometimes I feed the various birds with my hand. Here ducks, Guinea fowls, Partridges, and occasionally pheasants, daily look for my help. In the midst is a fountain, whence water flows from an urn supported on the shoulder of the statue of a man. . . . I have various fish-ponds, and one especially which forms a lake rather than a pond. It is situated in the midst of a wood, which is dissected by a number of paths . . . nor can I omit another fish-pond, or lesser lake, noteworthy for its position and solitude, which a poet only could describe. It is surrounded by hills and steep rocks, and no one can get access to it but by the mouth of a frightful cave. To those who enter therefore, first occurs the memory of the cave of the Cuman Sibyl, for the ruinous aperture, blocked up with stones and briars, strikes the eye. Then there comes upon the wayfarers a shudder, as they stand in doubt whether they are among the living or the dead . . . the form of this mournful cave, with its long and shady path followed by the light and prospect, make the exit more delightful. For suddenly the darkness disappears, and as if at the creation of a new world . . . the meadows are filled with every kind of field herbs, and watered with perennial streams. Therefore a multitude of tame animals, especially horses and oxen, are seen, not so much to graze as disport themselves.'

Meanwhile, Carmichael taught in Glasgow, and Hamilton of Bangour wooed his ladies in rhyme. In 1731 Edinburgh saw the beginning of a society that was the forerunner of the Royal Society of Edinburgh. It was instituted 'for the improvement of medical knowledge, by collecting and publishing Essays and Observations in the various branches of Medicine and Surgery, written by the members themselves or communicated to them.' The Secretary was Dr. Alexander Monro, the first professor of anatomy.

Eight years later Colin McLaurin, the professor of mathematics, enlarged the field of the society to include philosophy and literature. It then took the self-conscious title of The Society for Improving Arts and Sciences. The first president was the Earl of Morton, who was afterwards president of the Royal Society of London. The vice-presidents included Sir John Clerk of Penicuik.

The confusion of the '45 rebellion, and McLaurin's death put an end to this phase of the society. When it met again in 1752 David Hume was one of the secretaries, along with Alexander Monro (Secundus).

Another of the learned bodies that arose at the time, more immediately useful in its work, was the Society for the Improvement of Agriculture. This came into being in 1723. Though agriculture remained primitive until well into the second half of the century, a great deal of individual ingenuity was already paving the way for the transformation of the countryside. As early as 1710 fanners were introduced by James Meikle of Saltoun, but were not generally used for a considerable time. By 1720 carts were in use, taking the place of wooden sledges and pack-horses, but it took a long time for them to be accepted. Fifty years later Lord Kames wrote: 'Till lately our farmers had no wheel carriages; and to this day they are not universal.' It was not till quite far into the nineteenth century that the wheel became accepted in outlying parts of the Highlands.

In 1724 Cockburn of Ormiston was experimenting with potatoes and turnips. In 1732 Michael Menzies of Edinburgh made a primitive threshing mill. By 1735 the potato was beyond the experimental stage and small-scale cultivation had started. Turnips followed after a few years, in 1739, again in a small way. It was not till later that they provided winter feeding for animals and completely altered animal husbandry. In the same year, 1739, Hume published his *Treatise of Human Nature* which fell 'dead from the press'. In 1740 there was famine. 'About this time there began a very great dearth of provisions as was ever known in Scotland for above 40 years past.' – Sir John Clerk's memoirs.

1735 was also notable for the act that ended the death penalty for witchcraft. 'No person is to be persecuted for witchcrafts, sorcery, inchantment or conjuration, or for charging others with any such offence. Persons pretending to exercise witchcraft, tell fortunes, or by crafty science to discover stolen goods, are for any such offence to be imprisoned for a year, be pilloried once every quarter of it, and bound for good behaviour.' This was moderation indeed. In 1737 there was the first disruption within the Church of Scotland and the formation of the original church of secession.

In 1736 occurred the Porteous Riot, which began with the arrest of a couple of smugglers, involved Queen Charlotte, and showed that the ancient animosity between Scotland and England was not dead. Smuggling was a patriotic undertaking, a good thing in itself, and a defiance of the taxation imposed from London and enforced by English revenue officers who thought little of drawing blood. Walpole's malt-tax in particular was bitterly resented.

All the fishing villages of the east coast were centres of smuggling. Two smugglers, Wilson and Robertson, were caught and sentenced to death. An attempt was made to escape from the Tolbooth prison. Wilson, a huge and powerful man, went first and stuck between the bars of the window, and so prevented his colleague getting away. On the Sunday before execution both were taken, in custody of four of the City Guard, to service at the Tolbooth Kirk. At the end of the service, when the congregation was dispersing, Wilson made amends for his previous clumsiness. He seized a guard in each hand and a third between his teeth. Robertson dealt with the fourth and escaped.

'Jupiter' Carlyle was an eye-witness of what happened at the hanging of Wilson. In describing Captain Porteous, a half-pay officer in charge of the City Guard, Carlyle said that 'this man, by his skill in manly exercises, particularly the golf, and by gentlemanly behaviour, was admitted into the company of his superiors, which elated his mind, and added insolence to his native roughness, so that he was much hated and feared by the mob of Edinburgh.'

Wilson, by his courageous conduct in allowing his companion to escape, had become a hero to the mob – and to others who saw him as a sacrifice to bad financial policy.

'When the day of execution came, the rumour of a deforcement at the gallows prevailed strongly; and the Provost and Magistrates (not in their own minds very strong) thought it a good measure to apply for three of four companies of a marching regiment (the Welch Fusiliers) that lay in the Canongate, to be drawn up in the Lawnmarket, a street leading from the Tolbooth to the Grassmarket, the place of execution, in order to overawe the mob by their being at hand. Porteous, who, it is said, had his natural courage increased to rage by any suspicion that he and his Guard could not execute the law, and being heated likewise with wine – for he had dined, as the custom then was, between one and two – became perfectly furious when he passed by the three companies drawn up in the street as he marched along with his prisoner.'

After the hanging, there was a demonstration by the crowd. Wilson's body was cut down. Stones and dirt were thrown at the guard. 'It was generally said that there was very little, if any, more violence than had usually happened on such occasions. Porteous, however, inflamed with wine and jealousy, thought proper to order his Guard to fire, their muskets being loaded with slugs; and when the soldiers showed reluctance I saw him turn to them with threatening gesture and an inflamed countenance.

'They obeyed, and fired; but wishing to do as little harm as possible, many of them elevated their pieces, the effect of which was that some people were wounded in the windows; and one unfortunate lad, whom we had displaced, was killed in the stair window by a slug entering his head. . . . We had seen many people, women and men, fall on the street, and at first thought it was only from fear, and by their crowding on one another to escape. But then the crowd dispersed, we saw them lying dead or wounded, and had no longer any doubt of what had happened. The numbers were said to be eight or nine killed, and double the number wounded; but this was never exactly known.'

There was a public outcry, and Porteous was tried and sentenced to death. Queen Charlotte, acting as regent in the absence on the Continent of George II, was advised to pardon Porteous. When this was learned in Edinburgh, there was great indignation. 'They regarded the royal intervention in his behalf as a proof that the unjust English Government were disposed to treat the slaughter of Scotsmen by a military officer as a very venial offence.'

On the night of 7th September a number of bands occupied positions in the city. The West Port was seized. Communication was cut between the magistrates and the Welch Fusiliers lying in the Canongate, and the gate between the Canongate and Edinburgh proper was held. The City Guard was disarmed and their weapons given to the crowd. Led by a drummer the assaulting party came to the Tolbooth, where Porteous lay. Sledge-hammers and axes were useless on the door. It was set on fire with tar, and when it gave way the keys of the cells were obtained from the warders, to whom no harm was offered.

The prisoner was found halfway up the chimney of his chamber, impeded by a grating.

'Porteous was allowed to entrust his money and papers with a person who was in prison for debt, and one of the rioters kindly and humanely offered him the last consolation religion can afford. The dreadful procession, seen by thousands of eyes from the crowded windows, was then begun, and amid the gleam of links and torches, that tipped with fire the blades of hundreds of weapons, the crowd poured down the West Bow to the Grassmarket. So coolly and deliberately did they proceed that, when one of Porteous's slippers dropped from his foot, as he was borne sobbing and praying along, they halted and replaced it. In the Bow the shop of a dealer in cordage was broken open, a rope taken therefrom, and a guinea left in its stead.'

The shop remained in existence for more than another 200 years, still purveying cord. Recessed in the shop counter was a coin reputed to be that left in payment for the rope that hanged Porteous. The shop finally closed for business on the last day of 1967.

Porteous was hanged from a dyer's pole to the roar of the crowd. Very quickly the organisers of vengeance dispersed, and by morning there was nothing to be seen but the corpse of Porteous and the cinders of the Tolbooth door.

This demonstration against government authority was not relished in the south. The provost of Edinburgh was put into gaol, but released in bond after three weeks. After outrageously severe punishments had been debated in parliament, the town was fined £2,000 for the benefit of Porteous's widow. The ringleaders of the riot, said to be men of substance and power, were never caught.

Into this Scotland of good claret and bad lodgings, of potatoes and turnips, schisms, moderation, riot and radical scepticism, Charles Edward Stuart precipitated himself with the impetuousness of his youth and the folly of his family. But the anti-English demonstration of the Porteous riot was not an exact portent of Jacobite enthusiasm.

In the summer of 1745 the *Elizabeth*, a ship of the line, and *La Doutelle*, a frigate with Charles on board, set sail from France to Scotland. The larger vessel was set upon by an English ship and forced to retire, but the frigate reached the Hebrides. Prince Charles came at his own expense. Lacking

French support, he intended to prove his case by showing that loyalty to a king would raise the patriots of Britain.

With the support of Cameron of Lochiel, the royal standard was hoisted and the march began. It took Charles to within 150 miles of London, and then to bitter years of exile in drunkenness and dissipation. There was an undoubted element of stirring and colourful endeavour in the rebellion, but lost causes supported by doomed people are tragic and not romantic. The Celtic tribes of Scotland were sacrified to the Jacobite cause, which had already dwindled in popular favour in south Britain to the extent of being no more a potent political force.

Jacobitism was a curious hangover from the past. The stolid whiggery of Georgian England was unlikely to respond to so dubious a stimulus. In the lowlands of Scotland there was a great deal of sympathy for Charles. A successful rebellion might mean the end of the increasing burden of taxes imposed from London. But the southern Scot was suspicious: he saw the Highlander as a wild and wily man. A stabbing dirk and a propensity for burning and pillaging were not regarded as the happiest allies in a readjustment of fiscal obligations. By 1745 Scotland had settled down under the Union, just as Britain had settled down under the Georges.

The long march to Derby and back again was the exit from history of the royal house of Stuart. It was the old story of initial success, insufficient preparation, indecision, and ultimate failure. There was the excitement of the Camerons rushing the gates of a reluctant and rather indignant Edinburgh. There was the proclamation at the Mercat Cross of the Old Pretender as King James the Eighth.

Sir John Clerk, no dreamer of Jacobite dreams but a true-blue Government man, wrote in his journal: 'As to the Young Pretender, he and the bulk of his Savage Army marched about from Bred's craigs [the Braid hills] to the east side of Dudeston [Duddingston] and the King's park, and took possession of the Abbey of Holyroodhouse.'

There was celebration by candlelight in the Palace of Holyroodhouse. There was music and dancing, the headiness of royalty, with women preening themselves in robes of antique splendour unhooked from their closets. And from the castle the guns of the Hanoverian garrison sent occasional mementoes of war hissing over the dwellings of Whigs and Tories alike. The smell of gunpowder, the brave words of the proclamation, the flash of tartan, considerably worried the citizens of Edinburgh who were anxious to live in peace, whichever king was on the throne. If only peace meant fewer taxes!

There followed the brilliant victory over General Cope at Prestonpans, when the entire Highland army changed its position by moving through a bog under darkness and mist. Cope rushed south on horseback, 'the first general in Europe who had brought the first tidings of his own defeat.' The following Sunday a brave minister, a Mr. McVicar, preached in the West Kirk of Edinburgh for King George and added, as a postscript to his prayer, 'As for this young man that is come amongst us to seek an earthly crown, we beseech Thee in mercy to take him unto Thyself, and give him a crown of glory.'

The temper of the country was against Charles, as he learned during his march south. People of wealth buried their family treasures in the ground and fled. The masses offered fear or apathy. Yet there was optimism within the army of the rebellion, a faith in reinforcements and the destiny of the Stuarts. An officer of the 'Savage Army,' the second son of Macdonald of Glengarry, wrote in a letter to his cousin in the north: 'Things seem to go on so quickly that all that are so far behind as you will be at a loss not to share in the happie events immediately to happen.'

It was all to no purpose. Only 300 recruits joined Charles in England, and at Derby he was advised to turn back. He did so, believing that Scotland could be held. In bitter winter weather the army re-crossed the border. 'The Esk was swollen sae red sae deep, but shoulder to shoulder the brave lads keep.' There was another victory, at Falkirk, over the troops of General Hawley who afterwards pointed out to his staff that the Highlanders, whom they had described as a parcel of raw vagabonds, were in fact the best disciplined militia that he had seen in his campaigns in Europe.

But that discipline served no purpose. It was in any case a discipline of battle and not of the march. The greatest enemy of Charles's army was in its own ranks. Desertion was frequent and in large numbers. Brigades and regiments lost over half their strength. The soldiers vanished into the countryside. Lord George Murray wrote to Atholl: 'For God's sake cause some effectual method to be taken about deserters; I would have their houses and crops destroyed for an example to others, and themselves punished in the most rigorous manner.'

In battle it was different. Charles's army had about 5,000 infantry, of whom 4,000 were Highlanders. The total strength was about 6,000. There were about seventeen regiments, including cavalry, and the largest single unit was Lord George Murray's Atholl regiment with a strength of 1,000, not counting deserters.

The clan regiments, which formed the greater part of the total strength, were commanded by their chiefs. 'In some instances in the absence of the chief, the regiment of the clan was commanded by his son, and, failing both, by the nearest kinsman of the chief.' – Keltie. Each company in a regiment had two captains, two lieutenants, and two ensigns, who were usually the chief's blood relatives.

> 'The pay of a captain in the army was half a crown *per diem*; that of a lieutenant two shillings; and of an ensign one shilling and sixpence. The front rank of each clan-regiment was composed of persons who were considered gentlemen by birth, though without fortune or means. The pay of these was one shilling *per diem*. The gentlemen in the front rank were better armed than the men in the rear rank. All the former had targets [shields], which many of the latter had not. When fully armed, as was generally the case, every gentleman of the front rank carried a musket and broadsword, with a pair of pistols and a dirk stuck

in the belt which surrounded his body. In some rare instances another dagger was stuck within the garter of the right leg, to be used in cases of emergency. A target, formed of wood and leather thickly studded with nails, covered the left arm, and enabled the wearer to parry and protect himself from the shots or blows of an assailant.' – J S. Keltie.
The Highlander in battle was truly ferocious.

'They advance with rapidity, discharge their pieces when within musket length of the enemy, and then, throwing them down, draw their swords, and holding a dirk in their left hand with their target, they dart with fury on the enemy through the smoke of their fire. When within reach of the enemy's bayonets, bending their left knee, they, by their attitude, cover their bodies with their targets that receive the thrusts of the bayonets, which they contrive to parry, while at the same time they raise their sword-arm, and strike their adversary.'

The narrator of this battle drill adds that 'the fate of the battle is decided in an instant, and the carnage follows, the Highlanders bringing down two men at a time, one with their dirk in the left hand, the other with the sword.'

Prestonpans was won in that manner. So was Falkirk. If the attack failed there was no redress, no second chance. It failed at Culloden because the Hanoverians were tactically prepared for it. One hundred years after Charles I had handed himself over as a prisoner to the Scots Presbyterian army at Newark, his great-grandson and natural heir to the throne, Prince Charles Edward Stuart, saw his own Scots army defeated and destroyed. The English general, George II's son, was not loath to reinforce his title of Butcher Cumberland. It was the long-awaited chance to solve the problem of the Highlands, and it was done by the sword, without mercy, long after the battle proper was ended. Women and children, the wounded and the sick, over a very large part of Highlands, learned the horror of being on the side opposing the redcoat soldiery.

On hearing of the outcome of the battle, Sir John Clerk of Penicuik wrote:
'The success of this Battle gave universal joy, especially to the friends of the Government, but there were even Jacobites who were at least content at what had happened, for peace and quietness began now to break in, whereas anxiety and distress of various kinds had possessed the breasts of most people ever since the rebellion broke out. All trade and business in this country were quite at a stand.'

Peace had come to Scotland.

I I

SCIENCE AND PHILOSOPHY

The scientist's role.   The relation of Scotland to other
countries and the work being done in them.   The position of
Edinburgh and the 'dual authority' of Edinburgh and
Glasgow.   'Learned and ingenious men.'   The universities and the scholastic tradition.   Every man to sell his
vote.   Hume *vis-à-vis* the natural scientists.

THE SCIENTIFIC GENIUS is often obscured because he rarely works in
isolation. He is smothered by his colleagues and successors. He plays his part in
a story that is always changing, and the story in the end is greater than any who
contribute to it. The genius in the arts is more likely to be remembered because
his work remains unique, and his reputation is an individual one. Scientific
concepts are disputed, accepted, become commonplace, may be controverted,
until generations later it is difficult to appreciate them with the sharpness of
revelation they possessed when they were first announced.

Of the four Scotsmen – William Cullen, Joseph Black, James Watt, and
James Hutton – only Watt has won a popular immortality, and even that is for
the wrong reason: Watt did not invent the steam-engine. These four were
outstanding amongst the many very able men who, in a short time, made great
changes in the natural sciences. Cullen the doctor-chemist, Black the first exact
scientist, Watt the engineer-inventor, and Hutton the 'discoverer' of geology,
were all blessed with what is called genius. There were others as brilliant, and
many of little less ability, but these four are to be credited with certain
achievements which illustrate a bold change in man's understanding of the
natural world.

The work they did, in fields which were closely related, was of such
importance that it is difficult, in describing it, not to appear to detract from
work on similar lines and of comparable importance being done elsewhere, by
other men in other countries, such as Priestley in England, Lavoisier in France,
Franklin in America, and Lomonósov in Russia.

The world was ripe for scientific discovery. Medicine and philosophy had
already separated, with benefit to both. The natural philosopher held the
intellectual balance. New sciences were born when a sufficient accumulation of
knowledge about certain kinds of phenomena defined new fields of study.
Joseph Black developed chemistry out of medicine and physics; Hutton made
the science of geology out of chemistry, physics, and farming.

'The Scotland, and especially the Edinburgh of that time was, after Paris, the intellectual centre of the world,' wrote A. T. Pledge. That there should have been a continuous chain of discoveries, beginning about the middle of the eighteenth century, was due to many circumstances coinciding. Watt's creation of a steam-engine that 'worked' was not a happy accident: it was part of a renaissance.

Political and economic thought was intermeshed with science and literature. Most of the work of the period was done within the two universities of Edinburgh and Glasgow, between which there were frequent exchanges of professors, lecturers, and students. Travel further afield was limited, and the physical bounds of the cities kept people very much together. The philosopher talked to the theologian and the chemist in the common language of educated men, usually expressed in broad Scots. Ministers wrote plays, scientists translated Homer (into English, the language of politeness), and through it all, a leaven and an irritant, was the genial scepticism of David Hume.

The ubiquitous 'Jupiter' Carlyle tells of a supper in 1759 when Benjamin Franklin was in Edinburgh: 'We supped one night in Edinburgh with the celebrated Dr. Franklin at Dr. Robertson's house, then at the head of the Cowgate . . . Dr. Franklin had his son with him: and besides Wight and me, there were David Hume, Dr. Cullen, Adam Smith, and two or three more.' With tea-cups by day and claret glasses at night, at breakfasts, dinners, and suppers, this momentous generation was in constant converse with itself.

It is again Carlyle who writes:

'The whole circle of learned and ingenious men who had sprung up together at this time was remarkable for the unbroken union which prevailed in it. There were circumstances relating to the capital at this time which contributed much to this fraternal concord; such as the small size of the city, though containing a great population, and the social and hospitable manners which then prevailed. It was peculiar to the city and to the period that there could arrive from the country in the afternoon and be almost certain of assembling such men as David Hume, and Adam Smith, and Robertson, and John Home, and Adam Ferguson, and others, in a tavern at nine, which was the hour of supper in those days, and the chief time of convivial entertainment till about the year 1760. These circumstances conduced not a little to that harmony which then reigned among an order of men said proverbially to be irritable minds.'

The Scottish universities were sympathetic to those who became its greatest adornments. The sons of middle-class merchants and professional men were the recruits of learning. This middle-class was of fairly recent growth. It was diligent, hard-working, and God-fearing.

Though a rugged individualism was shown by both laird and loon, democratic freedom was of course unknown. In parts of the country there was a heritage of feudalism that the south had long ago banished. The Scottish barons' rights of arbitrary trial and sentence had only recently been abolished by act of the London parliament. In the lowlands of Scotland hereditary slaves continued to work in the coal mines and salt pans. There was bigotry and dissension throughout the country, expressing itself in rival methods of worshipping God. Politically the country existed under a despotism. The plums of political and civic office were distributed by one man, and Scotland prospered under the pernicious system.

Sylas Neville, the diarist, made an interesting observation in 1772 when he dined with Dr. Hutton in Edinburgh:

'Dr. Hutton is for having all laws against bribery and corruption abolished & every man sell his vote as he does anything else. I knew that political principles here were none of the purest but did not imagine that they proceeded to this length. Dr. Black, too, who dined with us joined Hutton in thinking we enjoy perfect liberty & have no political evils to complain of. Gracious God, that men can be so blind!'

The Scottish scholastic tradition was sound. For half a century the university of Edinburgh had built on the progressive teaching of Pitcairn, and it now possessed a medical school that eclipsed Leyden. The university of Glasgow was growing on the liberal thought of Hutcheson, and on Cullen's efforts in medicine and science. Young minds which were moulded (possibly in church as they listened to the local minister) by the precise disputatiousness of Calvinist theology could, if independent enough, and in a congenial academic atmosphere, become brilliant intellectual instruments.

Hume, Smith, Watt, Cullen, Hutton, and their fellows were all products of their country. They were made familiar in their youth with a habit of thought which dealt in fundamentals. Whatever individual genius each possessed, it was nourished to maturity by the country into which they had been born.

The Church of Scotland was the first democratic institution, of national size, to arise in Britain. In spite of its schisms, its bitterness and narrowness (the new moderate party was by no means the whole church), it taught the self-sufficiency of the individual in reaching personal decisions. It made it possible for men, if not to spurn dogma (as the authority of the priests had been spurned), then to create their own dogma rather than accept it fully fashioned. With ordinary men this led to the splitting of the church into a number of contentious groups. In greater minds it led to a more complete liberation of the intellect.

Even so, intellectual freedom was conditional. Early stirrings of political democratic feeling were treated as sedition. And the church was powerful enough, in spite of its schisms, to exercise a general theocratic authority. Hume's religious views challenged this authority, and he never escaped the disgraceful charge of atheism. But in science, which had not yet provoked the established order of things, the mind was at liberty to rove where it might, and publish its findings, though it was inevitably accused of meddling impiously with God's work.

Amongst the liberal men of science the advance was not smooth. For every theory there was often a counter-theory. Discoveries were not always exact.

Observation by one group fell foul of the cherished beliefs of another. There were many absurd difficulties. Watt knew how to make an efficient engine before he could obtain the precision materials for constructing it.

The important men were often those who made quite small discoveries, but made them finally and incontrovertibly so that they could not be denied, thus altering the basis of knowledge which the philosopher and the metaphysician must use as his material, even against his inclination.

It was not chance that Hume, who criticised inductive reasoning, should be of the same generation as Black and Cullen, who perfected it. Hume admitted no more than that 'all knowledge resolves itself into probability', and elsewhere he stated 'that all our reasonings concerning causes and effects are derived from nothing but custom; and that belief is more properly an act of the sensitive, than of the cogitative part of our nature.'

It was in fact some years before Cullen and Black developed their laboratory techniques that Hume advance his philosophy of scepticism which denied not only the prejudices and inexactitudes of earlier thinkers, but appeared to deny the merits of the reasoning of the scientists. Yet there was no fundamental antipathy between the two points of view. Hume's teaching was directed against dogmatic certainty and the wrong kind of conclusion. His attitude, and that of Cullen and Black, were different aspects of the same intellectual progress.

None of these men, nor any of the best of their contemporaries, would accept in his particular sphere of work the validity of a phenomenon or relationship except after the most exacting scrutiny. They did not 'believe' easily. The scientific attitude arose with them. Black was the first to express it fully, and in so doing carried to its logical conclusion the earlier teaching of Pitcairn.

The scientists investigated the 'real' world to seek the facts within it. Hume, the sceptic, accepted what the 'real' world offered him, but reserved final interpretations. The scientists, having made their experiments, announced the 'principles' they discovered. Hume, dealing with other principles as well as those of the physical world, said that no 'reason' could be given for them 'beside our experience of their reality'. He knew that behind the facts there are other facts, that knowledge is never final, and that the ultimate arbiter of what is 'real' is not the test-tube or the microscope, but the dialectic argued until it is acceptable, though never conclusive.

12

TWO CHEMISTS –
CULLEN (1710–90) AND
BLACK (1728–99)

Setting up the Glasgow medical school.   'A medical faculty
in himself'.   Cullen on the importance of chemistry.
Black and the discovery of carbon dioxide.   Golden
guineas and the discovery of latent heat.   High thinking and
plain living

WILLIAM CULLEN and BOORHAAVE were the two leading teachers of
medicine of their age. Cullen was born at Hamilton in 1710, a son of the factor
of the Duke of Hamilton. From the local school he went to Glasgow university
and took arts classes before studying medicine, a subject that was not then
taught very seriously in the west. There was no medical school equivalent to
that of Edinburgh. Cullen did the usual thing, and apprenticed himself to a
practising doctor.

He afterwards sailed to the West Indies as a ship's surgeon, and spent some
time in London as an apothecary's assistant to learn more about drugs. When
his father died, he went home to provide for his younger brothers and sisters,
and entered into practice on his own. He met the Duke of Argyll, who had an
interest in chemistry, and supplied him with equipment. The Duke of
Hamilton was among his patients. Cullen knew the usefulness of patronage.

For a short time he worked with William Hunter, but the partnership ended
when Hunter went to London to become the leading obstetrician of his time,
consultant to Queen Charlotte, and the enemy of London's midwives, who saw
a masculine invasion of their feminine mystery.

For a year Cullen studied in Edinburgh under Alexander Monro (primus).
He decided to set up a medical school in Glasgow, and he moved there in 1744
to begin to lecture in medicine. Two years later a laboratory was established,
partly with money given by a professor of oriental languages. Cullen became
professor of chemistry. Some years later he became professor of medicine when
the seat fell vacant. It was in Argyll's patronage. By 1755 he had created the
Glasgow medical school, seen the start of serious investigation of the chemical
world, had Joseph Black as a pupil, and worked to such effect that he has been

described as 'a medical faculty in himself'.

Having done his job, he moved to Edinburgh, became professor of chemistry and physics there, and began to lecture in clinical medicine in the Royal Infirmary, a method of instruction that had been copied from Leyden and introduced to Edinburgh by Dr. John Rutherford, grand-father of Walter Scott.

Amongst his students was Benjamin Rush, whose name persists in the Rush Medical College of Philadelphia, and who wrote to Cullen from America: 'If I have been in any degree useful or successful in my profession, I owe all these things to you.' Rush was one of many American doctors who came to Edinburgh for their training, and the development of American medicine was partly shaped by Cullen.

In imparting his enthusiasm to his students, and in creating institutions of teaching and research, Cullen knew the unimportance of the individual: 'It is always by the successive labors of Several that an art is brought to perfection ... the Case is, a second improves upon it, a third puts it in execution; and all claim the honour of the invention.'

He himself, who opened up the study of chemistry, published only one paper on the subject, *On the Cold Produced by Evaporating Fluids*. Black took over the research and established Glasgow University's long interest in the problem of heat.

Cullen had the ability to communicate his vision, his belief in the importance of what he was doing. He saw chemistry as a 'vast department of the science of matter.' He was determined to wrest it away from the natural philosophers and their parlour-tricks; he believed that the science of chemistry would show itself to be 'founded on principles as immutable as the laws of mechanism, and which may be one day formed into a great system of doctrines, of various degrees of subordination and dependence.' In taking over the workshop knowledge of metallurgists and pharmaceutists he turned it into a liberal science. When he began his work, the chemical nature of matter was almost unknown. When he died, many of the elements had been discovered, and the complicated structure of chemistry and physics was in process of being unravelled.

Bower, in his *History of the University of Edinburgh*, wrote that Cullen was also 'a great master of husbandry, a consummate biologist, and possessed a correct taste in the fine arts. In the year 1758, after finishing off a lecture on chemistry, he delivered to a number of particular friends and favourite pupils more lectures on the subject of agriculture. In these few lectures, he for the first time laid open the true principle concerning the nature of soils and the operation of manures.'

He died an old and revered man in 1790, having lived through the greater part of the century. Years later Cockburn wrote of him: 'I only learned his look from the number of heads of him which, out of respect to his memory, were instantly set up as signs for druggists' shops; all representing him with a huge wig and an enormous under lip.'

Cullen's most illustrious pupil was Joseph Black, who has been described, in a tribute paid this century by Professor John Read, as 'the first of the scientific chemists as distinguished from the medical chemists.'

Raeburn's portrait of Black shows a pleasant, rather handsome face, well-proportioned, with a strong nose and very black eyebrows that contrast quite dramatically, as often happened in that age, with a neat white wig. The features are slightly aristocratic, and there is the faintest quirk of amusement in his lips. It is a well-bred face, expressive and reticent.

John Robison, who edited Black's lectures posthumously (and dedicated the work to James Watt), said that, as Black became older, 'his countenance continued to preserve that pleasing expression of inward satisfaction, which, by giving ease to the beholder, never fails to please.' Adam Smith wrote, less clumsily, 'no man had less nonsense in his head'.

Black was born in 1827 at Bordeaux, where his father George Black was a merchant of substance, an Irish-Scot from Belfast, and a friend of Montesquieu, who used to visit the family in order, he said, to contemplate their happiness and virtues.

At twelve, Joseph was sent to Belfast, where he had four years of schooling, mostly in Latin and Greek. At sixteen he went to Glasgow university – still called 'the College' – and took the arts course. He attended all the lectures on languages and philosophy, and then began to study medicine. In Cullen he found a teacher and a friend, and in Cullen's chemistry classes he became a laboratory assistant.

In 1751, he went to Edinburgh to finish his medical studies, by then thoroughly entwined with the new science of chemistry. He had a cousin, James Russell, who was professor of natural philosophy in Edinburgh. It was another three years before he took his medical doctorate. He could have accomplished this earlier, but he was anxious to take great time and care in preparing his thesis, and its eventual publication brought him immediate fame in Europe and America. At the age of twenty-six, he accomplished the first of his two major contributions to science – the development of chemical theory. In Bordeaux, after reading the paper, Montesquieu assured George Black that his family name would be illustrious.

The discoveries that Black explained in his paper *Magnesia Alba* were made at a time when almost nothing was known of 'gases' and of 'burning'. By experimenting with magnesia and chalk Black discovered what he called 'fixed air', now known as carbon dioxide. John Robison summed up the wonder of the scientists:

> 'What could be more singular than to find so subtile a substance as air existing in the form of a hard stone, and its presence accompanied by such a change in the properties of that stone. What bounds could reasonably be set to the imagination, in supposing that other aereal fluids, as remarkable in their properties, might exist in a solid form in many other bodies, which at present attract no notice, because of our ignorance of their nature and their composition?'

Cullen's vision of the 'vast department of the science of matter' was becoming real. *Magnesia Alba* was the initial step in the new understanding of gases that led to the work of Priestly and Lavoisier. The paper is one of the classics of science. Black's exposition is as precise as his investigation. Robison said that 'excepting the optics of Newton, there is not a finer model for philosophical investigation than the essay on magnesia and quicklime.' A modern comment by Andrew Kent says that 'it is difficult still to appreciate the full significance of Joseph Black's achievements in his *Magnesia Alba . . .* it spread from Edinburgh to become a bible to the following generations . . .'

There is a story that Black's experiments arose rather strangely and indirectly out of the health of Robert and Horace Walpole. Some years earlier the brothers had both suffered from 'the stone', and they believed that their complaint had been relieved by a secret medicine prepared for them by a Mrs. Joanna Stephen. This lady was persuaded, for the sum of £5,000 paid from the public purse, to reveal the ingredients of her preparation, and the recipe was duly printed in the *London Gazette* of 1739.

> 'My medicines are a Powder, a Decoction, and Pills. The Powder consist of Egg-shells and Snails, both calcined. The decoction is made by boiling some Herbs (together with a Ball, which consists of Soap, Swine's Cresses, burnt to a Blackness, and Honey) in water. The Pills consist of Snails calcined, Wild Carrot seeds, Burdock seeds, Ashen Keys, Hips and Hawes, all burnt to a Blackness, Soap and Honey.'

Cullen and his colleagues had little use for such a fashionable mystery, but they knew that somewhere in an old wife's recipe there often lay hidden an effective principle. They were interested in calcination, in burning, in heat, and in medicine. They thought that behind Mrs. Stephen's potion there might lie an alkaline principle. Joseph Black, the laboratory assistant, set out to discover a 'milder alkali' than that afforded by snails and carrot seeds. He found carbon dioxide.

He discovered the gas by his precision with weighing instruments. Part of the unscientific wonder at his work was caused by his ability to weigh the invisible. By the exact use of his scales he also disproved the popular theory that to burn lime into quicklime made it gain weight, due to the acquisition of the mysterious 'phlogiston'. Black showed there was an actual loss of weight, due to the release of carbon dioxide. (The scales he used may have been the same as the pair with which he weighed the golden guineas of his students, when they paid their fees. He had to be sure they were not clipped.)

After *Magnesia Alba*, Black went back to Glasgow, where he succeeded Cullen in the chair of chemistry. That was when Cullen moved to Edinburgh, where he took over the same chair. Black now became busy with problems of heat. Again by simple experiments he gave an accurate account of processes that had been misunderstood. He found that, contrary to popular belief, a far greater loss of heat took place than seemed necessary when water became ice. Similarly, much more heat than appeared necessary was 'absorbed' by water when transformed into steam. 'In both cases, considered as the cause of warmth, we do not perceive its presence. It is concealed or latent, and I give it the name of *Latent Heat*.'

The myth of phlogiston was destroyed, though it remained popular for years amongst people who would not accept Black's teaching. It had been propounded by Stahl (1660–1734), a pupil of Boorhaave at Leyden, and had been a false but necessary postulation to interpret the knowledge of the time.

Black was an extremely reticent worker. Perhaps because of this, and his reluctance to publish, Cullen in Edinburgh in 1766 knew nothing of latent heat. Even more astonishing was the situation between Black and James Watt. They met each other almost daily, were interested in the same problems, yet Watt had to discover latent heat independently before he learned that Black had been teaching it to his students. In 1776 Black showed a hydrogen balloon to some friends, but no mention of it was later made by him. His lectures were not published until after his death, when Robison edited them.

This strange, modest man – who played the flute as a hobby – went back to Edinburgh, again succeeding Cullen in the chair. Though he taught for another thirty years, his health was not good, and as he grew older his constitution weakened. Great mental effort in the laboratory produced a feverish condition that was near exhaustion. Amongst his last class of pupils was Brougham, the future English Chancellor. In Brougham's memoirs is a vivid impression of the elderly professor.

> 'I have heard the greatest understandings of the age giving forth
> their efforts in their most eloquent tongues – have heard the
> commanding periods of Pitt's majestic oratory – the vehemence of
> Fox's burning declamations . . . but I would without hesitation prefer,
> for mere intellectual gratification (to be once more present) while the
> first philosopher of his age was the historian of his own discoveries, and
> be an eyewitness of those experiments by which he had formerly made
> them, once more performed by his own hands. I remember him
> pouring fixed air from a vessel in which sulphuric acid had been poured
> upon chalk, and showing us how this air poured on a candle
> extinguished the light. He never failed to remark on the great use of
> simple experiments within every one's reach, and liked to dwell on the
> manner in which discoveries are made, and the practical effect resulting
> from them in changing the condition of mere things.'

Black died at the age of seventy-one in the last year of the century. He was at table, eating a plain meal of bread, prunes, and milk diluted with an exact proportion of water. He was seated with his cup of milk in his hands, which were resting on his knees. Death came without warning or disturbance. 'In this attitude he expired, without spilling a drop, and without a writhe to his countenance, as if an experiment had been required to show to his friends the facility with which he departed.'

13

JAMES HUTTON, GEOLOGIST
(1726–97)

An unwilling doctor.　　The country farmer.　　His secret work.　　When the world began.　　The discovery of end-less time.　　Theory of the earth.　　An ingenious machine. Plutonists and Neptunians.　　The development of geology.

PROFESSOR PLAYFAIR compared the two men, Joseph Black and James Hutton:

> 'They both cultivated nearly the same branches of physics, and entertained concerning them nearly the same opinions. They were both formed with a taste for what is beautiful and great in science, with minds inventive, and fertile in new combinations . . . ardour, and even enthusiasm with the pursuit of science, great rapidity of thought, and much animation, distinguished Dr. Hutton on all occasions. Great caution in his reasonings, and a coolness of head that even approached indifference, were characteristic of Dr. Black. On attending to their conversation, and the way in which they treated any question of science and philosophy, one would say that Dr. Black dreaded nothing so much as error, and that Dr. Hutton dreaded nothing so much as ignorance, that one was always afraid of going beyond the truth, and the other of not reaching it.'

Both had been pupils of Cullen. When Hutton, quite late in life, came to live permanently in Edinburgh, Black was his inseparable companion. Along with Adam Smith they founded the Oyster Club, though both Black and Hutton were extremely fastidious about food; it was fellowship rather than gustatory experience that they looked for.

Hutton was a kind and lovable man, ready to discourse on any subject under the sun – 'every eye brightened when Hutton came into the room'. He had been born in Edinburgh, the son of a merchant who held office as city treasurer. From the High School he went to the university to study under McLaurin, the mathematician, as well as under Cullen. An attempt at the legal profession was followed by the study of medicine. He was a medical student during the '45 rising; later he went abroad, to Paris for classes in anatomy and chemistry, to Leyden where he graduated doctor of medicine at the age of twenty-three, having written a thesis on blood and circulation in 'microcosmo'.

In 1750 he was back in Edinburgh, reluctant to make a career of medicine. He could not accept what was still superstitious and unsavoury in normal medical practice; he saw that the quickening of knowledge was far in advance of its application. It was a point of view he maintained. Neville, the mysterious student-diarist who knew Hutton well, wrote in 1771 that Hutton 'tells me that the more medical knowledge we acquire, the more we know how little efficacious that art is.'

Hutton's chief interest was chemistry. He became engaged in a successful project for extracting sal ammoniac from soot. Fortunately a way of life lay open to him by which he could further his special interests. He was heir to a small farm in the Borders, near Duns, and he chose to match his knowledge of chemistry with the development of his land.

In 1752, to prepare himself for agriculture, he went to Norfolk to live with a farmer, John Dybold, 'whose practical lessons in husbandry' he greatly valued. He travelled about England studying rocks. In a letter to Sir John Hall he said that he examined every ditch and river-bed he came across 'and that if he did not always avoid the fate of Thales, his misfortune was certainly not owing to the same cause.'

Hutton spent a short time in Holland, Brabant, Flanders, and Picardy, where he was very impressed by what he saw, but he never failed to give East Anglia its pre-eminence in horticulture and farming. 'Had I doubted it before I set out, I should have returned fully convinced that they are good husbandmen in Norfolk.'

In 1754 he was back in the Border country. 'A ploughman whom he brought from Norfolk set the first example of good tillage which had been seen in that district.'

His curiosity had taken him from problems of farming to those of the soil itself, to mineralogy, and so to questions of land formation. He spent about fourteen years on his farm, visiting Edinburgh occasionally, until in 1768 he came to live permanently in the city. As well as Adam Smith and Black, his circle of intimate friends included Russel, Adam Ferguson, Sir George Clerk, and Sir George's brother, the astonishing Clerk of Eldin whose theories on naval warfare had been accepted by the Admiralty and put into execution by the King's Navy. It was said that Clerk had never seen the sea, which is hardly credible, but it is certain he had never been a sailor or fought in ships.

Hutton travelled occasionally. He had already been to the far north of Scotland. In 1774 he returned south, and was accompanied by James Watt on a visit to the salt-mines of Cheshire. He was very secretive about the work he was engaged on, and would not discuss it generally. Joseph Black and Clerk of Eldin were two who knew the nature of his investigations, and it appears they agreed with his conclusions.

At that time man's knowledge of the earth, its structure, and its components, was a mixture of biblical teaching, casual observation, and imaginative speculation. The Mosaic teaching was generally accepted. Six days had God laboured.

The Creation could be established, by those who wooed both mathematics and the church, as having happened on a certain day in 4004 B.C. 'Magic' was still good enough for the uneducated, and for many of the educated there was enough reason in 'unknown forces', supernatural or not, to account for all things in heaven and earth. Explanations of phenomena such as tidal waves, earthquakes, volcanoes, were given and received in fantasms of invention which did immense credit to the natural philosophers who refused to let their imagination be thwarted by observation and reasoning. Black had already found that 'phlogiston' was too convenient a concept to be lightly discarded by all men who professed reason.

Hutton had no apparatus or facilities for research that were not equally possessed by his contemporaries, but he saw the world with dispassionate objectivity. It has been said that 'his work might well be taken as the perfect example of the four steps of inductive reasoning – preliminary observation, making of hypotheses, deduction, and verification.' Hutton accepted nothing that he could not prove. Yet what proof could be advanced for the concepts in his mind, requiring a time-scale that had never before been contemplated, and experiments for which the world itself was the only laboratory?

After he settled in Edinburgh, he was frequently in the company of his particular friends, Joseph Black and Adam Smith. Neville received great kindness from Hutton, whom he called an oddity 'but at the same time a mighty good sort of man. His study is so full of fossils and chemical apparatus of various kinds that there is hardly room to sit down.'

In 1785 his life-long work was ready, and his paper *Theory of the Earth* was delivered to the Royal Society of Edinburgh.

The paper began: 'When we trace the parts of which this terrestrial system is composed, and when we view the general connection of their several parts, the whole presents a machine of a peculiar construction by which it is adapted to a certain end.' There was little knowledge said Hutton, of the interior of the earth, but the surface was known and one could study it.

He surveyed the world, showed how its construction was suitable for plant and animal life. But it was not everlasting or stable. 'We are not to look for nature in a quiescent state; matter itself must be in motion, and through scenes of life are continued or repeated series of agitations and events.'

In putting forward his 'general or preparatory ideas' he said:

'A solid body of land could not have answered the purpose of a habitable world; for a soil is necessary to the growth of plants; and a soil is nothing but the materials collected from the destruction of the solid land. Therefore, the surface of this land, inhabited by man, and covered by plants and animals, is made by nature to decay, in dissolving from that hard and compact state in which it is found below the soil; and this soil is necessarily washed away, by the continual circulation of the water running from the summits of the mountains towards the general receptacle of that fluid. . . . The heights of our land are thus

levelled with the shores; our fertile plains are formed from the ruins of
the mountains; and those travelling materials are still pursued by the
moving water, and propelled along the inclined surface of the earth.'

Hutton told how the silt washed from land became spread over the bottom
of the sea 'towards the unfathomable regions of the ocean', and he showed that
the 'machine of a peculiar construction' might be working towards self-
destruction.

'We may perceive an end to this beautiful machine; an end, arising from
no error in its constitution as a world, but from that destructability of its land
which is so necessary in the system of the globe, in the economy of life and
vegetation.' Such a self-destruction was not haphazard, no whim of blind
nature, but – if it were taking place at all – was a self-destruction that had
meaning and purpose.

Immense time would be required for such a total destruction of the land.
'Time, which measures every thing in our idea, and is often deficient to our
schemes, is to nature endless and as nothing; it cannot limit that by which alone
it had existence.' Never before had time been framed in a scale of aeons instead
of centuries.

'We are, therefore, to consider as inevitable the destruction of our land, so
far as effected by those operations which are necessary in the purpose of the
globe, considered as a habitable world, and so far as we have not examined any
other part of the economy of nature, in which other operations of a different
intention might appear.'

Here were boldness and subtlety, a preliminary suggestion to his audience
of a world that had existed long before man appeared. At this early point of his
address, Hutton discarded the idea of the earth as a beautiful self-destroying
machine. He invited attention to the world as a body 'in which the necessary
decay of the machine is naturally repaired.' He wished to consider the possible
existence of 'a reproductive operation' giving duration and stability to the
machine.

'If no such reproductive power, or reforming operation, after due
enquiry, is to be found in the constitution of this world, we should have
reason to conclude that the system of this earth has either been
intentionally made imperfect, or has not been the work of infinite
power and wisdom. . . . Here is an important question, therefore, with
regard to the constitution of this globe; a question which, perhaps, it is
in the power of man's sagacity to resolve; and a question which, if
satisfactorily resolved, might add some lustre to science and the human
intellect.'

He discussed the Mosaic teaching by which man and his world had no great
antiquity. The relics of sea-animals in the solid earth suggested a different
concept of time. By examining the data of the natural world 'we shall thus
arrive at facts which indicate a period to which no other species of chronology is
able to remount.'

Not since Newton's *Principia* had such revolutionary ideas been offered to men of science. Newton had restricted his formulae to the mechanics of the physical world. The laws he announced might well be God's laws. Hutton seemed to be determined to explain the world itself, disprove the veracity of the Bible, upset man's simple understanding of time, and examine objectivity the wisdom of the Creator.

'In what follows, therefore, we are to examine the construction of the present earth, in order to understand the natural operations of time past: to acquire principles, by which we may conclude with regard to the future course of things, or judge of these operations, by which a world so wisely ordered goes into decay; and to learn by what means such a decayed world may be renovated, or the waste of the habitable land upon the globe repaired. This, therefore, is the object which we are to have in view during this physical investigation; this is the end to which are to be directed all the steps in our cosmological pursuit.'

Hutton then turned to the details of his work. Immediately after the words 'cosmological pursuit' he took his audience back to the world that was being examined. He proceeded: 'The solid parts of the globe are, in general, composed of sand, of gravel, or argillaceous and calcareous strata. . . .'

He discussed rocks, the known facts of chemistry, and concluded part one of his paper, the *Prospect of the Subject*.

In part two, he investigated the *Natural Operations employed in consolidating the Strata of the Globe*. In part three, he considered the *Natural Operations employed in the Production of Land above the Surface of the Sea*. Volcanic action hoisted the submerged lands so that they formed new continents above the ocean. He commented that 'a volcano is not made on purpose to frighten superstitious people into fits of piety and devotion.' In part four, he dealt with the *System of Decay and Renovation observed in the Earth*.

Professor d'Arcy Thompson, commenting on Hutton, said that 'Hutton considered the effect of heat, and in turn of pressure, on rocks lying deep below the surface of the earth, and came to look on the earth as a machine, driven by internal heat, with volcanoes to act as safety-valves.' Hutton's machine, in certain aspects, seemed to owe a great deal to James Watt's ingenious contraption.

In his final paragraph Hutton said:

'We have now got to the end of our reasoning; we have no data to conclude immediately from that which actually is: But we have got enough; we have the satisfaction to find that in nature there is wisdom, system, and consistency. For having, in the natural history of this earth, seen a succession of worlds, we may from this conclude that there is a system in nature . . . but . . . it is in vain to look for anything higher in the origin of the earth. The result, therefore, of our present enquiry is, that we find no vestige of a beginning – no prospect of an end.'

Two of the main conclusions of the paper laid the foundation of geology. First Hutton showed the process of erosion and the building up of detritus into new strata, and second he showed how strata, built at the bottom of the sea, were 'up-heaved' to form new continents. He claimed, erroneously, that there were no other kinds of rock, and it was his idea of endless wearing down and building up that found expression in the famous final phrase that there was 'no vestige of a beginning – no prospect of an end.'

It was this phrase, too, that prevented immediate recognition as someone who had revolutionised the history of the world. He did not compete with the purveyors of fashionable explanations of the 'origin of things'. Those who were dissatisfied with the Mosaic teaching wanted something more dramatic than Hutton's timelessness. The paper according to Playfair, 'drew attention to itself very slowly, so that several years elapsed before anyone shewed himself publicly concerned with it, either as an enemy or friend.'

Though Hutton, in this one paper, created and founded the scientific study of geology, he was not the first Scot who had turned his attention to the nature of the earth. The first book on geology had been published in 1672 by George Sinclair. It was called a *Short History of Coal*, and was a study on the formation of the ground based on practical mining in the Midlothian coalfield.

As people came to support Hutton's new theories, others wished to controvert them. The eventual result of Hutton's teaching was the emergence of two schools, the Huttonian and the Wernerian, more popularly known as the Plutonists and the Neptunians.

Abraham Werner, the major antagonist of Hutton, had progressed from a smelting-house to become curator of collections and teacher of mining at Freiburg. He made a very orderly study of the earth, and in his lectures he included observations on the distribution of minerals and the effect of this distribution on tribal wanderings, as well as on the character and nature of tribal civilisations.

Werner's explanation of rock formations leaned heavily on the role of the sea, so that his teaching was named Neptunian. The envelope of water that surrounded the earth affected chemical composition and mechanical sedimentation.

Volcanoes, he claimed, were recent, accidental, and irrelevant. There was no internal fire in the earth. Hutton, on the contrary, had reached the idea that inside the earth there might be 'a fluid mass, melted, but unchanged by the action of heat.'

The patient, erudite, and methodological German was led astray by his stubborn pursuit of his *idée fixe*. While Werner and his disciples were carrying the flag of Neptunism triumphantly, some careful geological work was being carried on unobtrusively in the British Isles which was destined to undo the mischief done by the Freiburg school, and to lead geology back to a more scientific path. The head of this counter-movement was Hutton. . . .'

The emphasis placed by Hutton on heat and subterranean fire was, of course, the reason he was dubbed a Plutonian. The two schools argued the matter out for a number of decades until a satisfactory compromise was reached. In view of the argument, which was fiercely passionate and partisan, it is interesting to recall that Hutton had at first become interested in soil movement by his observations on the action of water on land – observations he could hardly have failed to make on his Border farm.

Robert Jameson, who held the chair of natural philosophy at Edinburgh for fifty years, was an adamant opponent of Hutton's teaching. D'Arcy Thomson has said that his description and defence of the Wernerian teaching were the best ever written. (Charles Darwin sat under him and thought him 'incredibly dull.') He capitulated in his old age and gallantly admitted his error, but before then he had, with David Brewster, founded the Wernerian Society of Edinburgh, started the *Edinburgh Philosophical Journal*, and had made the collections that were to become the origin of the Royal Scottish Museum.

Meanwhile the finding of fossil fishes assisted the Scottish Wernerians, such as Dr. John Fleming, who examined the old red sandstone of Fife and discovered it was a fresh-water formation, somewhat older than the carboniferous. At Burdiehouse, near Edinburgh (reputedly Bordeaux House, a name given by members of the court of Mary Queen of Scots, when they lived there while the queen was at Craigmillar Castle nearby), Samuel Hibbert found fish fossils in limestone.

Playfair, the mathematician, was a supporter of Hutton, and published *Illustrations of the Huttonian Theory*. It was he who stood on the moraines of the Jura Mountains and saw that the boulders must be the deposit of vanished glaciers in an age of ice. Sir James Hall used Hutton's theories in his investigation of the 'crag and tail' formations, of which Salisbury Crags was a dominant example within Edinburgh itself, and also the Castle Rock, though on a smaller scale. The Scottish geologists were fortunate in their country being one of the most suitable for early geological investigation, and even the most prominent feature in the capital city offered itself as evidence in support of one of their more important conclusions.

The impact of both Hutton and Werner was considerable. It aroused the resentment of the orthodox, the displeasure of the clerical. But there were men to champion the new conception of the world and its tremendous implications. In his *Vestiges of Creation*, which was first published anonymously, Robert Chambers tried to show how inadequate was the unvarnished doctrine of the creation. In a pre-Darwinian age Chambers's work met with a great deal of resentful opposition, especially on the part of Huxley.

The Geological Society of Edinburgh was founded in 1834, and the same year the first geological map of Scotland was published and the geological survey of England and Wales was started. It was the year of the British Association's meeting in Edinburgh. William Nicoll exhibited his rock sections; Murchison christened the Silurian system; Lyell published the last volume of his *Principles of Geology*, the instrument which made Jameson capitulate, and which deeply influenced the thinking of Darwin when he was considering the origin of species.

Murchison of the Silurian system had been born at Tarradale in Ross-shire in 1792; he was with Wellesley in Galicia and later at Corunna. While in his middle twenties, he left the army to become a geologist. *The Silurian System* was published in 1838, and *The Geology of Russia in Europe and the Urals* in 1845.

Other Scots who narrated the story of the rocks were Benjamin Peach, John Horne, and Charles Lapworth. Peach and Horne showed the complexity of the geology of the north-west Highlands. Peach's father had been a naturalist, and his discoveries of fossils were of great assistance to his son, who unravelled the mysteries of paleaozoic crustacea and arachnids. Peach and Horne mapped the glaciers of the northern islands, and also made a survey of the southern uplands, a task done separately by Murchison. Lapworth made a further survey, correcting earlier errors. In D'Arcy Thompson's words, 'no more brilliant piece of surveying was ever done.' The entire southern region was shown in a series of sections with complicated faulting and overlapping.

Archibald and James Geikie were both students of Murchison, and carried on the exploratory work. Hugh Millar was born in 1802 at Cromarty, and became a stone-mason. His remarkable work *The Old Red Sandstone*, published in 1841, appeared originally as a series of articles in the *Witness*, of which he was editor. Millar was one of the last to show the width of interests that used to unite the arts and sciences. He published a volume of poems in 1829, and a volume called *Legends* in 1835. His poetic ability was inconsiderable, but the attitude of mind that he brought to a scientific understanding of geology was one of wonder at the natural world. He had a simple sense of adoration founded in religion. It was a godhead rather than a Calvinistic god that he saw behind the phenomena of the natural world.

Archibald Geikie, knighted by Victoria, became the Director-General of the Geological Survey of the United Kingdom. It was he who described the calf-country of his teacher, Murchison, as 'the oldest fragment of Europe. It goes back far beyond the age of the earliest of our fossiliferous formations.'

It is possible to comment on the ability of the Scots as geologists, in their role as creators and nurses of the science. Their own land favoured such investigations; their inheritance of the Calvinistic desire to understand 'totality', a desire sweetened by the passage of time and given a weapon by the Scottish scientific tradition, fitted them not only intellectually but in their deepest emotions to conduct such fundamental work.

14

JAMES WATT (1736–1819)

The kirk session is displeased. An awkward, dull schoolboy. The head of a child. To Glasgow and then to London. A quick course of instruction. Press gangs. The return north. Black and Robison. Steam and heat. An engine keeps stopping. Watt solves the problem. He builds an organ. Later discoveries

WATT was born in 1736, when Bonnie Prince Charlie was a youth of sixteen, and he died in the year of Queen Victoria's birth. He himself was as responsible as any one man could be for the vast changes that moved British society during his lifetime.

He was born in the west of Scotland, but his father's people came originally from the north-east. There had been a Watt in Aberdeenshire, killed during the Montrose invasion, whose son came south to the Clyde coast to be employed as a teacher in the village of Cartsdyke. There he prospered, bought property, was given public office, and when he died his tombstone described him as a 'professor of the Mathematicks'.

This man, Thomas Watt, was the grandfather of James. The west of Scotland – unlike the more mannered north-east where the great-grandfather perished – was severe in its sabbatarianism. Thomas Watt was a kirk elder, and on Sundays kept an eye open to see that the holiness of the day was not broken.

There is a kirk session record in which he figures: 'March 5th, 1696. Informed James Rae, skipper in Cartsdyke, had loosed his ship, being sufficiently moored in a safe road, on the Sabbath-day, which gave great offence, and its [*sic*] appointed Alexander Lees and Thomas Watt speak to him, and know what induced him to do so, and report to the next diet.'

The two men saw the skipper, and found him 'really affected and concerned for his breaking of the Lord's-day.' Before the end of the month James Rae came to the kirk session, acknowledged his guilt, and was 'censured with a Sessional rebuke, and admonished to carry on more tenderly on the Lord's-day for the future.'

Thomas, the 'professor', had two sons – John and James. John had an eye for business. As a builder, contractor, merchant, and ship-chandler, he helped to build Greenock and supply the ships that made the town prosperous. He married Agnes Muirhead, 'a fine-looking woman with pleasing graceful manners', and in time became chief magistrate in the town council.

John and Agnes were the parents of the inventor. James was the fourth of five children and the only one to survive into manhood. He was not a healthy child, and his mother, with three children already dead, kept him by her side at home and did not allow him to go to school as early as was customary. She gave him the groundwork of his first lessons. When he eventually attended school, he was a solemn and unsociable boy, a victim of headaches.

'Had he gone very early to school his sensitive nature might have been bruised, and his tastes forced into the narrow channel of things accepted by schoolboy opinion. As it was, by the time he was let out of the family circle into a wider world, his individuality and originality were already well developed, and he never showed any tendency to adapt himself to the type that was most admired by his schoolfellows.'

To begin with, he was dull at his lessons, awkward in manner, and the butt of schoolboy humour. About the age of thirteen or fourteen he began to brighten as a scholar and made quick progress in his grandfather's subject, mathematics.

His apparent backwardness was replaced by a passionate appetite for all kinds of natural and mechanical knowledge. What was not taught at school he pursued on his own. From geometry and mechanics he progressed to geology, botany, and astronomy. Anatomy interested him, and once, while still a stripling, he was caught hiding under his clothing the head of a child that had died of disease. He had hoped to dissect it.

His father had a fascinating workshop in which the boy worked and learned from the workmen. He made models of ships' gear, including a crane that was probably copied from the first crane ever seen in Greenock, made by his father. The workshop itself was a stimulant to his mind. A description of it says that 'In addition to most of the minor details of carpentry, we observe the carving of ship's figure-heads, the making of gun-carriages, of blocks, pumps, capstans, dead-eyes, &., &. The "touching" of ships' compasses is also done here, and

THE HEART OF MIDLOTHIAN

The centre of Edinburgh as it appeared in the eighteenth century. In the background is the stone crown of the High Kirk of St. Giles. In front is the Tolbooth, a strong building that was once used as a meeting place for the Scottish Parliament.

Repaired in 1561 it was used for a long period as a place for debtors and criminals and as quarters for the City Guard.

It was from the Tolbooth that Porteous was abducted by the Edinburgh mob. The Tolbooth was taken down in 1817.

2. ANDREW FLETCHER

3. ALLAN RAMSAY

4. JAMES THOMSON

5. JOHN HOME

6. JAMES WATT

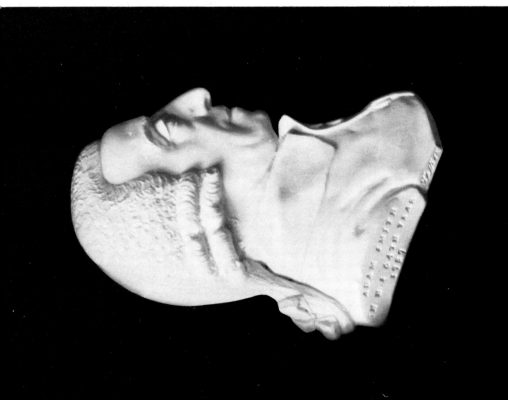

7. ADAM SMITH AND PROFESSOR GREGORY

8. DAVID HUME

9. ADAM FERGUSON

10. ROBERT FERGUSSON

(Scottish National Portrait Gallery)

11. JAMES MACPHERSON

12. THOMAS TELFORD

13. HENRY BELL

15. SIR WALTER SCOTT

14. JAMES HOGG

the adjusting and repairing of such nautical instruments as are yet in use.'

In his middle teens he was suffering from fits of ill-tempered moodiness that lasted his lifetime. As a youth he tried to cure himself by taking violent exercise or by hiding in the country. He had a habit of going to a high planatation behind Greenock where there was then a beautiful view of the Clyde estuary. 'To this spot he was wont to retire at night as well as by day; and, like another Ferguson, the astronomical herd-boy of Scotland, was known to spend hours lying upon his back, to watch through the trees the wondrous movement of the stars.' He was a voracious reader, and when mentally excited a torrential talker.

Watt worked for some time in his father's shop after leaving school, but the domestic pattern was broken when his mother suddenly died. He was then eighteen. This may have been a release for Watt. At any rate he knew exactly what he wanted to do, and went to Glasgow to train as an instrument maker. He lodged with George Muirhead, a relative of his mother and professor of Latin at the university. Watt did not intend to become an articled apprentice and was therefore barred from instruction by the Hammermen of Glasgow, a body as conservative as any modern trade union.

Watt was in a hurry to become as skilled as he could on the practical side of making things, and he was quite intolerant of slow years of apprenticeship. Muirhead introduced him to many members of the university staff, including Dr. Dick, of the chair of natural philosophy. Dick advised him to go to London, and he did so, travelling south on horseback in twelve days, in the care and company of another relative, a man called Marr, a captain of an East Indiaman returning to sea.

Watt found the same difficulties in London that he had come across in Glasgow. No one would accept him except on normal terms of apprenticeship. He wrote to his father: 'I have not yet got a master; we have tried several; they all make some objection or other. I find that if any of them agree with me at all, it will not be for less than a year, and even at that time [they] will be expecting

The Tron Kirk in the High Street, Edinburgh, prior to its being partly demolished to make way for the North Bridge.
It was the bell of this church that Robert Fergusson, who lived near by, called "a wanwordie dinsome thing".

some money.'

Through the office of a fellow Scot, James Short, he met John Morgan, mathematical instrument maker in Finch Lane. On the persuasion of Marr and the recommendation of Dick, Morgan took twenty guineas for a year's instruction, and Watt had to provide for himself. In a few weeks Watt was more competent in the workshop than the fully indentured pupil who had been there for two years. In August he made a Hadley's quadrant, in October he made rules, evidently a task of skill; in November he was busy with an azimuth compass, and by December he thought he could work 'tolerably well'. In the following April, 1756, he wrote to his father: 'I think I shall be able to get my bread anywhere, as I am now able to work as well as most journeymen, though I am not so quick as many.'

While he was in London he lived frugally. Food cost him eight shillings a week, and he could not spend less without pinching his belly. He went out seldom, partly because he was working hard, but also to avoid the press gangs. To his father he wrote:

'They now press anybody they can get, landsmen as well as seamen, except it be in the liberties of the City, where they are obliged to carry them before my Lord Mayor first; and unless one be either a 'prentice or a creditable tradesman, there is scarce any getting off again. And if I was carried before my Lord Mayor, I durst not avow that I wrought in the City, it being against their laws for any unfreeman to work, even as a journeyman, within their Liberties.'

Watt's ill-health would not have protected him, but his prudence saved him from being sent buccaneering against the French by Pitt.

In August 1756, a little over a year after he left Glasgow, he was ill, and felt he had learned all he could from Morgan. He went north, again on horseback, and rejoined his friends in Glasgow.

In October, Dr. Dick asked him if he would repair some instruments that had been left to the university by Alexander Macfarlane, a Scottish merchant in Jamaica, and an astronomer. Watt did the job and was paid five pounds. He was also given a workshop within the university, and was soon appointed its official instrument maker. This began his long connection with Glasgow university, kept him in daily touch with its professors who were curious about his busy workshop, and also kept him away from the jealous Hammermen, who resented his competition and thought him an upstart blackleg.

Joseph Black was amongst those who visited Watt and realised that the young man had a speculative mind and an extraordinary knowledge, as well as a knack for practical work. Black, so sparing of the written word, later wrote that he saw 'an originality, readiness and copiousness of invention which often surprised and delighted me.'

John Robison, then a student, was three years younger than Watt. He was a foil for Watt's moodiness: his quick sympathy and imaginative fancy were stimulants that Watt had great need of.

Robison's own career lay ahead. He became professor of natural philosophy in Edinburgh. Between his student days and his later university life he spent some years travelling. He was at one time attached to Admiral Knowles, who was president of the Russian Admiralty. He was at Quebec and heard Wolfe reciting Gray's *Elegy* before the assault on the Heights of Abraham. It is said that he put the idea of a steam-engine to Watt when he was still a student of twenty. He imagined a carriage on wheels driven by steam. Watt, though busy building up his business, made a model carriage with two cylinders of tin-plate. Nothing happened. It was not Watt but his pupil Murdoch who eventually built the first steam carriage. But Watt knew that steam could effect mechanical movement, and he began to study its properties. There was little enough to study and most of what existed was written in German and Italian. He therefore learned those languages.

He made a discovery about the nature of heat, and in discussing it with Black he found that the professor had for some time been teaching the same thing, describing it as the phenomenon of latent heat. Watt now felt himself committed to the investigation of steam and its use to drive an engine. The university had once possessed a model of the Newcomen engine; it had some time before been sent to London for repair. Watt urged its return. Meantime he experimented with apparatus made from apothecaries' vials, cane tubes, anything that could be turned to his purpose. It took two years, 1761–63, for the Newcomen model to be recovered.

Watt tackled it as a mechanic, repaired it, and found that it worked a few strokes and then stopped. The primitive engine required to be alternately heated and cooled, above and below boiling point. The continual stopping of the model interested Watt because he knew that full-sized models did continue to work, though part of the cycle was manual. The cylinder of the model was of brass (a good conductor of heat), whereas the full-scale models were of cast-iron (not so efficient a conductor). Watt realised from his knowledge of latent heat that the cycle of operations inevitably entailed a vast wastage of heat, and that the model was showing in an emphatic way what must be a considerable disadvantage in the full-scale engine. He argued that, if he could operate the engine without requiring to cool it, but always at the heat of steam, the increase in efficiency should be considerable. The solution to the problem occurred to him one Sabbath morning when he was walking across Glasgow Green. He devised the separate condenser. 'I had not walked further than the golf-course when the whole thing was arranged in my mind.'

At this time he was busy with the workshop, which had become 'a kind of academy whither all the notabilities of Glasgow repaired, to discuss the nicest questions in art, science, and literature'. In 1759, he had gone into partnership with a man called Craig. In five years the partners had a staff of sixteen men. Watt made and repaired everything, and any problem he met was dealt with by his technique of practical experiment and theoretical study. A Masonic Lodge, for example, had need of an organ. Could Watt build an organ? they asked. 'He sat down to study the theory of music, thoroughly examined the mechanism of the best organ he could find, and devised an exact method by which he could tune pipes by observing "the beat of imperfect consonances". By the time the work was completed, Watt had made substantial contributions, not only to the mechanics of organ design, but also to the theory of sound.'

After devising the separate condenser, there were years of work, of laborious make-shifts with imperfect materials. His ideas leaped ahead of the ability to translate them into mechanism. There was a succession of models, always amended and improved on paper before they had been completed. But his essential idea was so sound, and Watt so persistently fertile with secondary ideas, that the harnessing of power to industry followed with logical certainty. The Newcomen engine had been an elaborate toy, only workable when there was an unlimited and cheap supply of coal to feed the fire. By deciding to keep the cylinder hot, and establishing how it might be done, Watt raised the curtain on the industrial age. That he did so in a workshop where people discussed nice questions in art, science, and literature is a measure of the age that his invention helped to destroy.

Watt patented his steam-engine in 1769, and Boulton and Paul made it at Soho Ironworks, Birmingham. 'In 1783 came his double-acting rotary steam-engine, from which it may be claimed that the whole system of modern mechanisation and mechanical transport has sprung.'

15

ADAM SMITH (1723–90)

Childhood in Fife.   Hutcheson at Glasgow.   Penury
at Oxford.   Return to Glasgow.   Travel abroad.
Retreat to Kirkcaldy.   The Wealth of Nations.   Over-
production of humans.   Pessimism and optimism.   Vice
and virtue.   Comparison with Hume.   Social trivia.

EARLY IN THE EIGHTEENTH CENTURY the Fife town of Kirkcaldy
declined from prosperity to become an impoverished village. Its fishing
industry was crippled by the salt tax imposed after the Union.

Salt was the means whereby fish was processed and preserved in an edible
state. A tax on salt was a body blow to the fishing industry. In those dolorous
days Kirkcaldy possessed only one coaster of fifty tons and a couple of ferry
boats. A few ships sailed from its shore to fish the deeper seas, but herring
busses from Holland took the cream of the catch from within sight of the port
and, free of trade restrictions, sold their cargoes in those foreign ports with
which Kirkcaldy, and other Scottish towns, had done good trade in former
days.

In the seventeen-twenties the widow of Adam Smith, lately Writer to the
Signet and Comptroller of Customs (salary £30 per annum with perquisites),
lived in one of the few slated houses that the town possessed. Her husband had
died before the birth of their son, also christened Adam, in 1723. The name was
well-known in Kirkcaldy as the surname of a King's mason, whose family of
boys attended the local school with young Adam Smith.

In his infancy Adam Smith survived a kidnapping by gypsies. He was a
bright pupil, and in the thatched classroom he mastered the famous textbook of
the period, the renowned Ruddiman's *Rudiments*.

In 1737, young Adam went to Glasgow College, where his professors were
Robert Simson, the mathematician, and the famous Francis Hutcheson whose
domain was moral philosophy and who, when Adam was seventeen,
recommended that David Hume should send the promising youngster a copy
of the *Treatise of Human Nature*.

Three years later a Snell Exhibition, worth £40 a year, took Smith to Balliol
College. After the eager and searching vitality of Glasgow, he found himself in
the sterility of Oxford, where wages and board took a large part of his
scholarship, fees a small part, leaving little for books, clothing, and pleasure.
Gray Graham describes Oxford at this time: 'Scraps of antiquated philosophy,

tags of forgotten scholarship, were given by professors and tutors who taught as little as students cared to learn.' For six years Adam read in the little-used libraries and then returned to Kirkcaldy, where he spent the next two years with his mother, uncertain about his future. He had had thoughts, when at Oxford, of entering the Church of England, but his ties with the north were too strong. By ship he was able to cross the Forth from time to time to continue his friendship with David Hume, his elder by some years, and to meet others of the band of extraordinary men who frequented Edinburgh at that time.

In 1748 he began to establish his reputation, and to earn some money, by lecturing to the young lawyers, lairds, and ministers of Edinburgh.

In 1751 he obtained the Glasgow chair of professor of logic, and in the next year exchanged this for Moral Philosophy, teaching in the classroom where he had been Hutcheson's pupil just over ten years before. Here he made a great reputation. His classes and his opinions were fashionable, and as a teacher he broke new ground. There was then no portmanteau phrase to cover his subject. In Edinburgh he had talked on Jurisprudence; in Glasgow he developed the theme of Justice, but in effect he was talking about the development of civilised society, especially law and government. In 1753 he gave the first of his famous lectures on Justice, Police, Revenue, and Arms. Amongst his pupils were many destined to become famous, including John Millar (who is an astonishing bridge between Smith and Marx), and William Robertson, future historian and principal of Edinburgh University.

Glasgow in the 1750s was an active town. Its trade was flourishing and its university was eager, and these two vitalities worked on each other. Apprentices came to hear Adam Smith expounding the nature of human society as no one before had ever done. He found in Glasgow an unending source of material for examination. It has been suggested that the nature of Glasgow, and the Scotland of the '50s and '60s, made inevitable a close examination of society. Rapidity of progress, together with the facility for ready contrast with older forms of life, brought about the condition in which sociology and political economy became distinct studies, by logic out of moral philosophy, with law as the *accoucheur*.

In Glasgow he prepared his *Theory of Moral Sentiments*. He was teaching the principles that were later embodied in *The Wealth of Nations*. Glasgow's provost was president of a study society. David Hume had recently published his essay on the Balance of Trade. In 1754 the Select Society was formed in Edinburgh, one of a long number of 'improving' societies, devoted to the promotion of land cultivation, the arts, shipping, and the manufacture of linen.

Amongst Adam Smith's colleagues was James Moor, professor of Greek, a dapper and elegant man who wore an exquisitely powdered wig. In the street one day he passed two officers, one of whom said loudly to the other: 'He smells strongly of powder.' Moor replied: 'Don't be alarmed, gentlemen; it is not gunpowder.'

The *Theory of Moral Sentiments* was published by Andrew Millar in London in 1759, and was a success. Hume reported that 'three bishops called at

Millar's shop in order to buy copies and ask questions about its author.'

The *Theory* avoided conventional concepts of theology, and carried on the teaching of Hutcheson. The fresh optimism of the cleric-philosopher became a more wordly *laisser-faire*. 'This is a world where everything is for the best, under a great benevolent Being, who seeks to give the greatest possible amount of happiness here and hereafter.' If the optimism of Hutcheson and Smith seemed too good to be true, Hume administered the acid corrective, but without cynicism.

In 1763 Smith went abroad as tutor to the young Duke of Buccleugh, a post he obtained through the influence of Townshend. He relinquished his professorship (in itself a moral act, as many would have hired a hack to act as subtitute in order to keep the chair). Smith returned his fees to his students, wrapping them carefully in paper. His tutorship promised eventual leisure, as it carried a salary of £400 and a pension for life of £300.

He took the duke on a three years' intellectual tour of Europe, about which Gray Graham has this to say :-

'In fashionable circles which doted on "sensibility", after *La Nouvelle Heloise* and *Clarissa Harlowe* had touched the organs which their owners mistook for hearts, a writer like the author of the *Theory of Moral Sentiments* was sure of a welcome, especially from emotional dames, who fancied that when he had derived moral sentiments from sympathy, he had reduced morality to sentiment, so that one could be moral without the trouble of being virtuous.'

Before Adam Smith, Cantillon and the physiocrats (Gournay, Quesnay, Turgot, Mirabeau) were the most prolific and profound thinkers on economics. While he was abroad, Smith was in touch with Quesnay and Turgot, as well as d'Alembert and Helvetius. All this was preparation. When the tour was finished, he went back to Kirkcaldy in 1766. He worked there for ten years, while he lived with his mother, more or less in seclusion. In 1776 *The Wealth of Nations* was published.

In Adam Smith is found once again the method of approach that informed his Scottish contemporaries in their diverse fields – the seeking of universal principles through a close examination of factual detail. The recognition of his accomplishments was not delayed. Burke said of *The Wealth of Nations* that it was 'in its ultimate results probably the most important book that had ever been written', a statement which time might modestly modify, but which shows the *éclaircissement* it offered Europe and America at that time. More recently it has been said by V. A. Demant that Adam Smith 'did as much as any man to give a rational foundation for the emancipation of economics from religious or ethical control.' This emancipation was his achievement, but it was also a logical development on the teaching of his Glasgow professors, and not a revolutionary break-away. His work, in fact, arose directly out of his eighteenth-century Scottish background.

It was just before his retreat to Kirkcaldy, to work on *The Wealth of Nations*, that Alexander Webster made his census of Scotland, the first census taken in Britain. That was in 1755, two years after the House of Lords had rejected a proposal for an annual census of Britain. He calculated Scotland's population to be 1,265,380, of which he reckoned one-fifth were 'effective men'.

The significance of population had already exercised attention. In the seventeenth century, Sir William Petty had argued that the steady increase of world population contained an inherent peril. In the middle of the eighteenth century, Robert Wallace showed the Edinburgh Philosophical Society that the population would probably double in a third of a century. His pre-Malthus views were full of warning and apprehension, and he suggested that, until then, mankind had only been saved from over-population by its own errors and vices and by 'the defects of government and education'. He attacked Utopian visions of the future. The earth, by its nature, set limits to the peaceful expansion of the human race. In spite of 'sickly seasons of dreadful plagues', the result of mankind's fertility would be an overstocked earth 'unable to support its numerous inhabitants' – a view which the passage of some generations has not made less eloquent. He argued that, even if food production could be increased beyond imagination, the physical limits of the earth made it certain that, in time, man's capacity for multiplying would result in disaster. Though it was obvious that measures such as marriage limitation, sterilisation, infanticide, and geronticide, might stave off disaster, Wallace had no illusions about their being acceptable. 'Mankind would never agree about such regulations.'

Adam Smith, while deeply aware of the force of such arguments, to be developed with even more ineluctable foreboding by Malthus, was prompted to dispose of them by his conception of a world which adjusted itself, more or less happily, to its circumstances.

His *Moral Sentiments* and his *Wealth of Nations* were two parts, or two preliminaries, of an unfulfilled plan to write a comprehensive work on moral and political philosophy. Too much emphasis has been put on *The Wealth of Nations* by later generations, so that Adam Smith is not seen in his proper role as the complete philosopher-interpreter of society in all its aspects. He believed in man and mankind. This was the benevolence that Hutcheson had taught at Glasgow after the dethronement of the puritan concept of a divine malevolence. Smith believed that pity, compassion, love, gratitude, and friendship were ingredients in the make-up of every person, not absent from 'the greatest ruffian, the most hardened violater of the law.' In this he anticipated the attitude of twentieth century penal reform and psychiatric teaching, and continued the attitude of the New Testament.

The *Theory of Moral Sentiments* was constructed around the author's arguments about virtue and vice in human relationship. In *The Wealth of Nations* he developed the theme of self-interest as a social force. Self-interest was the unexpected obverse to the medal of social morality. Mandeville had argued that private vice – greed, for example – was in fact public benefit, through the stimulation of commerce. Adam Smith showed that this kind of vice, or self-interest, though it was expressed selfishly, did not deny the virtues of love and co-operation, nor was it a necessary impediment to the development of an enlightened society.

Smith argued that the dialectic was really one of common sense (in this he paralleled the philosophers who countered Hume): when abstract concepts and unreal philosophising were abandoned, this strange combination of vice and virtue interacting healthily with each other was what one really saw in society.

'Give me that which I want, and you shall have this which you want, is the meaning of every offer. . . . It is not from the benevolence of the butcher, the brewer, or the baker, that we expect our dinner, but from their regard to their own interest. We address ourselves, not to their humanity, but to their self-love, and never talk to them of our own necessities, but of their advantages.'

Adam traced the development of society from its most primitive forms to the involved industrial state with its division of labour. In arguing the importance of the division of labour – which in essence means that modern society demands a man do one thing reasonably well, rather than many things imperfectly – he was fully aware of the human disadvantage.

'The man whose whole life is spent in performing a few simple operations has no occasion to exert his understanding, or to exercise his invention in finding out expedients for removing difficulties which never occur. He naturally loses, therefore, the habit of such exertion, and generally becomes as stupid and ignorant as it is possible for a human creature to become.'

The ultimate custodian of man's welfare was the enlightened state itself. The worker was to be protected.

'His dexterity in his own particular trade seems in this manner to be acquired at the expense of his intellectual, social, and moral virtues. But in every improved and civilised society this is a state into which the labouring poor, that is the great body of the people, must necessarily fall, unless the government takes some means to prevent it.'

Adam Smith knew the cloddish miners, near-bestial in their slavery. But though he saw the dangers of the evolving state, he believed like Mirabeau that compulsory education would so develop man's faculties that brutishness would vanish, and the monotony of a repetitive job would be amply compensated by a more agreeable and fuller life.

In essence he was the first sociologist. 'Jupiter' Carlyle had a great admiration for his character and ability – 'perhaps second only to David Hume in learning and ingenuity.' The garrulous diarist was probably right. These two men, Hume and Smith, are the prime exemplars of the Scottish renaissance mind, enquiring into the great principles that appear to underlie the universe and human conduct within it. Their main conclusions, though so vastly different, are complementary and integrated.

Adam Smith's personality appears to have been charming in a rather helpless way. Carlyle describes him as conversationally awkward. 'He was the most absent man in company that I ever saw, moving his lips and talking to himself, and smiling, in the midst of large companies . . . His voice was harsh and his enunciation thick, approaching to stammering.'

Of a birthday party of the Duke and Duchess of Buccleugh, at which the fare was sumptuous and the company formal and stiff, Carlyle said that 'Adam Smith, their only familiar at table, was but ill qualified to promote the jollity of a birthday.' But Carlyle regarded himself as a bit of a dog socially, and Adam in all probability made a poor show beside the waggish cleric.

'I am a beau in nothing but my books', Smith said of himself. Like Hume, he was eminently sociable amongst his peers, but the foppishness of formal society meant nothing to him. His judgment on some things (and again he was like Hume) was appalling. Shakespeare, he claimed, had written 'some good scenes, but never a good play'. This gave Wordsworth the opportunity to say that Adam Smith was 'the worst critic – David Hume not excepted – that Scotland, a soil to which this sort of weed seems natural, has produced.' It is often possible to cavil at Wordsworth, but not in this instance.

16

DAVID HUME – PHILOSOPHER (1711–76)

Works on Hume. Spelling and pronunciation. Birth and childhood. A bare-foot boy. The Calvinist tradition. The law is uncongenial. Attempt at commerce. A triune of philosophers. Berkeley's chair. Reality a dream. Amazement, irresolution and confusion. A succession of perceptions. The insufficiency of logic. False reasoning. Natural instinct and ordinary living

IN HUME, the greatest of the individuals created by the Scottish eighteenth century, there is perhaps a clue to the formative processes behind the century's efflorescence of talent and genius. Hume, of course, stands alone. He was never popularly understood in his own time, and those who were competent enough to refute him failed to grasp the simplicity of what he said.

Bertrand Russell has written that 'Hume alone, among the great philosophers, denied substance altogether, and thus paved the way for modern discussions of the distinction between the mental and the physical.' Compared with his rowdy contemporary in the south, Dr. Johnson, who would talk cant as readily as sense provided he might talk at all, Hume was held in almost universal affection. His geniality, his sense of fun, his deep 'goodness', are still the attributes by which he is best remembered. He had no malice, nor any of the temperament of genius.

There has unfortunately been no study of Hume that deals imaginatively with the man and his background. Of the two modern works, the book *David Hume* by J. Y. T. Greig attempts an exposition of the extraordinary Calvinist background to his youth, but it does not relate Hume's own development to the *ethos* of his country. Indeed, Greig professes surprise that a man of Hume's stature should have arisen in Scotland at all. That he was a natural part of a Scottish process is not suggested.

The later book, *The Life of David Hume* by Ernest Campbell Mossner, is a work of scholarly devotion and precision. In both books the facts are plainly given. Even so, the story is not complete because much of the detail of his childhood is unknown. What is lacking is a study of Hume in relation to his day and age. His thoughts and writing were not the acts of a man living in a vacuum, and genius must be related to the events and influences that nourish it and determine its manner of expression.

The Scottish surname Home is pronounced 'Hume'. David was born a Home, and it was a reasonable decision as a young man that made him alter the spelling so that it coincided with the pronunciation. He was born in Edinburgh in 1711. His upbringing in a Border family of modest standing was without any spectacular event. He was brought up by his widowed mother, and he may have spent part of each year in Edinburgh and part at the family home of Ninewells in the Borders, nine miles from Berwick. He certainly knew Edinburgh as a child, though he knew Ninewells better.

The household was frugal of necessity, but not spartan. His dead father had been an advocate who had chosen his Border inheritance and the life of a laird in preference to the courts of Edinburgh. Hume's mother was the daughter of Sir David Falconer, who had been Lord President of the Court of Session in 1681. It is likely that David Hume lived the life of a bare-foot boy, keeping company and being educated with the sons of farmers and blacksmiths in a society which was in a way classless but by no means unaware of status and degree.

Brought up in a civilised and educated home, he was none the less exposed during his boyhood and youth to the rural Calvinist atmosphere in all its dreary severity, its long-windedness, its vindictiveness, and its stupidity. The savagery of Calvinism was part of Hume's youth. His upbringing in the Borders must have been very similar to that of James Thomson.

An uncle was the local minister at Ninewells. He was probably a benign enough man, but he was of the same age and breed and preached the same manner of sermons as the psychotic Thomas Boston. It was Calvinism that shaped Hume's powers so that, before he was thirty, he had summarily condemned its ethics and destroyed its logic. There is little doubt, too, that it was to the Calvinist tradition that he owed much of his ability for scrupulous argument.

What Greig views with horror as an astonishing and bizarre background for the philosopher was, in fact, the necessary background for the development of his thought. Calvinism was the anvil on which he forged his blade of reason: a blade which, if the metaphor be continued, became so tempered that in the end it was able to cut the anvil to pieces.

In 1723, in his early teens, Hume went to Edinburgh University and began the study of law. Already with a taste for setting his own course against pedantry and dogmatism, he found law uncongenial and restrictive. He also lost whatever serious belief in religion he had held as a boy. Amongst Edinburgh *literati* there was a taste for 'metaphysical disquisition', and Hume relished it. For four years he pursued the nominal study of law before deciding against it and leaving the university.

It was at this time that his mother, noting the apparent lack of application in her younger son, called him a 'fine good-natured crater, but uncommon wake-minded'. Weak-minded is an epithet that biographers and historians have seized on as inexplicable, and they have worried at it in unimaginative solemnity. Little can these solemn scholars know of the variety of apparently unsympathetic epithets bestowed on their children by Scottish mothers!

Aided by a very slender inheritance of money, Hume left Scotland, first of all intending to try commerce for a livelihood. He found this (in Bristol) to be no more congenial than law, and he went to France where, by strict economy, he was able to study in peace. At La Flèche he completed the *Treatise on Human Nature*, which had been occupying him for years. He became what he wanted to be, a man of letters. The book was published in 1739–40 and fell, as he said, 'dead-born from the press'.

1741–42 saw the successful publication of the *Essays Moral and Political*. From 1746 to '48, he was with General St. Clair on foreign missions. In 1748 he published his *Enquiry concerning Human Understanding*, an attempt to popularise the *Treatise*. Other publications followed, and the slow recognition of his *Treatise* turned him into a European figure. He was lionised in France when, in 1763, he became secretary to the ambassador there, Lord Hurtford. Four years later he was Under-Secretary of State. By 1769 he had returned to Edinburgh to set up house with his sister. Hume, the man, was a complex person bounded by a vast and unassuming simplicity.

His scepticism, his refutation of the philosophic truth of inductive arguments, was a product of an age when Scottish science was making its great strides by the application of such arguments to practical ends. Amongst Hume's friends were the most able scientists, such as Cullen and Black. Adam Smith was one of his closest companions. The simple subtlety of Hume's own arguments can be best appreciated against the work of his friends and contemporaries in the world of science, as much as against the rigid puritanical background into which he was born and in which he was brought up, but which, during his lifetime, greatly transformed its own outlook.

Locke, Berkeley, and Hume are a triumvirate, with Hume at the apex. He was the last of the three, and had benefited from the work of the other two. Locke, the empiricist, had carefully explored experience. He had accepted God as the prime mover and first cause in a system of causality. Matter, or substance, he had accepted as giving expression to qualities such as solidity and motion.

Berkeley, the churchman philosopher, dealt with materialism by showing that substance existed only in the mind of the beholder. He discovered the notorious 'chair' known to every schoolboy as existing only when it is seen. Berkeley believed that, if the material foundation of the world was shown to be, in fact, a false inference of prying scientific and atheistic minds, then atheism and scepticism would be dethroned. He managed to show that such qualities as solidity and motion might exist without the need of external material substance. If dreams sometimes appeared to be reality, then reality might well be a dream.

As Berkeley improved on Locke, by arguing him more closely, so Hume took Berkeley and sailed still closer to the winds of logic. Of Berkeley he said that, though he argued against sceptics and scepticism, yet the arguments were themselves sceptical, 'they admit of no answer and produce no conviction. Their only effect is to cause that momentary amazement and irresolution and confusion, which is the result of scepticism.'

Since man was limited to the experiences he felt mentally, Hume would allow no escape of comfort or convenience to an Eternal Spirit. 'Let us chase our imagination to the heavens, or to the utmost limits of the universe; we never really advance a step beyond ourselves, nor can conceive any kind of existence, but those perceptions, which have appeared in that narrow compass. This is the universe of the imagination, nor have we any idea but what is there produced.'

If the reality of the external world of substance could be rejected as unproved, then so should the reality of a mental soul or spirit. All that could be said was that man experienced a succession of perceptions, and from them he was entitled to deduce remarkably little in the way of beliefs. It was the continuity of rapid successive perceptions of the senses that gave an illusory notion of a personal soul, or self, or substance. The soul 'is only a system of floating ideas without any substance to support them.'

Hume showed with dry impeccability of argument that cause and effect were unwarranted inferences about the presumed connection of successive impressions. If these inferences could not be logically justified, then the elaborate arguments of Berkeley and Locke for a First Cause could not be upheld.

What Hume did was to show the insufficiency of logical reasoning, its presumptuousness in attempting to lay down conclusive 'beliefs' about the universe, the world, and about man himself.

Almost totally misunderstood, instead of being praised as the closest thinker of his age, Hume was seen as 'the damned atheist' who preached that immortal men, constructed in the divine mould, had no souls, no spirits, no pious and eternal union with the Father, the Son, and the Holy Ghost.

The idea of 'scepticism' – that anything is possible but very little can be proved by reason – was entirely foreign to the dogmatic temper of the times. It was this that led, in the beginning, to the *Treatise* being ignored. Only when time had passed did the few who were able to comprehend come to hear of the book and realise its importance.

Hume stated that a customary association of ideas, such as flame and heat, could not be shown rationally as one being the cause and the other the effect. He did not deny the possibility, nor the likelihood, of a causal connection. He argued only that it could not be proved by a logical process, that a cause was indeed not a reason, but only the habitual inference made from perceptions in constant association. 'The inference . . . depends solely on the union of ideas.' 'Perhaps 'twill appear in the end that the necessary connexion depends on the inference, instead of the inference's depending on the necessary connexion.'

It was a pretty argument. It showed there was no logical justification for physical or mental substance, for matter or for spirit, for causal relationships or for qualities. All that the rational mind could legitimately use in its philosophical cogitations were the impressions it gained from the senses, the ideas it presented to itself, and the associations of those ideas, made by itself. More than that there was nothing to be said except to deny false reasoning. And it was false reasoning that was to be attacked, not those things that were inexplicable or unassailable by the instrument of reason.

Such simplicity was not to be brooked. To the stupid, Hume was an atheist, a denier of God. To the more intelligent, he was the iconoclast of reason, the one faculty by which men differed from brutes. To a few, he was a man who cleared away the inherited intellectual lumber of centuries and set man free of prejudice by clearly defining the power of his mind. And he defeated the supernatural which was the essence of Calvinist thinking.

He was quite aware of the limtations of the philosophical approach. While seeking to propagate these limitations, he was accused of bringing the godly order of the universe crashing about the ears of the faithful. He said of the scientific approach that what it proved would be probabilities rather than ascertainable facts, but the probabilities were certain enough to be sufficient for ordinary life and living. The scientists, better trained in thinking than the theologians, accepted this and went ahead with their science.

17

THE RESPONSE TO HUME

The uncerntainty of certainty. Behaviour more important
than philosophy. £40 a year. A dance in emptiness.
Marischal and King's The reply to Hume. The
School of Common Sense. Hume's backgammon. A
cul-de-sac. Kant's dogmatic slumbers. The puritan
tradition

THE 'HERESY' OF HUME was his reluctance to see that there was any
necessary connection between the benefits of a moral society and a belief in a
godhead. To use the mind as an instrument of exact argument was a deplorable
novelty to many of his contemporaries, as it would be today to their
descendants.

Hume carried to its conclusion the attempts of the Calvinists to strip man's
attitude to the world of all obfuscating prejudices, false loyalties, and
misleading emotions. That the Calvinists leaped from one set of prejudices to
another was, in part, an intellectual progress, and in part their inevitable
inadequacy as tyros. What they were seeking, in any case, was not a credible
philosophy but the right to worship God in their own way, not necessarily the
same thing. To be free to worship God is presumably better than to be unfree to
worship him, or to be forced to worship him in what, to a mind occupied with
its own conception of freedom, appears to be an unfree way. God remains the
postulate, the presupposition.

It seems hardly necessary to affirm that Hume was not an atheist, nor need
much fuss be made of it one way or the other. Names mattered little to him. It
would also be unjust to suggest that he had no need of the comforting emotions
that arise out of beliefs confidently held; he simply refused to bowdlerise his
thoughts to acquire such beliefs. He maintained his rigorously sensible
approach to morals and metaphysics without becoming an intellectual ascetic.
His scepticism was rich, never the bare bones of disbelief. He did not accept the
contentious disputations of his day, the religious and philosophic ideologies
that framed the universe, as being any more than the smallest and most
imperfect glimpses of truth. Nor was it possible to say that truth and reality
were understandable. It was certainly impermissible for an honest thinker to
patch together the message of his senses and proudly weave the complete fabric
of truth. Nothing was certain; certainty least of all.

Meanwhile, said Hume, since it is both pleasant and beneficial to behave quietly and reasonably in an orderly society, it behoves everyone to be polite and civilised; one can always argue about God and First Causes and Survival after Death over a bottle of claret. He knew that emotions were important, especially emotions of kindliness and love, but they were of little use as instruments in mental exploration. The Christian Calvinists, or the more bitter of them who survived, had long before thrown love and kindliness to the devil, and would have flung Hume too if they could.

It was a kindly cleric who was most able to answer Hume. He was Thomas Reid, the son of a minister. He went to Marischal College Aberdeen when he was twelve, and joined the class of the regent, George Turnbull, by whom he was instructed in a shabby ill-lit room. Turnbull, a remarkable teacher, was paid the sum of £40 for instructing his pupils in every subject required by the curriculum.

Reid became a minister and was licensed to preach at the age of nineteen. He was presented to a living at New Machar, and this presentation was contrary to the principles of his aggressively democratic charges, so that the induction took place under the protection of a military guard with naked swords.

When he left this church after fifteen years, those who had opposed his coming wept at his depature. 'We fought against Mr. Reid when he came; we would have fought for him when he left.' He had a quaintly trafficking attitude towards his God, and on an occasion when his wife was ill he tried to requisition divine intervention by promising and covenanting 'through grace to turn from my backsliding, to express my thankfulness by a vigorous discharge of my duty as a Christian minister, and master of a family, and by an alms of ten pounds sterling to the poor in meal or money.'

He philosophised, botanised, sermonised, and in the year of the last Stuart Rebellion his *Essay on Quantity* was read before the Royal Society in London. This was his major effort at authorship, and in it he wrestled with a theory of Hutcheson.

He came upon Hume's *Treatise* some years after it was first published, and he was appalled at the succinct manner in which the Berkeleian structure of philosophic truth was shattered. 'I see myself and the whole frame of nature' he wrote, 'shrink into fleeting ideas, which like Epicurus's atoms dance about in emptiness.' (Reid's natural horror of Hume's philosophy is underlined today, as is Hume's philosophy itself, by the teaching of twentieth-century scientists who inform us that the universe may indeed be a dance of atoms in emptiness.)

Reid resolved, by way of empiricism and the neglected 'natural instinct', to create a habitable human house in this emptiness. His approach to Hume was that of a man of common sense who would have none of the idealistic nonsense and specious argument that led nowhere.

When he left his charge of New Machar, he returned to Aberdeen and became regent in the university's other college, King's, distinguished by its monastic discipline from Marischal College, whose students had freedom to lodge anywhere in town. The discipline at King's had been instituted by an earlier principal, the historian Row the younger. Reid insisted that King's students live within the college, as they would then be secure from such temptations as were afforded by Aberdeen. They were locked inside the walls of their college from nine at night until six in the morning.

The subjects that Reid taught included logic, moral philosophy, natural philosophy, hydrostatics, and astronomy. He took his place in the professorial fraternity that met informally over eighteen-penny meals to discuss and debate the whole range of knowledge and affairs.

Reid composed and wrote his reply to Hume, and through the medium of Dr. Hugh Blair he submitted the work to Hume so that his philosophic antagonist could have the opportunity of correcting, not Reid's arguments, but his literary style. Hume had a reputation for spotting Scotticisms.

Andrew Millar published the work in London under the title *Enquiry into the Human Mind on the Principles of Common Sense*. Reid had taken twenty years to compose it, and from Millar he received a flat sum of £50. This was in 1762, over thirty years after the first appearance of Hume's *Treatise*. In 1764 Reid took over the Glasgow chair of Moral Philosophy, left vacant by Adam Smith. He taught there for sixteen years. He listened to Black talk on latent heat; he knew Alexander Wilson's famous type-faces; he was enthusiastic about the studies of optics and astronomy. He was regarded by Hume as the only worthy opponent to have contested the *Treatise*.

Reid was the major figure in what became known as the Scottish School of Common Sense Philosophy. He had the greatest admiration for Hume's work. 'I shall always avow myself your disciple in metaphysics. I have learned more from your writings in this kind, than from all others put together.'

He had felt the inadequacy of philosophic doubt, stretched to Humeian scepticism. It was unsatisfactory. The light it shed was brilliant, but so concentrated, such a thin pencil of light, that it hardly illumined the human scene or the cosmos. He felt that Hume had not given enough attention to 'natural instinct'. Hume's own diffidence about scepticism had been illustrated by his famous passage: 'I dine, I play a game of backgammon, I converse, and am merry with my friends; and when after three or four hours' amusement I would return to these speculations, they appear so cold, and strained, and ridiculous, that I cannot find in my heart to enter into them any farther.'

He argued that an idealist philosophy was bound to lead to almost total scepticism, an arid, unfruitful, and unhelpful outlook. The fault was not in the argument but in the 'doctrine of ideas'. In discussing the solid material world, Reid totally reversed the Berkeley-Locke-Hume attitude; he claimed that 'those things do really exist which we distinctly perceive by our senses, and are what we perceive them to be'. A very sensible comment.

Of Hume's inability to decide about the source of impressions, whether they had an origin in objects, in the mind, or were derived from God, Reid suggested that Hume had ignored the possibility 'of their arising from any cause'. It was a fair blow, even though Hume had indicated that he was sceptical of scepticism. Reid completed Hume's argument by taking it into a cul-de-sac from which, in the nature of culs-de-sac, there appeared to be no exit at the far end.

Common sense, he argued, was the alternative to this kind of sceptical frustration. But the principles of common sense could not be logically proved; they could however be supported by the 'consent of ages and nations, of the learned and the unlearned', an old argument made to do duty again.

Reid was soon eclipsed by Kant, who had spent the earlier part of his life working on problems in the manner of Leibnitz and Locke, until Hume's *Treatise* 'wakened him from dogmatic slumbers'. It seemed unrealistic to Kant that the validity of the physical sciences could not be accepted. Transcendentalism and his *Critique* were his answer to Hume. But Kant himself was dogmatic in his abuse of Reid.

In this way Reid was the quintessence of the practical learned outlook. He lacked genius, but his hard, competent and far-ranging mind was eminently kindly and civilised; he was enthusiastically curious, and in the puritan tradition he was without affectation or frills of manner. Again in the tradition, while unendingly interested in humanity and indefatigably curious about the physical world, he kept an eye on eternity. His Common Sense School exercised a considerable influence in its day, especially in New England, and his arguments have not lost their savour nor their importance.

18

EDINBURGH AND ROBERT FERGUSSON

A triple centre. Whimsicals and Sootymen. The town
expands. The clapper of the bell. Robert is insulted.
Ruddiman's magazine. Lyrics from Tenducci. The
Cape Club. Tom Sommers is a gloomy man. The poet
in distress. In Bedlam. Robert Burns and Robert Louis
Stevenson.

IN 1760, WHEN GEORGE III began his long reign, about 70,000 people
lived in Edinburgh. The city had changed little since the beginning of the
century; it remained antique and malodorous. It had a triple centre – the
church of St. Giles, the jail of the Tolbooth, and Parliament Hall where the
lawyers nested. A child might toss a stone from one of these buildings to the
next; they were the triangular heart of the city – spiritual power, judicial power,
and prison cells for those who had neither.

The city was without factories, but many books were printed, and near
Holyrood a family called Younger was busy with the brewing of beer. No great
expansion had happened to Edinburgh, in the way that Glasgow had expanded
in the previous thirty years on the profits of its American trade; nor had the
port of Leith grown as, in the west, Greenock had developed to the commercial
advantage of James Watt's father. Edinburgh remained a tight mediaeval
fortress, and the gates in its massive walls were shut every night.

Allan Ramsay had been dead only a few brief years. The rose bushes he had
known outside the 'goose-pie' still offered their annual flowers. Edinburgh's
high tenements, decorated with pepper-pot turrets and crow-step gables,
stretched from the castle past St. Giles to the Netherbow Port. From there the
separate burgh of the Canongate continued the Royal Mile as far as the gardens
of Holyroodhouse.

The city had spread a little towards the south, to incorporate the
countryside around the university. This busy and now famous college was
reached by a mean alley-way. In its buildings Monro, Cullen, and Black
pursued the investigations of rational men.

For half a century, since the time of Sibbald and Pitcairn, there had been
plans to extend Edinburgh northwards by building on a small ridge that rose
beyond the Nor' Loch. On the north side of the ridge there was a gentle descent
for a few rural miles of farmland and woodlands to the shores of the Forth.

Nothing had come of the plans, and the Union had made them unnecessary
by draining people away from the city. But now after mid-century Edinburgh

was once again overcrowded, and the idea of expansion was a popular topic. Trade was prospering, the country in general was enjoying belatedly the greater trade that had been promised by the Union fifty years before, and Edinburgh was uncomfortably full. 'Gentle and simple lived within the compass of a single close, or even a single stair, knew and took an interest in each other. Acquaintances might not only be formed, Pyramus-and-Thisbe fashion, through party-walls, but from window to window across alleys, narrow enough in many cases to allow of hand coming to hand, or even lip to lip.' – George Chalmers. In 1763 James Craig, nephew of the poet Thomson, published his plan of the new town, and the first building was started a few years later.

George Chalmers's description of Edinburgh in the late '60s is cosy and somewhat couthie:

'Every forenoon, for several hours, the only clear space which the town presented – that around the Cross – was crowded with loungers of all ranks, whom it had been an amusement to the poet Gay to survey from the neighbouring windows of Allan Ramsay's shop. The jostle and huddlement was extreme everywhere. Gentlemen and ladies paraded along in the stately attire of the period; tradesmen chatted in groups, often bare-headed, at their shop-doors; caddies whisked about, bearing messages, or attending to the affairs of strangers; children filled the vennel with their noisy sports. Add to all this, corduroyed men from Gilmerton, bawling coal or yellow sand, and spending as much breath in a minute as could have served poor asthmatic Hugo Arnot [the historian of Edinburgh] for a month; fisherwomen crying their caller haddies from Newhaven; whimsicals and idiots going along, each with his or her crowd of listeners or tormentors; sootymen with their bags; towns-guardsmen with their antique Lochaber axes; water-carriers with their dripping barrels; barbers with their hair-dressing materials.'

This crowded Edinburgh vanished abruptly after the building of Craig's new town, but before it came to an end there grew up in it a young poet who was later called by Burns 'my elder brother in misfortune, by far my elder brother in the Muses', a compliment which stated the relationship picturesquely, though too modestly.

Robert Fergusson (1750–74) was born in the Cap and Feather close, a little east of the Tron Kirk. The close vanished in 1770 when an approach road was made to the North Bridge. The house was next to the kirk, and the clapper of the holy bell rang the hours of Fergusson's childhood years, 'wanwordy, crazy, dinsome thing'.

His parents were humbly genteel, the father a clerk, the mother a 'very superior being from whom he inherited both his genius and virtues'. The Fergussons had come from the north-east of Scotland, that fecund district which also provided the forebears of Robert Burns, James Watt, Joseph Black, and the long line of Gregories. William Fergusson, the father, had been a clerk to an Aberdeen merchant, Dean of Guild Burnett. On Burnett's death

Fergusson came south to Edinburgh where he found employment at a modest wage, but never had the drive or influence to 'improve himself'.

Robert Fergusson spent four years at the High School, and then won a bursary that took him to the University of St. Andrews. There he met David Wilkie, professor of natural philosophy. Wilkie had a farm and the boy went there, probably finding as much good in the fare of the farm as in Wilkie's discursive conversations. When Fergusson was at university, his father died and his mother was left almost destitute. Robert paid a visit to a maternal uncle near Aberdeen, a man of affluent circumstances, from whom Mrs. Fergusson expected assistance in her distress. It was no sense of begging charity that made her send her son north; gentility, pride, and her own sensitivity prevented that, but blood ties were strong and 'the family' meant much. In her desperation she felt she was entitled to seek the advice of her nearest male relative.

Robert was well received and stayed for some months, but took offence at what he imagined was a slighting remark of his uncle about the state of his clothing. The insult, as the boy considered it, was delivered in the presence of the local laird. Whether it was an insult or blunt untactful humour, Robert was bitterly wounded; he left the house, and without money he walked to Edinburgh, which he reached 'debilitated in body and depressed in his mind'. He was seriously ill for some weeks, while his mother made ends meet by taking in boarders.

In spite of his education he was unable to find tolerable employment. He took a job as a copying clerk, where the work was below his abilities and the pay was meagre. The rest of his short life was spent in routine employment.

He began to contribute poems to the *Weekly Magazine or Edinburgh Amusement*, published by Ruddiman, son of the Ruddiman whom Pitcairn had introduced to Edinburgh. Fergusson's work was in the English pastoral style, of no merit. It was a young man's work; it brought attention and the kindness of the Ruddiman family, with whom he used to share a box in the Theatre Royal. Once, with the youngest Ruddiman on his knee, he listened to Tenducci, the Italian tenor, singing lyrics that he had written.

In 1772 he began a series of poems in Scots. *The Daft Days, Caller Oysters, Hallowfair* were published by Ruddiman, and Fergusson was hailed as the successor to Allan Ramsay. The new voice was authentic:

> 'Now mirk December's dowie face
> Glowrs owre the rigs wi' sour grimace,
> While, thro' his *minimum* of space,
>   The bleer-ey'd sun,
> Wi' blinkin' light and stealin' pace,
>   His race doth run.'

He became a member of the Cape Club ('their principal regale is the best London porter, entire from the butt'), where he was injudiciously flattered and 'assiduously courted by the literati of every description, who found in him an uncommon flow of *Hudibrastic* humour, expressed in the peculiar dialect of his native country.'

Fergusson had the melancholic's craving for society; he immersed himself in the tavern life to the distress of his friend Thomas Sommers; 'he was insensibly led into a circle of associates and flattering admirers, who frequently enjoyed over a bottle his witty conversation, by way of spending the evening, but who never thought of serving him further.'

Amongst Sommers's acquaintances was Alexander Runciman, who painted the Ossian scenes in Sir John Clerk's house at Penicuik. Runciman had a partly finished canvas to be called 'The Prodigal Son', but had not found a suitable model. Sommers suggested Fergusson 'on account of his sprightly humour, personal appearance, and stricken features'. Runciman painted the poet 'in the character of a *prodigal*, sitting on a grassy bank, surrounded by *swine*, some of which were sleeping, and others feeding; his right leg over his left knee; eyes uplifted, hands clasped, tattered clothes, and with expressive countenance bemoaning his forlorn and miserable situation'. The picture went to London and was bought by 'a gentleman of taste and fortune'.

Of Sommers, who had a glazier's shop, Fergusson wrote deliciously:

> 'Tom Sommers is a *gloomy* man,
> His mind is *dark* with sin,
> O holy Jesus, *glaze* his soul,
> That *light* may enter in!'

A new series of poems appeared, including *Leith Races, The Tron, Kirk Bell, The Election, Auld Reekie*. Of their kind they were perfect. Fergusson had established his place in what was to be the eighteenth-century triune of Scottish poets – Ramsay, Fergusson, Burns.

There was nothing more. Early in 1774 he became dangerously ill and depressed. He doubted the world and his own sanity. He destroyed his unpublished poems. There was a nervous breakdown, a resumption of his dull work, and still more desperate search for the obliteration of his fears with his Cape Club friends.

In February the *Caledonian Mercury* carried a notice. 'The admirers of Mr. Robert Fergusson, the celebrated poet, will be sorry to learn that he has had a very dangerous sickness.' In July the same paper recorded that he had been 'seized with a very dangerous illness', and the Cape Club made a collection for the poet 'who has for a considerable time past been in distress.'

One evening he fell on a steep stair and wounded his head. When he recovered consciousness, his brain was disordered 'so that three men could hardly restrain his violence.' Being put in a sedan chair in the pretence that he was being taken to visit a friend, he was brought to the city Bedlam where, on recognising the place, he cried aloud in terror, to be answered by the demented yells of the other inmates. When he recovered, he earnestly discussed his religious visions with his keeper.

Sommers let nearly two months go past before he found courage to visit the poet. He went with Dr. John Aitken, a well-known medical man, and they had both to go to some pains to obtain a magistrate's mandate of admission. They found Fergusson 'lying with his clothes on, stretched upon a bed of loose uncovered straw'. He was in a bare stone cell, and he was hungry. He was quite lucid when they saw him, and Sommers noted that he 'was very anxious to obtain his liberty'.

The three men walked in the garden of Bedlam. Aitken assured Fergusson that he was normal, and release would be only a matter of time. An odd incident took place before they parted:

'The sky was lowering, the sun being much obscured; led by curiosity, and knowing his natural quickness, I asked him what hour of the day it might be? He stopped, and looking up, with his face towards the south, while his hands were clasped, paused a little, and said, it was within *five* minutes of twelve. The Doctor looked his watch, and exclaimed, "It is just *six* minutes from twelve".'

His mother and sister visited him shortly before he died, and Grossart gives an account in which Fergusson asks:

'"Might you not frequently come and sit by me thus – you cannot imagine how comfortable it would be – you might fetch your seam and sew beside me?" An interval of silence was filled in with sobs and tears. "What ails you? Wherefore sorrow for me?" he said. "I am very well cared for here – I do assure you I want for nothing, but it is cold – it is very cold." Again he said, "You know I told you it would come to this at last: yes, I told you." The keeper gave the signal for retirement, and his mother and sister rising, he cried "Oh, do not go yet, mother! I hope to be soon – Oh, do not go yet – do not leave me!"'

He died that night, and was buried in the churchyard of the Canongate in the presence of 'a numerous company of friends'. His grave was unmarked until Robert Burns, thirteen years later, arranged for the erection of a stone.

Fergusson's clear but limited genius was almost forgotten in the riot of acclaim that soon greeted Burns, but he has survived as a master of miniature in Scots poetry. Burns honoured him. Thomas Carlyle paid cautious tribute. But it was Robert Louis Stevenson, a century later, who revered Fergusson as a kindred spirit; in a letter to Craibe Angus he showed the depth of his feeling.

'. . . surely there is more to be gleaned about Fergusson, and surely it is high time the task was set about.

'I may tell you (because your poet is not dead) something of how I feel. We are three Robins [Fergusson, Burns, Stevenson] who have touched the Scots lyre this last century. Well, the one is the world's. He did it, he came off; he is for ever; but I, and the other, ah! what bonds we have! Born in the same city; both sickly; both vicious, both pestered – on nearly to madness and one to the madhouse – with a damnatory creed; both seeing the stars and the moon, and wearing shoe-leather on the same ancient stones. . . . He died in his acute and painful youth, and left the models of the great things that were to come; and the man who came after outlived his green-sickness, and has faintly tried to parody his finished work . . . you will never know, nor will any man, how deep this feeling is. I believe Fergusson lives in me.'

19

OSSIAN

On the bowling-green at Moffat. A poor Highland tutor.
The Death of Oscar. 'Vast antiquity and rare genius.'
The lost epic. Travels in the Highlands. The lost
epic found. And another. European success. The
farce of authenticity. Accusations of forgery. Macpherson
serves the government. Dr. Johnson buys a
cudgel. Speculation and profits. Highland revelry.
Unto Westminster.

ST. BEUVE SAID OF LAMARTINE, 'reading Ossian, he feels his tears
congealing on the fringe of his eyelids'; of Napoleon he wrote, 'He ascribed
some of his genius to Ossian and would like to have put him into his box, as
Alexander did with Homer.'

The genesis of the Ossian poems was as alarming as their influence. It began
on the bowling-green of Moffat, a small watering-place in the south of
Scotland. Taking the cure there, in the autumn of 1759, were the usual lairds,
lawyers, savants, and merchants; amongst them was John Home, the clerical
playwright of *Douglas*, and his companion George Laurie, a fellow minister.

'Jupiter' Carlyle was on his way home to his Eskside manse after a visit to
Dumfries (where he had decided to engage the assistance of the Duke of Argyll,
Lord Bute, and others for the preferment of his friend Dr. Wight to the chair of
history at Glasgow). Carlyle stopped at Moffat, and on the bowling-green he
was introduced by Home to a gentleman whom he described as 'good-looking,
of a large size, with very thick legs, to hide which he generally wore boots,
though not then the fashion.'

The young man was James Macpherson, a poor Highlander, and tutor to
Graham of Balgowan. Macpherson had come to Moffat with a letter of
introduction to Home. Carlyle went on his way, his tidy and faithful mind
recording his impressions of the unknown young man. It was the month after
his supper in Edinburgh with Wight, Benjamin Franklin, Hume, and Adam
Smith.

Macpherson was reserved; Home was pleasant and agreeable, and took the
conversation to the young man's own interests. They discussed Gaelic
customs, folklore, traditions, and poetry, especially poetry.

Home wanted to see specimens of Gaelic verse, but as he knew no Gaelic he
hoped that the young man, in kindness, might care to translate some lines so

that he could 'form an opinion of the genius and character of Gaelic poetry.' After proper reluctance Macpherson agreed, and in a few days he brought to Home a fragment which in its translated state, was called *The Death of Oscar*.

Both Home and his friend Laurie felt they had discovered writing of great importance. In Edinburgh they took the English lines to their colleague in the cloth, Dr. Hugh Blair, the arbiter of literary taste.

'The three friends agreed that here was indeed a literary revelation of transcendent importance, poetry of vast antiquity and rare genius.' Dr. Blair insisted on meeting Macpherson, who at the age of twenty-two showed a young man's modesty before the important man of letters. After a great deal of coaxing, the diffident Macpherson agreed to search for further Gaelic originals and render them into English.

The following year there appeared in Edinburgh, with a preface by Dr. Blair, a volume called *Fragments of Ancient Poetry collected in the Highlands of Scotland, and Translated from the Gaelic or Erse Language*. It had an immediate success. It was championed by Hume and Home, Principal Ferguson of the university and Blair, Lord Elibank, Lord Kames, Lord Hailes. The bench, the pulpit, and the professorial study, insofar as they were occupied by *literati*, announced the discovery of ancient genius, preserved by the people of the Highlands since the fifth century. 'All Scotsmen were delighted at being able to boast that even the most barbarous parts of their despised country had been possessed of genius before England had risen out of savagedom.' The *Fragments* went south; Gray, Shenstone, and Walpole were charmed.

Macpherson, the happy producer of the book, let it be known that there was an oral epic in the Highlands, far superior to the *Fragments*. Edinburgh listened to him. Had he not been born near Kingussie, on the far side of the Grampians?

It was not the first time Macpherson had been in Edinburgh. As a youth he had studied there, as well as at Aberdeen, before going back to his birthplace to be the poorly paid master of the local school. For three years, before obtaining his tutoring job, he had spent his leisure writing 4,000 verses, as well as a poem of six cantos called the *Highlander*, which 'crept into light in 1758, and at once crept back into obscurity'. It was already obvious that the *Fragments* would not suffer from obscurity. Edinburgh was madly enthusiastic; London politely approved.

The rumour of a lost epic brought about a dinner party, presided over by Lord Elibank, to persuade Macpherson to seek out the poem. After more hesitation and reluctance Macpherson agreed. He would try. A subscription was raised to finance him; the Faculty of Advocates, aware that the law's place is behind letters, gave sixty pounds.

In September, Macpherson rode north, travelling with another Macpherson, a 'friend and kinsman'. The two Macphersons traversed the Highlands, four months later James came back to Edinburgh, declaring that the epic had happily been recovered. With a fine appreciation of the mood of the times, he quit the city where he was 'discovered', packed his saddle-bags and rode south, to find a printer in London and a patron in parliament.

At the end of 1761 there appeared, under the patronage of Lord Bute, a volume entitled *Fingal, an ancient Epic Poem, in six books, together with several other poems composed by Ossian, the son of Fingal, translated from the Gaelic language by James Macpherson.*

The response was excellent. Another book was published – *Temora, an ancient Epic, in eight books, composed by Ossian, son of Fingal.* An epic had been promised; two were delivered.

The Ossianic poems were a huge success; they were new and yet they were old; they were of mysterious parentage; best of all they were different. Within a remarkably short time they were translated into many European languages. Caesarotti, financed by Bute, made the first and most important translation, into Italian. In London, Macpherson found that he had many enemies. He was a Scot; it was a time of strong anti-Scottish feeling that was not mitigated by Bute, the Scottish Prime Minister, being quite tactless in advancing his compatriots. Macpherson himself, his modesty somewhat abated, became pushing and overbearing. In addition, there was the suggestion that the translations from Gaelic were less ancient than the translator had claimed. The voices that maintained Macpherson to be more author than translator grew loud in denigration.

The situation that Lady Elizabeth Wardlaw carefully avoided began to develop around Macpherson in a solemn farce. The merit of the poems was in their antiquity; if they were the recent products of a Highland school-teacher, they were of little significance; that the school-teacher might have been cunning enough to gull the critics was an insult that could not be tolerated. It was no more than prudent of Macpherson to insist he was only the translator, and it was essential for those who believed he was the only begetter to brand him as a forger and charlatan.

He was publicly accused of forgery. He could reasonably claim inability to produce the ancient Gaelic manuscripts; had he not obtained the poems from an oral tradition? There were a few pieces of manuscript – mere unintelligible land-leases and household accounts, said his detractors – which he placed with his bookseller for the examination of any who cared. Surely, writes Gray Graham, there was excellent humour of a sardonic sort in this proposal that Englishmen should satisfy themselves of the genuineness of a translation of a Gaelic epic by looking at documents without a history, manuscripts without a date, in a language which they knew as little as a Hottentot.

The doubt about the poems spread to Scotland, even to David Hume who usually distinguished between philosophy and the affairs of daily life. Macpherson would not give way; his accusers would not cease their attack. The affair was bitter, angry, and unresolved, and those who had complete faith in Macpherson, such as Dr. Blair, were astonished at the obtuseness and pettiness of the critics who squabbled over so fair a thing as the poems of Ossian.

Macpherson meanwhile urged the cause of his own advancement. As Surveyor-General and secretary to Commodore Johnstone he went to Florida, where he quarreled with his fellow Scot, but back in London retained a pension by serving the government as a hack. It was probably inevitable that he should translate Homer. Hume by this time had lost patience, and on the appearance of the Homer he said he did not know whether the attempt or the execution was worse.

Macpherson continued to scorn those who abused him, adding very rightly that those who doubted his veracity complimented his genius. But in private, as well as in his preface to the 1773 edition, he made many oracular remarks: 'All the polite nations of Europe have transferred them [the poems] into their respective languages; and they speak of him who brought them to light, in terms that might flatter the vanity of one fond of fame'; 'In this country men of genuine taste abound; but their still voice is drowned in the clamours of a multitude, who judge by fashion, of poetry, as of dress'; 'The making of poetry, like any other handicraft, may be learned by industry.' The last sentence of the preface is a gem of equivocation: 'A translator, who cannot equal his original, is incapable of expressing its beauties.'

When Dr. Johnson published his *Journey to the Hebrides*, Macpherson was not the only Scot to take umbrage at some of the remarks in it. Forewarned of the nature of certain of the passages, Macpherson had written politely to Johnson before publication, requesting that injurious remarks might be omitted. As his request went unheeded, he wrote again, after publication telling Johnson curtly that 'his age and his infirmities alone protected him from the treatment due to an infamous liar and traducer.' Johnson replied roundly:

> 'Mr' James Macpherson, I have received your foolish and impudent note. I will do my best to reply to it, and what I cannot do for myself, the law will do for me. I will not desist from detecting what I think a cheat from any fear of the menaces of a Ruffian. I thought your book an imposture. I think it an imposture still. For this opinion I have given my reasons to the public, which I dare you to confute. Your rage I defy, your abilities since your Homer are not so formidable, and what I hear of your morals inclines me to pay regard not to what you say, but to what you shall prove. You may print this if you will. – Samuel Johnson, 20th January, 1775.'

Johnson despatched the letter and bought a cudgel, or so it said.

Macpherson continued his career of letters; his pen was at the service of the government. He became agent to the Nabob of Arcot. At the time of the East India Bill he was able to speculate profitably. Soon he was a rich member of parliament, with two houses and a handsome carriage – and he affected to despise the English. When his persistent champion, Dr. Blair, taxed him with staying in London when he hated John Bull, Macpherson had a Boswellian answer. 'Sir, I do not like John Bull, but I love his daughters.' Gray Graham remarks, 'He was not married, but he was not without children, for whom he provided well.'

When he grew older, he spent part of his time in the Highlands to which he was deeply devoted. Robert Adam designed a house for him near Kingussie, called Belleville.

'People long remembered the great man from London, who came every year bedizened with rings and gold seals, and clad in a fur-edged coat. They told stories of the grand state he kept up as a Highland chief, his splendid table, his home filled with guests; of his sallying forth in the morning and bringing bibulous lairds from houses far and near, who in the dining-room, from whose walls portraits by Sir Joshua Reynolds looked down, kept high revelry till they and the nights were far spent.'

He spent lavishly on his tenants, refused the government offer of the forfeited estate of Cluny Macpherson, and was beloved by the neighbourhood for his kindliness and generosity.

When he died in 1796, he left money for the erection of a monument to himself, together with instructions about his burial in Westminster Abbey where, after a funeral procession down the length of Britain, lasting eighteen days, he was interred in the presence of an important gathering, to lie near the remains of his inveterate enemy, Samuel Johnson.

The disputed poems were then famous throughout Europe. Caesarotti's translation had been used for a further translation into French. The translation into German was done by a Jesuit, Denis of Vienna. The influence of the Ossianic Legends continued to spread far and wide. The kings of Sweden called themselves Oscar. The poets Herder and Klopstock drank avidly at the dark fount of antiquity. Macpherson was their inspiration to seek, as he did, in the folk-song of a country to unearth the treasures of the past! Lady Wardlaw had been an unknown intimation: Thomson had been the precursor of the romantic dawn in the sky of letters: Ossian Macpherson was the flush of dawn itself!

In London the poems were a constant *divertissement*. Macpherson made Ossian give a picture of savagery transformed to a divine sensitivity. The heroic grandeur was favoured in a sophisticated society that had acquired a taste for the sweet sentimentalism of Rousseau's *Nouveau Héloise*. Though the Highlands were still unknown – except through such books as Dr. Johnson's *Journey* – they were becoming romantic; they were tamed and brought to heel. In *Humphrey Clinker* Smollett made Bramble say of Loch Lomond, 'Everything here is romantic beyond description.'

How pleasing it was in the tiresome bustle of London for a young lady to pretend weariness with the sharpish entertainment of Mr. Sheridan, and, while awaiting her *cicisbeo*, to experience in imagination the romantic passion of Tinthormod and Oina-morul, safely and picturesquely dead those thousand years and more in the romantic Highlands of North Britain. And to think that Mr. Macpherson may have invented it himself – how extravagantly exciting!

Many years later Saintsbury said that Ossian 'gave, just as the ballads gave, something *different* – the necessary twist and alternative to the actual course of poetry – and that is enough.'

20

THE ASTRONOMERS

A pantheistic psalm and a metaphysical digression.   Poverty
and curiosity.   An outrageous ambition.   Strings of
beads.   Star papers.   Discovery of the world.   The
gentry are kind.   Models on gateposts.   The Astronomical Rotula.   The nebular theory.   Contemporaries.   Sun spots and the parallax.   Short's telescope.

'I TO THE HILLS WILL LIFT MINE EYES' runs the first line of the
metrical version of Psalm 121, sung many times a year in nearly every Scottish
kirk. It is, to the Scots, one of the most moving songs of worship. The uplifted
eyes see the hills, near and far, and at night the stars, very distant. There is
something pantheistic in the psalm, and a sense of searching and seeking. It is a
motif that is familiar to all brought up in the worship of the Scottish church,
and it has its place in any narration of Scottish endeavour.

Metaphysics and mathematics were both at the birth of astronomy. Napier
of Merchiston had given his country men and the world the mathematical tool
of logarithms. The Scottish church was nothing if not mathematical.
Generations of mathematical kirk-goers made astronomy inevitable, though it
might be more realistic to give some credit to long dark nights and a clear
atmosphere. The technical adjuncts such as Gregory's reflecting telescope had
also been developed by Scots. Then one man's intellectual curiosity,
confronted by the awe and wonder of the heavens sought an explanation in
analytical observation by pinning the indescribable to a formula of numbers.

The story of James Ferguson, shepherd boy and fellow of the Royal
Society, is an object lesson to those who are impressed by the outlook and
teaching of Samuel Smiles. He was a child of no advantage who made good,
with nothing to help him but his native talent. Ferguson's life is so much a
parable of self-help that, if it were not true, it would seem a parody.

The facts are these. Ferguson was born in 1710 in Banffshire, the son of
peasants. At seven he taught himself to read, and his surprised father then gave
further instruction. For the next three years he developed in the rural pattern of
utter poverty and growing literacy.

By the time he was ten years old, the poverty was such that his father could
no longer support him. The literacy was such that – his mental teeth sharpened
on the catechism – young Ferguson became curious about the mechanics of
nature, and decided to investigate them.

In later years he wrote: 'As my father could not afford to maintain me while I was in pursuit of these matters, and I was rather young and weak for hard labour, he put me out to a neighbour to keep sheep, which I continued to do for some years, and in that time I began to study the stars at night. In the daytime I amused myself by making models of mills, spring-wheels, and such other things as I happened to see.'

There is an obvious parallel with James Watt, who also made models as a child and was fascinated by the sight of the heavens. But Watt had many advantages and a good deal of encouragement. He had a wealthy and influential father; he had a devoted mother with university 'connections'. Ferguson had nothing, and his entire world in his early teens was what he could see. The books from which he learned to read appear to have petered out, for further literary instruction was negligible. But he was fascinated by the stars. Because a state of fascination was not in itself intellectually profitable or satisfying, Ferguson decided with no tutors and no text-books to make his own direct observations.

This is perhaps the most outrageous part of the Ferguson story. The boy who had no formal education, who was unaware of even the most elementary facts of the world he lived in, decided to make a personal assault on the nature of the universe. Such effrontery deserved success.

Even before his voice had broken he devised a string threaded with beads. With this device, together with paper, candle, pen, and ink-horn, he went to the fields at night, and – lying on the ground – he laid his beads across the firmament. He tied the ends of the string to bushes and moved the beads so that each obscured a star or a planet from his point of vision. The difference between stars and planets was unknown to him, but it was the individual behaviour of the planets that specially attracted him.

The position of the beads on the string he then recorded on his paper. The technical difficulties of doing this might have daunted anyone with an inkling of the immensity of what he was attempting. It is just possible to appreciate the persistence of this stripling, examining the sky in such a way, dealing with candles and gusts of wind, with slithering beads, cold and rain, in order to make a record of the relative positions of the stars, not knowing at all what use he might make of his information, yet feeling that what he was doing was necessary and with purpose.

It is recorded that another self-educated man, Alexander Cantley, a butler to a Highland gentleman, instructed Ferguson in decimals, algebra, and geometry. In time Ferguson acquired a number of star-papers recording planet movements. At the age of seventeen he took his papers to a minister in the town of Keith. The minister explained to him that the world was round, which the boy had not known before. For the first time in his life he was shown maps. Because he now had access to maps, and because he had been told that the world was round, Ferguson made a ball of wood, covered it with paper, and on this he traced the maps. With the help of a 'geographical grammar' he constructed the first terrestrial globe that he had ever seen.

It was already obvious, though there was no one to record it, that Ferguson had a self-sufficiency somewhat above normal and that the deprivation of a formal education was hardly a handicap.

It was in the natural course of things that he should now be encouraged by the local gentry, who were as kind to humble talent as they were to their dogs and horses. He was not of course given material assistance, but the ladies of the lairds' houses discovered that young Ferguson had a bent for design, and they paid him small money in return for patterns to be used on their needle-work tambours. In this way Ferguson entered his majority, still undestroyed and undisciplined by schooling.

Of the year 1733, when he was twenty-three, he wrote in his memoirs: 'All this while I could not leave off star-gazing in the nights, and taking the places of the planets among the stars by my above-mentioned thread. By this I did observe how the planets changed their places among the stars, and delineated their paths on the celestial globe.'

On two stone balls that ornamented the gateposts of Durn House he painted in oil colours a globe and a representation of a planisphere. The poles of the stone globes pointed to the poles of the heavens so that the sun, shining on the small globe of the earth, 'answered to the like enlightened parts of the earth'.

In 1734 he was able to go to Edinburgh, and stay for two years as a humble non-paying guest in the town house of one of his lady patrons. He was foolish enough to wish to be an artist. He tried to become apprenticed to Edinburgh painters, 'but they would do nothing without money.'

He turned to medicine, studied anatomy and midwifery, then went north to marry and practise as a doctor. This failed completely, and he went to Inverness where, for some months, he was accepted as a painter.

It was then that he produced an astronomical rotula, which he sent to the minister who had explained about the roundness of the earth. The minister sent the document to Maclaurin at Edinburgh, who recognised its importance and wrote to its author, pointing out the one error, of less than a quarter of a minute – the only flaw in Ferguson's table of the stars in their courses, the rise and fall of the tides, and the eclipses of the sun and moon, covering every year until 1800. Maclaurin sensibly summoned Ferguson to Edinburgh, and the university was at last able to claim its own. Ferguson's career was afterwards brilliant but more orthodox. He enunciated the nebular theory, some time in advance of Kant who is usually credited with it, and so he at last explained the movements of his beads.

The attention of mathematicians had been directed to astronomy mainly as the result of Newton's *Principia*, in particular his theory of gravity and his teaching of a series of orderly relationships in the physical world. The 'harmony of the spheres' was known – though not by young Ferguson. Might not this harmony be explained in terms similar to gravitational discipline? Once he had properly learned the problem it was Ferguson who found the answer, and one of the quirks of history that Kant received the main credit.

Ferguson's published works included a great many on astronomy, an introduction to electricity, and a number of books and papers on machines.

Amongst Ferguson's contemporaries was Alexander Wilson, who became the first director of Glasgow Observatory and was the first person to make a scientific study of the sun. He dealt with meteorology on scientific principles, and was the first man to make exhaustive examinations of sun spots.

Wilson had been an apothecary's assistant in his youth, at St. Andrews. Later he was a type-founder at Glasgow, where he was financially helped by the university (at six and a half per cent) in setting up a type-foundry within the precincts of the university, obtaining the university's protection and patronage in much the same way as James Watt did. He became a printer, and it was his press that published the famous *Homer* of Robert and Andrew Foulis. His appointment as the first professor of astronomy took place in 1761.

Near the end of the century, in 1798, Thomas Henderson was born in Dundee. He became a lawyer's clerk, and spent his spare time as an astronomer. Later he was employed as secretary to Francis Jeffrey (the editor of the *Edinburgh Review* and, from 1830 to 1834, Lord Advocate), and with Jeffrey he went to London. In the south he was appointed government astronomer at the Cape of Good Hope, where he was succeeded by John Herschel. Henderson was the first man to measure the distance of stars, or, more technically, to determine the parallax of a fixed star. He came back to Scotland as Astronomer-Royal, and died in his forties.

It was an Edinburgh man, James Short, who helped to develop the instrumentation that astronomy required.

The refracting telescope had been invented in Holland, it is said by a happy accident when children were playing with lenses made by the spectacle-maker, Hans Lippershey. Quite by chance the children found that two lenses, one behind the other, made distant objects appear near.

Out of this discovery Lippershey made the first refracting telescope. Only a year later, in Italy, Galileo Galilei – having heard of the discovery – began to construct his own telescopes, and his knowledge of theoretical optics allowed him to improve on the Dutch invention. A few years later Galileo created a new astronomical picture by discovering the satellites of Jupiter, the mountains and craters of the moon, the phases of Venus sunspots, and the clusters of the Milky Way.

The telescopes used then, and for some time after, relied only on glass lenses to capture, condense, and transmit to the eye the light from objects in space. In order to achieve high magnification and reduce 'spherical aberration' and 'chromatic dispersion', faults born of an insufficient understanding of convex lenses, telescopes had to be very long. Some exceeded one hundred feet, and there were obvious problems in the construction and management of such instruments.

In 1663 James Gregory, of the illustrious Aberdeen family, had published a book on geometric optics. The book included a design for a reflecting telescope, using convex mirrors instead of lenses. While in London for the publication of his book Gregory tried to have his new mirrors made by the instrument makers of the day. The task was beyond their capacity and Gregory died in 1675, still a young man, without having seen a physical example of his invention.

Meantime Isaac Newton came independently to rather similar conclusions and the first Newtonian reflecting telescope was made in 1668. The great advantage of the reflecting telescope, apart from optical improvements, was its much more modest size, one or two feet compared with a hundred feet.

Soon there were three variations of the reflecting telescope – the Gregorian, the Newtonian, and the Cassegrain. In due course the refracting telescope came back into favour, due to improved methods of manufacture and a better understanding of optics.

But by then the reflecting telescope had been developed to a high degree of precision, and made available in large numbers largely by the work of James Short.

Short was born in 1710. He was the son of an Edinburgh burgess in the Corporation of Wrights (a joiner to trade) and was educated at George Heriot's, the High School, and the university – a succession of institutions which might well destroy one who did not possess a strong and unique talent.

When he was a young man his grandmother tried to persuade him to become a minister, a status career. This did not please him – nor presumably his grandmother – and it was Professor Maclaurin who turned him towards science. (Maclaurin, in the chair of mathematics, was a man of exceptional ability in the 1730s and '40s. He was a Jacobite which meant that, like many of the Scottish savants of his age, he had small appreciation of political realities. His genius was to teach and encourage the talented young.)

Maclaurin allowed Short to use one of his college rooms as a work-shop. By trial and error he worked on the making and improvement of mirrors for reflecting telescopes. In two years Maclaurin was able to report on Short to Robert Smith, professor of astronomy at Cambridge, and master of mechanics to George II.

In 1736 Short spent some months in the south as mathematics tutor to the king's fifteen-year old second son, the Duke of Cumberland. This young man was soon to earn the title of 'butcher' in his dealings with the Scottish Highlanders.

Short published his first work *Optics* in 1738, and in the same year he moved permanently to London. 'Though the son of an artisan his good Scottish education and his generous nature permitted his ready acceptance into the scientific and social world of Scotland and England.' – D. J. Bryden's dissertation on Short.

He was equipped with a patron, the Earl of Morton who had estates in the Orkneys. He prospered so well that at the end of a long and busy life he left £1,000 for a mourning ring to Lady Mary Douglas, his patron's daughter. He became a man of considerable influence in London. It was due to Short that James Watt was able to find employment there when he was avid for instruction but unable to break through the guild system. He also assisted his fellow-countryman Thomas Melville, the pioneer of spectrum analysis.

Short's main work was to construct a vast number of telescopes, mostly of the Gregorian type, for private individuals and universities at home and abroad. Russia, Sweden, France, and America all purchased his work. Banjamin Franklin acknowledged him. The most expensive instrument he made was a twelve foot reflector which the King of Spain purchased for £1,200, but the vessel taking it to Spain was wrecked and the telescope lost.

Before leaving for London Short had been a founder member of the Edinburgh Society for improving the Arts and Sciences, later the Philosophical Society of Edinburgh. He was back in Scotland in 1748 to make observations on an eclipse of the sun. He was accompanied by the Earl of Morton and Pierre Le Monnier, France's astronomer royal. Though handicapped by the fact that Maclaurin's meridian line had been lost in the recent Prince Charlie affair, observation posts were set up in Kirkwall, Ayr and Dundee. At Aberdour he conducted his own observations.

Le Monnier was impressed, and ordered telescopes. Short's six-foot reflector (made in 1749) is now in the Conservatoire National des Arts et Metiers in Paris, and his four-foot reflector (1752) remains at the Paris Observatory.

He was active in collating observations made on the transit of Venus in 1761. He was involved on behalf of the Royal Society, along with Robert Ferguson, in making preparations for the transit due in 1769, but he died the year before. Captain Cook took two of his telescopes to Tahiti where they were used to observe the transit.

The Imperial Academy of Sciences at St. Petersburg, and the Macfarlane Observatory in Glasgow, also ordered Short telescopes for the transit observations.

James had a brother, Thomas, also an instrument maker (though of lesser reknown) who may be remembered for devising a means whereby two people could look through a reflecting telescope at the same time.

21

THE BACKGROUND OF TECHNICS

English Whigs and Scots Mechanics.   Eotechnics.   The
Stuarts look for gold.   Father Damien, Alchemist.   Fowls'
feathers.   The northward march.   Communications.
Leyden   and   Boorhaave.   The   medical   schools.
Teachers and pupils.   Early industries.   Improvements in
technics.   Turning water to flint.   The Lunar Society.

FROM THE LATE 1740s until the 1790s there was political stagnation and
apathy in Scotland. The country's affairs were managed from London, and
there was little in the way of internal disruptions to upset the peace. This is one
factor that may have contributed to the amount of technical work done by Watt,
Black, and their colleagues. English Whiggery was of great assistance to the
mechanics and the scientists in the north, and the reaction after the American
War of Independence was, if anything, beneficial to Scotland.

In *The Chemical Revolution* Archibald and Nan Clow make reference to the
'significant contribution which Scotland made to the development of social
technology, especially during the eighteenth century.' They also mention 'a
galaxy of Scotsmen who gave scientific direction to the Industrial Revolution,
particularly to its neglected non-mechanical aspects. The vital contributions of
these men were made for the most part between 1750 and 1830.'

Part of the contribution has already been surveyed. Before proceeding
further it is necessary to sketch very briefly the record of the eotechnic phase in
Scotland. This concerns the technology that man developed, the tools and
methods of using them that he created to deal with the material side of his life
before the Industrial Revolution. In Scotland the eotechnic phase lasted,
approximately, until the time of Watt.

'The history of eotechnics in Scotland is not dramatic. Little is
known of the personnel taking part: less even of the undertakings
established. No names shine out against a European background as did
those of Cullen, Black, and Home [Lord Kames] in the late part of the
eighteenth century. Yet it was on the solid foundation of eotechnic
economy that the Scottish intellect reared a culture comparable, for
many generations, with anything to be found on the Continent of
Europe, with the possible exception of France.'

There were, as *The Chemical Revolution* adduces, special conditions
operating in Scotland to allow the country to emerge 'from a state of

comparative obscurity to become one of the intellectual foci of Europe, with a world-wide reputation for fertility of invention and eminence of academic teaching.'

An argument advanced is that the poverty of Scotland made the study of alchemy a national necessity to help in solving financial difficulties. This is possibly an exaggeration, as none of the leading states was backward in this intriguing research, but a happy alchemical outcome might have benefited Scotland more than most. The country was poor at a time when other European countries, including England, were relatively wealthy. The Stuart dynasty, whatever its disadvantages, was not corrupted by riches nor tempted to use the armies that wealth might command.

It was certainly of advantage to Scotland to encourage alchemical research, especially the manufacture of gold from base metals as was then considered possible. This was less a desire to keep up with the Jones's in the comity of nations than to keep out of national bankruptcy. Gold-mining was undertaken in the Border hills and in the north as a practical contribution to the exchequer, and there is a record of a porringer of Scottish gold being presented to Queen Elizabeth of England. But nature was not generous and the mines were abandoned.

Under the Jameses, especially the most brilliant of them, James IV, there was in the Edinburgh royal court of Holyroodhouse an early efflorescence of science in pleasant liaison with the arts. It was in the court of James IV that the celebrated Father Damian, a man of many parts (one part being charlatan) was given treasury assistance to establish an alchemical laboratory. In this project Damian worked with the Master of the Mint.

A familiarity with laboratory work thus became established in Scotland, and in the cities there was a permanent nucleus of craftsmen used to handling precious and base metals, making instruments, dealing with mensuration, all skills that made possible the erection of the later superstructure of discovery and invention.

The reigns of James V and VI continued experimentation and semi-mystical research, at a sufficiently high level to maintain a body of learned men of international reputation, such as John Napier, the discoverer of logarithms, George Erskine, David Lindsay, Ruthven, and Scott. Neither Charles I, during his misguided ventures to Scotland, nor his successor, Oliver Cromwell, nor indeed the intriguing zeal of the Covenanters, could interrupt the experiments or the writing of books. Pitcairn, Cullen, and Watt had their natural predecessors.

The problems that occupied them had an everlasting fascination for the educated speculative mind. The problem of flight, for example, had persuaded Damian to cast himself from the embattlements of Stirling Castle, equipped with wings made of fowls' feathers, to escape with no worse injury than a broken thigh, and to blame both injury and failure on his own stupidity in choosing, for the act of flight, the feathers of so humble and unethereal a bird as the domestic hen. Had he chosen the pinions of an eagle, then success, he thought, might well have been achieved.

The matters to which Leonardo da Vinci applied himself with prophetic acumen were problems common to European scholars. Many of those problems were ultimately solved by the rapid advance of technics and understanding in the north, after the bright spark of inventive genius had been quenched in the Mediterranean. This northward movement – which has today spread westwards across the Atlantic – of skills and understanding at the sharp edge of discovery is one of the interesting phenomena of European history.

Before the end of the seventeenth century, men such as Pitcairn had brought the sharp edge to Edinburgh, and helped to create the scientific attitude of experiment and hypothesis. Though the universities awakened and created centres for experimental work, the country itself was most backward. Little social order had been imposed on it. The Highland Line still divided Scotland into two territories, entirely different in administration, social usage, culture, and language. Communications were poor. Wheeled carriages were rare, and such roads as existed were barely passable. The journey between Edinburgh and Glasgow, a mere forty miles, was more difficult in a purely mechanical sense than the journey to London. Highland chiefs and lowland lords controlled their own peoples in a sparse countryside, and in the towns the theocrats exercised an unenlightened authority.

In considering some of the advances made in the less spectacular fields of science, and in putting them in historical perspective, it is necessary to emphasise again the importance of the relation between Edinburgh and Leyden. When pre-eminence in Europe had passed to Leyden from Paris and southern Europe, the influence of that university was immense. Boorhaave, the most famous of Leyden's teachers, had a personal influence that came down the generations, especially in the development of chemistry, which was the most vigorous, the most necessary, and the most influential of the exact sciences. Across Europe, from Vienna to Dublin, Boorhaave's teaching moulded the growth of new university faculties except when, as in England, the seed fell on stony ground. Pitcairn had, of course, been for a brief period a colleague and teacher of Boorhaave. The influence was reciprocal. According to the Clows, Boorhaave's teaching was 'perhaps nowhere . . . of greater significance than in Scotland'.

The medical schools of Edinburgh and Glasgow were founded by men derived from Leyden. Amongst those who studied there were the early Gregorys, Chalmers and Gordon, all of Aberdeen, and Brisbain, Johnstoun, Dick (who sent James Watt to London), the Hamiltons, all of Glasgow. Roebuck (the Englishman who worked in Scotland as industrialist, ironmaster and colleague of Watt), Hutton the geologist, and Plummer also studied at Leyden.

Chemistry as an independent science reached Edinburgh when John Rutherford and three others began extra-mural lectures. They were soon absorbed into the Town's College. Rutherford had been a pupil of Boorhaave, and was one of the medical men who insisted on chemistry having the status of a separate and distinct study.

Plummer, one of Rutherford's colleagues in the extra-mural adventure, was an outstanding teacher. (His praises were sung by Oliver Goldsmith, who had attended both Leyden and Edinburgh universities.) Plummer had as pupils Roebuck, Cullen, and Black. Hutton too was his pupil, also Keir who began the manufacture of soda and soap at Tipton.

About the middle of the eighteenth century, after forty or fifty years of gestation, chemistry sprang from the universities of Scotland fully born and began immediately to influence the outer world. In distinction to the previous isolation, there was a close relationship between the teaching of chemistry in Edinburgh and Glasgow and the early metallurgical industries that sprang up near those cities, such as Prestonpans on the Firth of Forth and Carron near the town of Falkirk. To those industries Roebuck contributed immensely.

Throughout the century the interrelationship of medicine, botany, physics, and chemistry continued, so that a man of science could converse with his colleagues on all matters covered by these subjects. Specialisation had not set in to divorce a scientist, not only from his near colleagues, but from the world of philosophy and the liberal arts.

The new sciences remained within the ambience of natural philosophy. As the natural philosophers were on friendly terms with the moral philosophers, science did not lose its virtue.

Equally important with research and discovery was the influence of the professors on their classes of international pupils. On one occasion, out of fifty-nine of Black's chemistry students, only three were Scottish. This was in the eighth decade of the century and is an indication of the teaching role that Edinburgh, to which Black had by then returned, had taken over from Leyden, though the relevance is a little obscured when it is noted that, in this instance, fifty-three of the students were Irish.

Amongst Black's pupils was Thomas Beddoes, founder of the Pneumatic Institute at Bristol where, with apparatus made by Boulton and Watt, he put into practice his ideas on inhalation therapy. This is an excellent example of the recurring interconnection between the Scottish universities, the developing industrial Midlands of England, and such isolated activities as those of the Bristol Institute. Beddoes married a daughter of Richard Edgeworth, one of the 'Birmingham philosophers'.

During his stay in Cornwall, James Watt came upon a boy who had an obvious talent for chemistry, and he asked Beddoes to accept the youth as a pupil. The boy was Humphrey Davy, inventor of amongst other things the safety lamp, and investigator of the anaesthetic properties of nitrous oxide (laughing gas).

Black's pupils, from the lecture rooms of Edinburgh and Glasgow, were scattered throughout the world. Some followed him in his own chairs; Aberdeen secured Ogilvie; Glasgow's rival institute, the Andersonian, had Garnett; Smithson went to Cambridge to invigorate the classes there; Rush and Morgan began teaching chemistry in Philadelphia, where the Rush

Institute continues today.

After so much preparation, the third quarter of the century saw the start of the astonishing fulfilment. The results of the labours of two generations suddenly emerged to so adjust the technical competence of men that a new age was born. Yet it was not a new age that was sought by the men involved. The industrial revolution was not the purpose of the work, though it was the inevitable by-product. What impelled them was their training in a philosophic appreciation of natural truth.

In Scotland the branches of technics that were improved, or were created, during this relatively brief period included the use of fuel, the technics of bleaching and of dyeing, improvements in textile manufacture, the discovery and application of artificial gas light, the engine and its multifarious machinery, road building, bridge building, canal building and all aspects of civil engineering, the production of industrial chemicals, and the application of mechanical power to ships.

Much was done imperfectly, but some of the pioneers wrought better than they knew. Watt's invention gave power to industry and transport for over a hundred years until the electric motor arose as a rival, and in that time the steam engine created the modern world. It was Watt, the most enduring, who best showed the innocent enthusiasm that left few stones unturned. The pattern of discovery did not always distinguish between the probable and the possible. In a letter to Black, Watt once asked: 'I hear of an acid somebody has discovered that turns water into flint; do you know anything of it?' Black did not reply.

The importance of Scottish work in the sciences and technologies is far more than the sum of the individual discoveries. The diffusion of ideas was a fertilising influence in Europe and America, but perhaps it was nowhere of greater importance than in the Midlands of England where, in the Lunar Society (so called because it met by moonlight so that members might see their way home), industry and science met to lay the foundations of the new industrial civilisation, with its centre in Birmingham. Boulton, the versatile entrepreneur, a man of immense commercial and technical ability, was the leader of the Lunar fraternity. With Watt, who joined him after parting from Roebuck, with Black and Cullen, with Wedgewood and Davy and Priestly, the Lunar Society during its period of existence was a most astonishing example of scientists and men of commerce aiding each other in a serious yet free-and-easy intercourse of ideas.

The Clows write of the Lunar adherents, also known as the 'Birmingham philosophers': 'Some were English by birth and education; some were Scots, but the intellectual power behind their achievements was the direct offshoot of the cultural renaissance in eighteenth-century Edinburgh.'

The Lunar Society is interesting, too, as it showed, in the interplay between the two countries, that the Scots came from their universities in the north, but the English were working outwith the interest, advice, or encouragement of either of their own institutions of learning. Professor Merz has written:

'Whilst in England modern science was cultivated outside the pale of the universities by Priestly, Davy, Wollaston, Young, Dalton, Faraday, and Joule – to whom we may even add Green and Boole – all eminent Scotch men of science, such as Gregory, Simson, Maclaurin, Playfair, Black, Thomson, Leslie, Brewster and Forbes, were university professors, many of whom did not confine their labours to one centre, but spread the light of their ideas and researches all over the country. Whilst England has been great in single names, Scotland has certainly in proportion done more to diffuse modern scientific knowledge.'

22

COLLEAGUES OF WATT

Heather on fire. A bucket of bull's blood. Salt and the Earl of Bothwell. 'A state of slavery'. Highland smelting. The Carron pioneers. Dr. Roebuck. Archibald Cochrane and his coal tar. A 'Scots job.' Gas lighting. A steam-driven Evil One. The Lunar Society again. Towards the welfare state.

COAL HAS BEEN MINED IN SCOTLAND from early times, certainly in the Middle Ages, but its use was limited to those who mined it. For the rest, who did not know coal, there was something magical in stories of a hard black stone that could be burned.

For a long time coal did not take the place of wood, either domestically or in trade. Like the rest of Europe, Scotland looked to wood and peat for its ordinary fuel. As there was sometimes a dearth of wood near the cities there was recourse to substitutes. Heather was once stored in such quantities in Edinburgh, where brewers used it as fuel, that the Scottish parliament passed an act against the practice because of the danger of fire.

In the seventeenth century the ancient forests of the lowlands were either denuded or the remnants so inaccessible that an impetus was given to coal mining. Coal had been used by some metal smelters. It became the fuel in the salt-pans. By the end of the seventeenth century coal was used in Scotland by brewers, salt makers, sugar boilers, soap boilers, alum makers and gunpowder makers. This last was something of an innovation: gunpowder was once imported from England, but the Scottish Privy Council considered this an imprudent practice and persuaded some Englishmen to set up powder mills in Scotland.

Salt panning was an industry that developed rapidly. It had been an important part of the Scottish economy since the twelfth century. In the seventeenth century the coast of the Firth of Forth was a daily smudge of dirty smoke from the burning of coal at the salt-pans. Though improved techniques during the eighteenth century diminished the vast number of small panning establishments, there remained in 1798 as many as ninety-eight salt-pans on the Forth littoral. A large part of the production was exported to the Low Countries.

Strange methods were used to purify the salt. When the brine had been evaporated to a concentrated thickness, a bucket of bull's blood was added. 'On mixing with the liquor it changed colour and by a sudden transformation the seething white liquor became overspread with a thick variegated and brown bubbling scum.' The coagulated albumen was intended to carry off impurities.

A manuscript note to Pennant's *Tour* shows the hideous scene: 'Nothing ever exhibited such an idea of the infernal regions as this horrid furnace and the poor naked wretches attending it.' Even at its birth the Industrial Revolution showed its predilection for satanic and bizarre squalor.

Cullen – the doctor, chemist, and biologist – studied this ancient basic industry from the point of view of industrial use. He held the belief that salt, or impurities in its manufacture, might be the cause of scurvy. Dr. Roebuck, the English entrepreneur from Sheffield who gave massive assistance to the development of Scottish technology, built huge salt-pans at Bo'ness near the Carron undertaking, and burned ten thousand tons of coal there annually.

Salt was also manufactured in the west at Saltcoats, and as far north as Brora, where the discovery of an outcrop of coal made panning possible in the bare land of Sutherland. Lady Jean Gordon, Bothwell's divorced wife, built the salt-pans at Brora. (It is probably not attributable to uxorial revenge, but in 1955, when the mummified corpse of Bothwell was discovered to be 'sweating' in Denmark – whence he had fled to die after the murder of Darnley – part of the remedy administered in Copenhagen was salt solution!)

At Port Seton, near Edinburgh, coal was delivered to the pans by means of a railway of wood, built in 1719. Strictly it was a 'tramway', a tram being the Norse word for the lengths of wood that made the rails. Along these trams or rails the bogies of coal were pushed.

The railway was about two miles in length and crossed the ground that became the battlefield of Prestonpans where Bonnie Prince Charlie won his victory and Sir John Cope departed on horseback to announce his own defeat in the south. It is perhaps a small corrective to the romantic view of Prince Charles to realise that he fought this battle across a railway track.

The coastal manufacture of salt from sea water disappeared in the nineteenth century when an industrially developed Britain could concentrate production in rock-salt mines, as in Cheshire, where the yield was very much higher.

As in the collieries the conditions for workers in the Scottish salt-pans were usually inhumane. The workers were slaves, a fact bluntly acknowledged in an Act of Parliament in 1755 which began: 'Whereas many colliers, coal bearers, and salters in Scotland are in a state of slavery or bondage, bound to the collieries and saltworks where they work for life, and are sold with the mines . . .'

Any Highland soldiers who tripped over the rails at Prestonpans were not necessarily making their first contact with developing technology. There is a small but interesting glimpse of the Highlands earlier in the century when iron-smelting plants were built amidst the Gaelic speakers at the very time the Stuarts were planning their return to the throne.

The English iron industry had already been driven from the south of

England to the midlands and the north. It was seeking new sources of wood to fuel its furnaces. It set up its smelting furnaces in Derbyshire, Yorkshire, and Lancashire, always pressing north towards new sources of timber and leaving behind a waste where the forests had been felled.

Because Britain was a single country the English ironmasters turned their attention to the Highlands. The lowlands had already been stripped. The smelters were quite prepared to accept very long lines of communication. 'It was more economical to transport the compact ore to the wood than to carry the bulky wood to the ore.'

From the north-west of England money and labour went to the Highlands. At Invergarry in Inverness-shire, at Taynuilt and Invergaray in Argyll, the early furnaces were built. (The township of Furnace still exists on the shores of Loch Fyne near Inveraray.)

The first was the Invergarry furnace, and it began work in 1729 – between the '15 and the '45 risings, and only a decade after the Spaniards had made their abortive invasion of the west coast of the Highlands.

A contract made with Macdonell of Invergarry gave a lease of his woods for thirty-one years. The ironmasters had the right to erect their ironworks, and construct the necessary waterways and roads, with whatever wharfs and dams they required. Local labour was employed, but all skilled workers came from Yorkshire and Lancashire, masons from Edinburgh. The iron ore came from England by boat to Corpach. It then went by land to Loch Lochy, along the loch by water, and by land again to Invergarry.

The project was not very successful and the furnace went out of existence in seven years. It is noteworthy that when the operating company felt it necessary to dispense entertainment to 'The Company's Friends' the strong drink was brandy and not whisky. Much of the produce was shipped south again to Bristol, but General Wade and the Governor of Fort William were supplied with iron castings for beams and lintels.

Another ironworks was started at Abernethy on Strathspey using local ore from Tomintoul, only twenty miles away. This was operated by the unchancy York Buildings Company, notorious for its lack of business success, and did not last long.

The other furnaces did not begin operating until after the '45. At Taynuilt smelting was carried on for about a hundred years. A self-contained company's colony was built – houses, farm, church, school, and a public house – in much the same way as the trading colonies in other wild countries, such as Canada, were to develop. Not until 1775 was the Inveraray furnace opened at Furnace, and this enterprise lasted until 1813.

These events are of interest as they show that the Highlands were not a distant inviolable part of Scotland, that they were open for the exploitation of natural resources with no thought of the consequences of deforestation, and that Scotland was not entirely a treeless waste. These Highland furnaces were 'bloomeries' where the fuel was charcoal. Even as they were contributing their smoke and flame to the Highland scene they were doomed by new methods arising elsewhere.

The English ironmasters had developed the use of coal in smelting. The start of the Seven Years War in 1756 made it necessary to forge large quantities of cannon. Larger and more efficient works were required.

It was no coincidence that Scotland's most significant iron works, the Carron Iron Works, were built in 1759 and opened for production in the beginning of 1760. They were pioneers at Carron. For a time it swung between success and failure. In the '70s, when it was desperately trying to raise money, it was saved by the American War of Independence. It had great technical problems to overcome.

Carron itself was the product of English skills and workmen, allied with Scottish needs and enterprise. By the '80s it was a vast and busy place, its fortunes founded on weaponry. The famous carronade cannon, probably invented by Miller of Dalswinton, was one of its main products. It exported its weapons to Russia, Spain, Denmark, wherever there was a market. It purchased bar iron from Sweden and Russia for further processing. It built its own satellite factories, the most important at Cramond, the Roman station near Edinburgh. It absorbed and developed the techniques invented in the south – such as Cort's puddling process and the grooved roller. It benefited immensely from James Watt whose rotary engine allowed the operation of forge-hammers by steam.

Though the needs of warfare were a spur, its contribution to peace was substantial. It provided boilers, stoves, grates, kettles, cylinders, and anchors, to growing markets at home and abroad. It was an exemplar to others. By the end of the century there were eighteen blast furnaces in Scotland. Five were at Carron, and of the remainder two were the more primitive charcoal furnaces at Furnace on Loch Fynne and at Taynuilt on the River Awe at Bonawe.

Carron was a major development in setting the stage for the sudden and immense proliferation of industry in central Scotland. Coal, iron, steam power, and chemistry transformed the country. The site for the Carron works had been carefully selected. It was a bleak and sparsely populated location, not far from where General Hawley had been defeated by Prince Charlie's soldiers at the Battle of Falkirk a few years before. The River Carron was a small stream that rose in the Campsie Fells south of Stirling and made a short easterly journey to enter the Forth at Grangemouth. The stream was needed to drive the machinery to create the blast for the furnaces.

The site was not too far from Glasgow; it was within easy distance of sea-going ships on the Forth; it was beside iron-ore and coal. And in the change-over of techniques, it was also handy for wood and charcoal from the Highlands.

The Forth and Clyde canal, partly built by James Watt to make an income in his early days, was begun in 1768 and finished in 1790. It helped the development of the Carron works so that by the end of the century they were pre-eminent in Europe.

Dr. John Roebuck was largely responsible for founding the works. He was born in 1718, the son of a Sheffield cutler. His importance in the Scottish scene is partly explained by the fact that he was educated at Edinburgh and Leyden and so fitted into the tradition of scientific thought applied to practical developments. Again he played the traditional role and became a physician, a training which was a springboard into all the developing sciences and industries. In Birmingham, where he first settled, he met Samuel Garbett. This became a vital partnership that led firstly to discovering better ways of refining gold and silver and a cheap method of making sulphuric acid. This paved the way for the creation of the sulphuric acid plant at Prestonpans, near Edinburgh, and the beginning of the partners' involvement in Scotland.

Roebuck worked with both Black and Watt. He assisted Watt financially – Watt was frequently pressed for capital – for the very practical reason that he knew Watt's invention of a separate condenser, with which he was busy in the 1760s, could make it possible to work coal mines that would otherwise remain flooded through the inefficiency of the Newcomen engine. By then the Carron enterprise was well under way. His assistance to Watt was in return for a two-thirds share in the invention. Roebuck himself got into financial difficulties, and control of Watt's patent passed to Matthew Boulton, another Birmingham man of greatness, and it was in Boulton's works – the Soho Works, Birmingham – that the engine began to be manufactured in 1769.

Watt and Roebuck also experimented with the making of soda from salt but they were incompletely successful, partly due, it is said, to the duty on salt making their process uneconomical. The soda problem was solved by James Keir (1735–1820) working with George Lind, Lord Provost of Edinburgh. At the same time the Edinburgh graduate Thomas Melville was conducting his pioneer work in spectrum analysis. He burned various salts in spirits and examined the colours through a prism.

In the bleaching industry great advances were made in the latter part of the century. Roebuck's commercial production of vitriol at Prestonpans paved the way for the abolition of the primitive methods of bleaching in which sour milk, lye of ashes, apple juice, and urine were variously used. Dr. Francis Home of Edinburgh University is said to have introduced the use of sulphuric acid immediately after Roebuck produced it at a low price. The French chemist, Berthollet, had previously shown the action of the acid in bleaching. By 1756 Francis Home's *Experiments on Bleaching*, authorised by the Board of Trustees, was published. On the advice of Lord Belhaven and Lord Kames the board had liberally decided on publishing details of the new method, in spite of the fact that this would give the knowledge to all. The time of bleaching had been reduced from months to days. Home, a colleague of Cullen, was also the first professor of *materia medica* in Edinburgh, demonstrating again the interplay of interests that would in due course cease to exist when each man became his own specialist.

The poisonous and suffocating nature of gaseous chlorine used in bleaching brought many problems. Watt's difficulty over the handling of chlorine had been real. Charles Tennant of Ochiltree patented a process for making a bleaching liquor by combining chlorine with a sludge of lime. The germ of the idea appears to have been French. There was a great deal of opposition to this patent. In the following year (1799) he took out another patent, this time for a dry bleaching powder, so that both the problem of gaseous chlorine and of transporting a liquid bleach were solved. It appears, however, that though the second patent was in Tennant's name it was Charles Macintosh – of waterproof fame – who was the actual deviser of the process. Tennant founded the St. Rollox chemical works which rapidly became one of the largest in Europe.

Those who were anxious to further scientific knowledge for the general good (and who published their results) can be contrasted with those who found secrecy more profitable. In the second part of the century great advances were made in finding new dyes. In 1771 a dye-works was built in Glasgow where everything was conducted in privacy. Highlanders speaking only Gaelic were employed within a screen wall ten feet high. George Mackintosh was in charge, and he – with his son Charles – made huge strides in developing the techniques of dyeing. George was a highly able and practical chemist. His son, next century, was the waterproofer.

Meanwhile, new uses were being found for coal, of which central Scotland had abundance. Attempts had been made for a hundred years, in many European countries, to 'crack' coal to obtain coke, which was accepted as a better industrial fuel, and to extract tar and other products.

The principle was known – the problem was to make the operation commercial. Becher in Germany in the previous century, experimenters in Liège, Newcastle, Coalbrook Dale, Wentworth (where the Marquis of Rockingham undertook an extraction project), Edinburgh, and elsewhere, had forwarded the techniques to a point near to breakthrough.

Success came to the ninth Earl of Dundonald, Archibald Cochrane (1749–1831). It was in fact a family affair. Cochrane's mother Lady Dundonald was a formidable woman in her own right, with a profound understanding of the practical sciences and their relation to industry. There was his brother Captain Cochrane, at one time in charge of iron ore interests at Lamancha, to the south of Edinburgh. A son, Thomas Cochrane, wrote that his father, while serving in the navy, had noted the ravages caused by 'worms' to ships' bottoms and had thought that tar, extracted from coal, might arrest this.

The main family property was at Culross on the north coast of the Firth of Forth. Coal had been worked there for generations. In 1781 the Earl of Dundonald, back on the family estates, had done his preliminary work and obtained Letters Patent under the Great Seal of Scotland, granting privileges to exploit his invention for extracting tar, pitch, oils, acids, and cinders from pit coal. This privilege was granted for fourteen years. In fact Dundonald did not claim to have invented the process; he improved it and made it commercially workable, just as Watt did with the steam engine. His work led directly to a new industrial chemical industry, and in due course to coal-tar dyes and the more sophisticated industrial processes of the following century.

Like Watt, Dundonald suffered from financial difficulties. Only a year after his Letters Patent were granted he was forced to join with others, who had the capital, to form the British Tar Company. Again, as Watt with Roebuck, he had to relinquish a major interest in his project. The arrangement was successful, but unfortunately, the success pertained solely to the process, and Dundonald's personal affairs remained in a tangle. A creditor insisted on settlement and he resigned his remaining two-fifths.

Even so, Dundonald was concerned with the expansion of his work, far beyond the twenty kilns then operating at Culross. Meantime Lady Dundonald called in the services of her brother, Andrew Stewart, an influential Member of Parliament who was shrewd enough to know the difficulties of dealing with Scottish affairs in the south. He wrote in 1783 that if a project requiring legislation had the reputation of being a 'Scots job' it would be immeasurably prejudiced in the House of Commons.

Sir John Dalrymple, a landower and sympathetic entrepreneur, asked Dundonald to provide him with the company's books that 'Doctor Black, our friend Adam Smith, and me' could examine them. One of the Culross products was sent by Black to Messrs. Hutton & Dairy, a firm engaged in the manufacture of sal ammoniac which they were making from chimney soot. The Hutton was James Hutton, the geologist and the writer of *Theory of the Earth*, still at that time two years short of delivery. Black produced some interesting figures, comparing profits in time of peace and time of war. In time of war the profit doubled.

In his own field, which was as wide and varied as an old run-rig, Dundonald made major contributions to many industrial processes. His tar on ships' bottoms was an immense success, and when ultimately bottoms began to be copper-sheathed it was another Scot, William Forbes of Aberdeen, who made a dubious double profit out of the Admiralty by manipulating stocks of copper.

Dundonald's work produced coke, lamp black, ammonia, sal ammoniac, Glauber's salt and alkali, phosphatic fertiliser, and lead carbonate. He made possible the preservation of wood – in ships, carts, wheels, roofs – and prevented corrosion in anchors, guns, shot, and other metal products. He came near to discovering gas lighting, and in fact burned a 'vapour' as waste so that the vivid flame could be seen on the other side of the Forth. He was conscious that his work did not bring the personal profit to which he was entitled, and at one time he wrote of 'the most cruel and oppressive usage from individuals and neglect on the part of the government.' He spent his life and his money pursuing scientific knowledge, and his son wrote that this 'scientific knowledge, as often happens, [was] unaccompanied by the self-knowledge which would have taught him that he was not, either by habit or inclination, a "man of business".'

Though William Murdoch (1754–1839) is usually credited with the invention of gas-lighting it is proper to add a qualification. He developed gas-lighting and was the first to persevere with its application to large-scale illumination, but it is unlikely that it was his unique brainchild. Lord Dundonald in Scotland and Bishop Watson in England had experimented earlier with gas made from heated coal, and it is almost certain that Murdoch knew some of the details of this. Dundonald had visited Watt at Birmingham and discussed gas-lighting.

There was also a letter dated 1790 from John Champion of Bristol to Boulton, in which Champion related how the gas he had made from coal was suitable for lighthouses, and that Trinity House, at its own expense, had experimented with it. The letter was occasioned by Champion's wish, at the age of eighty-six, to sell an interest in his discovery, for which a patent was 'going forwards', to someone who could take over from him.

This, too, is likely to have been known to Murdoch, and may have encouraged him to go forward with his own experiments. It was in 1792 that he succeeded in lighting his own home in Redruth, leading the gas over seventy feet through iron and copper tubes from his retort. Industry was ready for extended hours of working in factories and offices, and Murdoch devised methods for the large-scale production of gas, not giving a thought to the exploitation of the proletariat.

In 1802 gas lighting was introduced to the public when the factory at the Soho works at Birmingham was illuminated by gas to celebrate the Peace of Amiens. On the roof a crown burned, and on the facade PEACE and G.R. blazed in raw flame. The *Birmingham Gazette* said that 'every house in the neighbourhood was splendidly lit, and all the workmen belonging to the manufactory were regaled at public-houses.'

In 1805 the mills of Phillips and Lee of Manchester were lit by almost a thousand burners, and this installation allowed Murdoch to demonstrate the economy of his invention. To light the mills by candle-power 2,500 candles were required, and the total annual consumption cost £2,000. Gas lighting cost no more than £600. The gas age was in being. Private companies arose all over the country to exploit, at a good profit, this major advance against natural darkness.

Some years later the Glasgow Gas Company had as its manager James Neilson, the inventor, in another field, of the 'hot blast' and the designer of the 'batswing' or swallow-tail gas burner. 'The world was indebted to two Scotsmen, Murdoch and Neilson, for the advance which had been made in artificial lighting.' – Clow: *The Chemical Revolution*.

It was also the Glasgow company that Charles Mackintosh approached, in 1819, to purchase the by-product of coal tar. He was able to utilise the ammonia and pitch that he got from it, but the naphtha he did not know what to do with until he heard of using it as a solvent for caoutchouc or india rubber. With this solution he was able to make textile material waterproof, and so immortalise himself as a raincoat. (James Watt, in a letter written many years before, mentioned an earlier venture in waterproofing. He wrote of 'a truly chemical Swiss dyer' who promised to make him a coat 'that will not wet, though boiled in water'.)

Murdoch came into the Watt sphere of influence when he was a young man and obtained employment with Boulton and Watt in Birmingham. He was born in Auchinleck in Ayrshire, where his father (a miller) is said to have been the first to use iron-toothed gears in milling. Murdoch spent the greater part of his life in the south and the spelling of his name changed from Murdoch to Murdock, better accommodated to the English tongue.

From Birmingham Murdoch was sent to the Cornish mines as an engineer manager, and it was there that he did his early gas experiments. It was difficult to make the contemporary unscientific mind understand that while gas was a product of coal it was not the same as smoke. Walter Scott found humour in the idea of 'lighting London with smoke'.

Once when Murdoch was visiting Boulton there was a loud clatter when he laid his hat on the floor. Boulton enquired about this, and Murdoch explained that he had turned the hat on a lathe and it was made of wood. He was a prolific inventor. He invented the hydraulic lift, and also a model carriage to be propelled by steam. In his later years, James Watt had a strange dislike of the idea of propulsion on land by steam, and tried to smother the idea.

Murdoch devised his contraption to move between the Cornish mines. He frightened the wits out of a clergyman whom he encountered on the lonely Cornish roads, and who thought 'he was at last face to face with that Evil One of whom he was accustomed to make such uncomplimentary remarks in the pulpit.'

The French engineer, Nicholas Cugnot, had made a steam-carriage in 1763 which moved at a very modest speed, slower than a man walking, but a miracle none the less. To him the honour of being first is due. Robison had persuaded Watt to develop the steam-engine for locomotion, and Watt included plans for this in his 1784 patent, but later he lost interest. Erasmus Darwin had also asked Boulton to develop an engine for locomotion. Murdoch's contrivance in 1784, while workable, was neglected because of Watt's extreme stubbornness and possible jealousy. He claimed there was no point in pursuing the idea.

In 1797 Trevithick made another model, and in the first decade of the next century he made a number of full-size engines, but they met with one drawback after another, including the greatest of all – apathy. Although he demonstrated a locomotive hauling a passenger coach on a track laid down in Euston Square no one was prepared to encourage him. It was not until James Stephenson (son of a Scottish immigrant to northern England) put his Rocket on rails that steam traction became accepted.

Chemicals and their industrial application, artificial lighting, steam power, were a few of the practical results of the scientific attitude taught so rigorously down the generations by Pitcairn, Cullen, Black, and their pupils. Their influence helped to create the Birmingham Lunar Society, and through this the practical and catalytic influence of Watt was widespread. One of the Watt-Boulton entourage was William Playfair, brother of John Playfair the geologist. He devised the method of presenting statistics in visual form, by inventing the graph.

No apology is needed to give an extensive quotation from the Clows, those dedicated chroniclers of the period:

'Phlogistians and anti-phlogistians dined at the same table: Watt
and Priestley vied with Cavendish and Lavoisier over the discovery of
the composition of water: Keir achieved the manufacture of alkali
where Watt, Black, and Roebuck had failed: Murdoch's gas-light
illuminated the mills powered by Boulton and Watt's engines:
Wedgwood supplied chemical utensils for Priestley's experiments:
Priestley in turn analysed minerals of possible utility in pottery: a
leaven of wit and philosophy was added by Darwin and Edgeworth.
Indeed there was not an individual, institution, or industry with
pretensions of contact with advancing technology throughout the
length and breadth of the land, but some member of the Lunar Society
group had connexions with it. Behind many of them was the inspiration
of the environment in which they had passed the formative years of
their adolescence, the Scotland of Cullen, Black, and Hope, faithful
guardians of embryonic science who remained in the north while their
pupils moved south to plant and nurture in English soil the seeds of the
chemical revolution and reap their often rich reward.'

But the reward was not yet for all. The working people moved from
poverty to penury. The 1775 Act of Parliament had made gestures towards the
emancipation of Scottish serfs. This was not for humanitarian reasons, but
because the use of labour under the slave system was not sufficiently
productive. Serfdom was inefficient. It was observed that they managed things
better in England with a 'free labour' system.

Next century when all bondages were totally removed the Scottish worker
became 'free'. Though his personal condition was little better, he was more
economic within the system.

Conditions were being created whereby further generations of men would
live in the most appalling degradation and suffering, so calling into being the
immense Victorian efforts towards liberal charity and the lightening of the
working man's burden. The satanic mills, the deadly city slums, were aspects of
society that the cool minds of Pitcairn, Hutcheson, Adam Smith, and other
were unable to foresee. Innocently they paved the way. But they also pioneered
the means whereby, many generations later, a welfare state could be created.

23

THE BUILDERS – ARCHITECTS

Early skyscrapers.   A horse and a handsome lass.   The
Adam family.   Life in Edinburgh.   Journey to Italy.
'A very remarkable improvement.'   Bute is uncivil.   'I'll
fell him dead.'   Tea-urns and candle-snuffers.   The
Emperor Diocletian.   The Adelphi.   Sold by lottery.
Achievements and frustrations.   Chambers and Gibbs.
The Empress Catherine.   Pistachio porcelain.   A treatise on
chimneys.

SCOTLAND HAS NEVER HAD, and is now unlikely ever to achieve, a
distinctive tradition in architecture. The primitive 'black houses' of the north
and of the islands, like upturned boats of stone and thatch, cutting the winds as
a keel cuts the sea, were rational developments out of primitive necessity, as
exact climatically as an Eskimo's igloo.

In the lowlands of Scotland the L-shaped country house, developed from
the pre-Reformation 'keep' or fortress-tower, was characteristic and not
unseemly. (One example of the early 'keep' is the house in which Napier lived
at Merchiston in Edinburgh.) In the town of Edinburgh necessity again had
mothered an early form of skyscraper, forcing the builders to build upwards as
there was no room to spread laterally within the limitations of the defensive
walls and natural valleys.

Such things were the oddities rather than the adornments of a country that
had no real feeling for architecture, where the mediaeval abbeys were more
squat, more stolid, closer to the earth than in the south, perhaps bespeaking
those who worshipped in them or fought around them or pillaged them,
according to the theistic mood of the changing times.

The Scot knew how to handle masonry as the material of building. In this
he was expert, but of the art of shaping for pleasure as well as for function he
knew little. This reluctance to express himself in the shape and design of his
buildings may be allied with the dearth of visual and plastic arts. That Scotland
in the eighteenth century should have produced one architect of great genius,
and a clutch of architects of vast ability, is another of the inconsequent
surprises of the period.

Blackfriars Bridge in London, the Radcliffe Camera at Oxford, St. Martin-
in-the-Fields, the Pavlosk Palace, are some of the constructions of Scotsmen quite
outwith the astonishing Adam family. Robert Adam was the genius in whom

there flowered a new expression of classical qualities. Though he gave his name to a style of building and of decoration, it is not a Scottish style, and it is difficult to say why a Scot should have been the instrument. It is tempting to suggest that a simple but clear logic, a pertinacious search for first principles and an invincible determination to apply those principles, are as much the foundation (given the necessary genius) of an architect as they are of a philosopher.

When Robert Adam was a young man he had a horse called Piercy. One day Robert dined at Carlyle's house at Inveresk, along with John Home the playwright, and others. After dinner everyone except Robert went to drink wine with a neighbour. When they returned, Robert was 'galloping round the green on Piercy like a madman, which he repeated, after seeing us, for at least ten times.'

He stopped this raffish display at Home's express bidding, and the two chatted together. That night, Home and Carlyle being alone, the explanation came. Robert Adam had stayed away from the drinking party to make advances to Carlyle's maid Jenny, described as 'a handsome lass'. He had offered to take her to London and set her up there. Jenny had rebuffed him, and he exorcised his disappointment, so he said, by his wild horseback ride on Piercy.

That was in the summer of 1754, when he was leaving Scotland for Italy. Had Jenny been willing, there is the interesting possibility that Robert Adam might not have gone to Italy and the Adam style would have been an amorous flourish. But ambition was probably too strong, whatever Jenny's answer, and it is doubtful if the family would have stood for it. Robert Adam's career was calculated; his genius was led by a business shrewdness that planned every move in advance. In this he was not by himself: there was the Adam family.

The father was William Adam, a hard-working builder and architect, who was the first man in Scotland to design and build in the Palladian style. He excelled in business, drew money from coalmines – those same mines where the hewers were bonded – and had the ear of men with government contracts to sell. Some of the military works in the Highlands were built by him. He acquired a substantial estate, which he did not hesitate to call Blair Adam. When Robert was a boy, he was given a ruined castle by his parent, a gift more apt than any other recorded between parent and genius offspring.

The four sons of William senior – John, Robert, James, and William junior – came into the world as inheritors of substance. What was of more importance, three of them had, in different degrees, a flair for building and an ability in business.

The eldest, John, was the stolid successor to the family fortunes. He inherited the estate, which became his chief concern, and he followed his father as Master Mason to the Board of Ordnance in North Britain, building still more forts in the Highlands to keep the Hanoverian peace.

James, who is bracketed with Robert in 'the brothers Adam', had no genius. He reflected the sound qualities of Robert, but without fire. He was Robert's business partner and chief assistant.

William, the youngest, was appointed to something in the nature of an accountant's role in the family business. He lived nearly thirty years after his older brothers had died, and he himself appears to have died in penury. He was the unsuccessful one, in whom talent as well as genius was lacking.

Robert was born in 1728, and attended the same school in Kirkcaldy as Adam Smith, who was five years older. They may have sat together in the same thatched room and drummed their heels on the earth floor. Robert later went to the High School in Edinburgh and to the University, the normal pattern of education. On the death of the father in 1748, the family moved to the capital and became part of the inner circle of Edinburgh life. William Robertson, principal of the University, was a cousin. John Home, the cleric who introduced James 'Ossian' Macpherson to Edinburgh, was a particular friend.

About David Hume there is a story that Mrs. Adam, an orthodox woman, warned her son: 'I shall be glad to see any of your companions to dinner, but I hope you will never bring the Atheist.' Robert introduced Hume to the house, along with others, without revealing his identity. The occasion was a huge success, and when the guests had left Mrs. Adam said: 'I must confess that you bring very agreeable companions about you, but the jolly man who sat next to me is the most agreeable of them.' Robert reported that this was the Atheist. 'Well, you may bring him here as much as you please, for he's the most innocent, agreeable, and facetious man I ever met.' The story has a contrived flavour, but it smacks very much of the period, and illustrates the quiet authority which Mrs. Adam exercised over her grown-up family. The sons were devoted to her, and appear to have been always aware of her apron-strings.

When Robert went to Italy in 1754 he had £5,000 set aside for his Grand Tour, and he stayed away for three years, writing home regularly. He was much with Clérisseau.

With young Allan Ramsay the artist, and a few other Scots, he formed a Caledonian Club in Italy. He cultivated the English milords, possibly for their own worth, certainly as potential clients; he filled three years with immense work and considerable amusement. He was then ready for London.

Writing of the year 1758, Carlyle said that Robert Adam 'had been three years in Italy, and, with a first-rate genius for his profession, had seen and studied everything, and was in the highest esteem among foreign artists. From the time of his return – in February or March 1758 – may be dated a very remarkable improvement in building and furniture, and even stoneware, in London and every part of England.' Though Carlyle had a habit of writing like a fulsome schoolmaster penning a report on his outstanding pupil, he was not wrong in suggesting a sudden and urgent change. James Lees-Milne calls it the 'revolution of 1758'.

It is possible that the four brothers had formed a family partnership before Robert went abroad. If so, it is probable that Robert was selected as the most promising of the family, on whom no expense was to be spared, in order that he might equip himself for the future. Little is known of the internal arrangements of the Adam family. They were more than reticent: they were silent on personal matters. Even the numerous letters of Robert and James throw little light on the mechanics of their arrangements, and less on their thoughts and feelings.

1758 saw the setting up of a London office and the further encouragement of potential patrons. There were new friendships. There was a strange game of golf with the Garricks when Carlyle drove a ball through a tunnel under the road at Molesly Heath. There was a journey northwards on horseback to Scotland, accompanied part of way by the Adam sisters. Three of the brothers were in the party, with John Home and Carlyle. They called on Shenstone. They visited Blenheim, where (according to Carlyle) 'James admired the movement' of Vanbrugh's building. What Robert said then is not known, but this was the first mention of the idea of 'movement', which became the theme of the two brothers in the *Works in Architecture*.

1758 also saw the episode of Lord Bute, the able and disliked Scottish Prime Minister of George III. John Home had by this time resigned his pulpit to become Bute's secretary. Through Home and the assistance of Lady Mary Wortley Montagu, who had met Robert in Rome and had written to her daughter, Bute's wife, that 'a man of genius' would like to meet her, the introduction to the Prime Minister was effected. Bute was at his clumsy worst – haughty, withdrawn, and barely civil. Robert was furious at the way in which he was received, and, once outside, 'fell a-cursing and swearing. What! Had he been presented to all the princes in Italy and France, and most graciously received, to come and be treated with such distance and pride by the youngest earl but one in all Scotland!'

It was not long till Bute and Adam were reconciled, but not before Robert had written a fantasy of revenge in a letter to McMillan of Dunmore, Deputy Keeper of the Signet. It was rococo rather than post-Palladian in content.

'I shall certainly be revenged on Bute for his conduct. I have a great mind to go out to K- [Kew] and when he and Madame P [the Princess of Wales] are living together, I'll have them put in a boat naked and brought down the river, like Adam & Eve, and I'll fell him dead with Piranesi's 4 folio volumes from Westminster Bridge as they are going to pass under the Yoke & Robt. Adam. If you disapprove, write me a better scheme.'

1759 saw the beginning of the buildings. His screen at the Admiralty was commissioned, and he started work on Castle Ashby, Shardeloes, Harewood, and Croome. In 1760 he was engaged on Compton Verney, Kedleston, Goodwood, and Alnwick.

It was now time to send brother James to Italy, where he lived and travelled in as affluent a way as Robert had done a few years before. On a tour to Sicily he had to trim his retinue to a draughtsman and two servants. The draughtsman was Clérisseau, and this seems to scotch the long prevailing opinion that Clérisseau was in some way the tutor and inspiration of the Adams.

It is astonishing that two such men as James and Robert should leave so faint an impression of their personal lives. They were certainly agreeable; they were soon famous, and, after the episode of the Adelphi, even notorious. Yet their character as individuals has left no impression at all in the letters and diaries of the period. Even Carlyle's many references are hardly perceptive, and the story of the horse Piercy and Jenny the maid is almost the only indication of Robert Adam as a man rather than an entrepeneur and designer.

In Italy James was a 'noticing' person, but in a casual way, and much more concerned with buildings than with persons, though he does mention a certain Signora who 'was served by Hamilton when here', and records his departure from Pisa where he left a Mrs. Elliott 'with pain, as she is easy and agreeable.' Apart from these few emotional reactions, the lives of the Adam brothers might have been monastic, a difficult feat to accomplish in the Europe in which they travelled, and in the eighteenth century Britain in which they worked laboriously for over thirty years. Their reticence is unnatural, their discretion too complete. Outside the jealousies of their profession and the occasionally acid comments of Johnson and Walpole, references to them are fair and pleasing, but give no depth to the men.

During James's sojourn in Italy, the firm of Adam was already acting for the 'highest in the land', and James purchased the Albani collection for George III. Robert was elected a Fellow of the Royal Society and appointed joint architect of His Majesty's works. The fellow appointee was Sir William Chambers, another Scot, and Bute can be seen behind the division of office between two countrymen, a sardonic Bute because Adam and Chambers had little use for each other.

The Market Hall in High Wycombe, plans for Bowood, the designing of Osterley, Syon, Shelburne House, Moor Park, were some of the buildings Robert was concerned with during the following years. He was a decorator and designer as well as an architect, and when possible would control everything, exterior and interior, ceilings, tapestries, furniture, tea-urns, and candle-snuffers. He hired the finest workers to execute his designs – Chippendale for furniture, Boulton for metalwork, Wedgwood for pottery.

Shortly after James returned to London, Robert published a monumental and sumptuous work on which seven engravers were employed, *Ruins of the Emperor Diocletian's Palace at Spalatro*. Five years later, in 1768, much of his greatest work had been done. He was at the peak of his career, and he entered the House of Commons where he sat, not very actively, as Tory member for his native Kinross-shire. In itself this was a sign of the times, showing how power was passing from the great Whig landowners who, a generation earlier, would have been an architect's most influential patrons.

His parliamentary duty entailed resignation from the office he held jointly with Chambers, a resignation which probably suited him, as he had found no good in it. In any case Chambers was so jealous that it was as well not have have him as a colleague. Because Chambers was treasurer of the Royal Academy, Adam was not elected a member. London, always amused by the Scots, must have delighted in these muted passions and stubborn strivings.

Adam gave up his seat after the Adelphi fiasco, the name of which was intended to immortalise James and Robert, though they did not allow for the eclipse of classical education – the brothers brought the censure of Horace Walpole as the 'affected name'. This vast project on the Thames front caused the Adams serious financial embarrassment: for once Robert was too ambitious, and his desire to be identified with a great public or semi-public building (as Wren was with St. Paul's) overran his prudence and his business sense.

How far this was due to a miscalculation about his enemies is a moot point, but the king-pin of his arrangement was that the government would rent the huge vaults in the base of his building. The government did not do so and disaster followed. Even so, the building was erected. Wedgwood wanted a show room there, and Garrick rented a house from 'my dear Adelphi.' There was the added hostility of the City of London, which declared that land reclamation in front of the building would ruin the interests of the city down-river. The brothers made the best of a bad job by arranging, by Act of Parliament, to sell the Adelphi by lottery. This raised over £200,000. The greater part of the Adelphi has now been demolished, but the vaults that remain are a curiosity worth exploring. The Embankment, part of the reclamation, is the traditional roosting-place of London vagrants, and an unintended memorial to the Adelphi.

After this fiasco, Robert turned to building in his native Scotland. Culzean Castle, a strangely designed castle, the beautiful Mellerstain in the Borders, and Newliston, were all built before 1780. This turn northwards did not follow on any lack of favour in the south, but from the lack of money and of confidence brought about by the American War of Independence, the impeachment of Warren Hastings, the Gordon Riots, and the King's insanity. Life was too troubled for people to build vast country houses.

To some extent Adam gave his attention to town houses, less expensive and presumed to be essential whatever the state of the country. In 1776 he designed the auditorium of Drury Lane Theatre. He also embarked on more considerable schemes, so ambitious in conception that they were never fulfilled. His Cambridge University scheme never went beyond paper. His Edinburgh University scheme was started, stopped, and later (long after Adam's death) completed in so mutilated a way that it is more a caricature than a monument to his genius. He was fated never to build the one great building that would be his permanent glory.

His life was an extremely active one. In all seasons he travelled the length and breadth of Britain, and, at the time of his death from the sudden bursting of a blood vessel, he was busy with eight public and twenty-five private buildings.

He was buried in Westminster Abbey under a plain slab, and his pall-bearers were the Duke of Buccleugh, the Earl of Coventry, the Earl of Lauderdale, Lord Stormont, Lord Frederick Campbell, and Mr. Pulteney. John died later the same year. James, his fellow-worker and closest intimate, died two years later. William, the dull dog, survived for many years. In the year of Robert's death the Register House in Edinburgh was completed, and is now the only surviving building that was supervised by the architect from start to finish, and even that has been meddled with since.

Before the Adam brothers descended on London and Robert, with painstaking preparation, brought about his revolution, a number of compatriots in the same profession had preceded him. Sir William Chambers, of an older generation, was established in the Roman and Patrician tradition, with a strange whiff of the Chinese which he had brought back from eastern travels. James Gibbs of Aberdeen had by then built, much in the style of Wren, the churches of St. Mary-le-Strand and St. Martin-in-the-Fields, as well as the Radcliffe Camera. As was Adam later, Gibbs was consulted about a huge project at King's College, Cambridge, but only the west block was built. The domestic works of Ditchley and Sudbrook Park were his.

James ('Athenian') Stuart was born in 1713, the son of a Scottish mariner. He had a strange and chequered career, beginning as a painter of fans in Rome and ending as a dissolute, procrastinating, untrustworthy, and utterly amiable old man. He built the Doric Temple at Hagley, more or less as a stone-by-stone reproduction of the Temple of Theseus at Athens, and important as the original neo-Georgian building in Britain. Stuart was involved in many structures, and though he had no importance as an original artist or architect, he appears in an uncreative way to have been in tune with the principles of Robert Adam and to have been an enthusiast for what they signified.

Charles Cameron was a countryman of Adam, twelve years his junior. According to Professor Talbot Rice, Cameron was 'an architect of outstanding ability, and his name is worthy to rank beside those of his better-known [British] countrymen, the Adam brothers, Chambers, Wren, Vanbrugh, or Inigo Jones.' Who Cameron was is uncertain. A bookplate of his, in Russia, bears what is recognisable as the arms of Cameron of Lochiel, but the Lochiels are unable to trace him. It is possible that he was the son of a Dr. Archibald Cameron. He was almost certainly patronised by Bute. He was a Jacobite, and attendance at the court of the Young Pretender in Rome may have introduced him to the Roman architecture that was the foundation of his success. At the end of the 1760s and the beginning of the '70s he was in London, living near Piccadilly, but no known work of his was built in Britain. Among the plans he exhibited at the Free Society and the Society of Artists were his drawings for a reconstruction of the Baths of Caracalla. In 1772 he published *The Baths of the Romans* which included, in the full measure of the day, a 'dissertation upon the state of the arts during the different periods of the Roman Empire.'

This book came into the hands of Catherine the Great. It dealt with the buildings of Imperial Rome, and it awakened an imperial empathy and ambition. Catherine summoned the author to Russia, and he went there in 1779, not then forty years old. In a letter, Catherine described her find as *'écossais de nation, Jacobite de profession, grand désignateur, connu par un livre sur les bains romains.'* Above all things, said Catherine, her intention was to build. *'La fureur de bâtir est chose diabolique, cela dévore de l'argent et plus on bâtit, plus on veut bâtir, c'est une maladie comme l'ivrognerie.'*

It was a heady opportunity for Cameron, who knew Adam's earlier work and was very much influenced by it. He built, with every possible material at his command. 'In the use of his adopted materials, the agate and porphyry for his entablatures, the mauve and pistachio porcelain for his columns and columnettes, the ormolu for his capitals and ceiling inlays, and the milky glass for his walls, Cameron's genius was free to revel in sources of dream-like quality unknown to the sombre lands of western Europe.'

While Cameron, Adam, and the rest were interpreting the Graeco-Roman inheritance, more immediate domestic matters were being attended to by others. The development of domestic heating led to improvements in fireplaces, a subject to which Benjamin Franklin gave his attention, as did Count Rumford. In Edinburgh in 1776 James Anderson published his *Practical Treatise on Chimneys*, in which he demonstrated the advantage of high chimneys and low grates, his conclusion being proved daily by the windy vagaries of his native town. He examined the deflection of winds bouncing from the gables of high buildings and then driving down the chimneys of lower buildings to blow soot and sparks into the rooms. He took this wind and diverted it through a by-path on the chimney-top. His chimney cowl increased the 'draw' of the fire beneath. It is possible that Anderson's contribution to domestic comfort and pleasure was of greater importance than the works of his more celebrated compatriots and their colleagues.

24

THE BUILDERS – CANALS,
BRIDGES, AND ROADS

A dynasty of masons. The Thames bridged at Blackfriars. A consulting builder and engineer. 'All his life an adventure.' The New River Company. Alaric on the Flaminian Way. The first threshing-machine. Canals and docks. The Thames bridged at Westminster. The Thames bridged at Southwark. The new London Bridge. The Gotha Canal. Macadamising.

JAMES WATT, of course, gave part of his time to civil engineering in order to make money. But it was Robert Mylne, much less known to posterity, who left his mark on the century as one of the first civil engineers.

In 1754, the year when Robert Adam left Scotland for Rome, Robert Mylne sailed from Leith, also bound for Rome by way of Paris, Marseilles, and Civitavecchia.

From the time of James III the family of Mylne had provided Master Masons to the crown of Scotland. As builders they had worked on the palaces of Stirling, Linlithgow, and Holyrood. They had served Mary Queen of Scots, James VI, and both the Charles's. In the reign of Queen Anne their descendants emerged as architects.

Robert Mylne, probably the greatest and certainly the most prolific of this dedicated family was the eldest son of the man who, during the '45 rebellion, built the Edinburgh Infirmary for the new medical school. He built in the solid style of William Adam.

In Italy Robert spent five years studying what was visible and perceptible. He attended the usual classes in the Academy of St. Luke. Like James Adam, though with less of a flourish, he visited Sicily. But it was Roman engineering that specially interested him, and in 1758 he was awarded first prize in an international competition 'in the presence of a number of cardinals'.

He came back to Britain in 1759 and entered a competition for a bridge over the Thames at Blackfriars; one of his sixty-eight fellow competitors was Sir William Chambers. At the age of 27 Robert Mylne was successful, and became responsible not only for the design but for the entire building of the bridge. It took him ten years. 'Stage by stage', wrote his biographer A. E. Richardson, 'he built up his own methods of constructing this great work, learning to overcome difficulties by hard experience: by sheer improvisation developing a new building technique. And so, by constant application, he convinced himself as he convinced others on matters which had hitherto been obscure.' After an altercation with Dr. Johnson, who disliked the shape of the arches of the bridge but soon capitulated, the two became friends. In 1760 he became engineer and architect to the City of London.

Mylne went ahead rapidly; he acquired a powerful mercantile and ecclesiastical patronage. He was appointed engineer to the New River Company, surveyor to St. Paul's Cathedral, to the Palace at Croydon, to the Abbey Church of St. Albans, and to Canterbury Cathedral. 'He designed the tablet inscribed with the epitaph to Sir Christopher Wren, and superintended the arrangements for all public ceremonies that took place during his tenure of the surveyorship, including the funeral of Lord Nelson.' He designed Almack's club house in London, and the exquisite St. Cecilia's Hall in Edinburgh. (Almack was a Scot called Macall who inverted his name to disguise his nationality – a prevalent practice to avoid the dislike in which the Scots were held.) Mylne designed the City of London Lying-in Hospital, and made some innovations in the building of country houses. (The internal decorations at Wormleybury, attributed to Robert Adam, were probably done by Mylne.)

His reputation as a bridge-builder brought commissions at the Tyne, the Clyde, and Yarrow. He reported on the bridge at Kelso (later reconstructed by Rennie and the prototype for Westminster Bridge). Mylne worked for the Duke of Argyll at Inverary Castle, and both castle and town remain as one of his most forceful works. He built The Wick on Richmond Hill for Lady St. Aubyn.

He was consulted on innumerable projects, reported on the harbour and bridge at Great Yarmouth, was appointed Clerk of the Works to Greenwich Hospital. He designed and built the gracious single-arch bridge in the grounds of Warwick Castle, built the bridge of nine arches at Hexham, worked at Southampton Docks, on the reservoirs in the Pentland Hills near Edinburgh, and designed a hospital for Belfast. He advised on Bognor, Arundel, and Chichester. He built a London town house for Coutts the banker (a fellow Scot) and remodelled the Stationers' Hall.

Such activity suggests a very busy man. But his notebooks give an impression of more than mere busyness: he was so quick, so multifariously occupied, so bursting with work, that a man today would be regarded as exceptional if he accomplished a part of it with the assistance of twentieth-century travel and facilities. 'All his life was an adventure, and judging from his personal sketches he was interested equally in Gothic architecture, field gates, and machinery.' He was used to travelling to Scotland in four days by post-chaise. He might leave Inverary, and a week later have begun and completed a report on waterworks in the south of England, having on the way advised on a bridge in the Midlands.

He died in harness at the age of seventy-nine in 1811. He was a man of transition. In him can be seen the change from architect-designer to architect-builder and builder-engineer. His long working life covered a period of great technical development which made voracious demands for bridges, docks, factories, and waterways, and for the proliferation of cities. Mylne contributed to it all, and was entirely responsible for an astonishing part. So vast were his preoccupations that it was almost incidental that, for the New River Company, he controlled 250 bridges, about forty sluices, covering thirty-eight miles of waterways, as well as lakes and rivulets, a job which in a less vigorous age would require a considerable department of officials.

'He planned with clarity and constructed with foresight. He possessed neither the skill for composition and planning exercised by Sir William Chambers, nor the versatility for decoration enjoyed by Robert Adam. On the contrary, he worked upon the whole standard of every day practice, perfecting the ordinary and demonstrating that a precision in construction had a purpose to fulfil.'

He led naturally to his fellow-countrymen – the great civil engineers, Rennie, Telford, and Macadam. Agnes Muir Mackenzie said that the last two 'brought road-making, quite suddenly, to a level that it had not reached in Europe since the barbarian tribes under Alaric came marching down the Flaminian Way on Rome – that is to say, for about fourteen hundred years.'

John Rennie (1761–1821) had a career rather similar to Mylne, but he leaned even further towards engineering. His father was a farmer at Phantassie, in East Lothian. His brother George was sent, at the age of sixteen, to make a survey of agriculture on Tweedside, was later associated with Meikle in the construction of the first threshing-machine, and had a son who became governor of the Falkland Islands.

John Rennie, twelve years junior to George, went to the parish school, worked for two years on the land with Meikle, and then went back to school at Dunbar, where he later had the chance of becoming a teacher. He refused this to return to Meikle, the engineer farmer. When he was twenty-two he went to London, and was employed by Boulton and Paul in the construction of steam engines in a flour-mill near Blackfriars Bridge. He then installed machinery in Whitbread's brewery, and was soon in business on his own account.

By the time he was in his early thirties he was one of the major civil engineers in Britain. He designed and executed canals, bridges, docks, and machines. He built Ramsgate harbour, London Docks, East and West India Docks at Blackhill, Prince's Dock at Liverpool, the docks at Hull, Dublin, Greenock, and Leith, and the breakwater at Plymouth. By following the principles of Smeaton at Eddystone, he constructed the Bell Rock Lighthouse in the North Sea. His bridge over the Tweed at Kelso was the model for his Westminster Bridge. He also built the Thames bridge at Southwark. He superintended the construction of the Great Western Canal, and flung an iron bridge – daring in its day – over the Witham in Lincolnshire. He designed the new London Bridge, which was built by his son Sir John Rennie.

Thomas Telford the roadmaker was born in 1757 at Eskdale in the uplands of Dumfriesshire. His parents were poor and he attended school at Westerkirk, where instruction was limited, and afterwards taught himself to read Latin, German, French, and Italian. The pattern of his growing-up was indeed quite normal.

At fourteen he became apprenticed to a builder and learned the trade of stone-mason. Later as a qualified tradesman he studied architecture. When he was twenty-five he went to London, and with the help of Sir Robert Chambers he worked on the building of Somerset House. His unusual merit was rewarded with an appointment to superintend government works in the dockyard at Portsmouth. Within five years of his going south he became county surveyor in Salop, an appointment he held throughout his life.

The British Fishery Society employed him to inspect their harbours. At Wick, in the north of Scotland, he built the harbour extension known as Pulteneytown. Early in the nineteenth century he was appointed by the Parliamentary Commissioners as engineer in charge of the building of bridges and roads in the Highlands. Under his direction, 1,100 bridges and 860 miles of new road were constructed. He completed the Caledonian Canal, on which James Watt had worked earlier. He put the Dean Bridge over the Water of Leith in Edinburgh. He surveyed mail-coach roads in the south, engaged in numerous public works, and built the Menai Suspension Bridge. At the invitation of the Swedish Government he constructed the Gotha Canal system.

In his early Edinburgh years he had been a versifier and contributor to *Ruddiman's Magazine*. He was driven by a belief in the fundamental worthiness of his work. With the liberal faith of Hutcheson and Smith, he believed that, through the techniques he introduced and developed, the life of his fellows would be made better.

Macadam, who put the surface on roads, grew up in America, where his father had taken him at the age of six, following a depletion of the family fortunes in the west of Scotland. The father died when the son was still a youth, and Macadam grew up during the American Revolution, later making a fortune as agent for the sale of prizes.

He came back to Scotland to become Commissioner of the Peace and deputy lieutenant of the county of Ayrshire, where he was also a trustee of roads.

He moved to England, and, after an appointment as victualling agent to the navy, he became surveyor-general of the Bristol roads. He had been interested in roads from his boyhood in Scotland when he had made a model of a section of a local road at Girvan. Public roads were becoming quite inadequate for the increasing demand for travel – ruts and potholes in summer, a quagmire of mud in winter.

Macadam's idea was to construct a road on a base of carefully laid stones, so that they would become even firmer by the impact of traffic. The bed was well-drained.

So successful was this system that it was soon adopted throughout the country. When a top dressing of tar was added the modern tarmacadam road was in being. The House of Commons examined his methods, with the result that the streets of the major cities were Macadamised. He was voted £10,000 for his services, and he refused a knighthood (which was conferred on his second son, Sir James Nicoll Macadam, general surveyor of metropolis turnpike road.)

The traffic in engineers was not always one way, from north to south. The great Smeaton, an Englishman from Leeds, came to Scotland to construct the Forth and Clyde Canal, and to reinforce the North Bridge at Edinburgh which had partly collapsed owing to the incompetence of the local builder.

25

THE BUILDERS – STEAMSHIPS

The banker-gunner.   'A plurality of masts.'   A gift of
turnip seed.   Five miles an hour.   Seven miles an
hour.   Lord Dundas shows interest.   The *Charlotte
Dundas*.   The Admiralty prefers the wind.   *The Comet*
on salt water.   Clydeside begins to build.   Napier's
engines.   The sea is conquered.

JAMES WATT'S STRANGE RELUCTANCE to harness steam power to
transport was not shared by his fellows. The Scots engineer Murdoch made
early attempts to create a steam carriage, but it was not until many years later
that Stephenson, a north of England man and the son of a Scottish emigrant,
was successful. Steam was successfully applied to ships before it was used in the
movement of people and goods on land.

There had been a number of unsuccessful attempts to develop steamships
with atmospheric engines of the Papin and Savory-Newcomen type. In 1763 a
Lancaster mechanic, William Henry, was the first to try to use the Watt type of
engine, but he made little progress. The Frenchman, Perier, tried with both
duck-foot paddles and a paddle-wheel. Fitch, an American, experimented in
1785 with Watt's engine for ship propulsion, and is believed to have killed
himself in disappointment.

Miller, Taylor, Symington, and Bell were the four Scots who created the
steamship, and in their hands it developed from an experiment on an inland
sheet of water to a small vessel capable of a brief sea voyage.

Patrick Miller was a retired banker with an estate at Dalswinton, in
Dumfriesshire, and a passion for boats. As a young man he had been to sea. He
had his own ideas about propelling a ship mechanically, and at Leith he had
made a vessel by joining two small boats with a paddle-wheel slung between
them. The wheel had been turned by hand and the contraption moved at
'several miles an hour'.

Miller was a 'lad o' pairts' and had made his own fortune. His brother
became Sir Thomas Miller, Lord President of the Court of Session. His
youthful seafaring life had taken him to the West Indies and America. Later, as
a successful banker (deputy governor of the Bank of Scotland for thirty years),
he indulged in his hobbies of navigation, artillery and agriculture, and in all
three he made his name.

As a gunner he invented guns with chambers which he had made at the

Carron foundry. (He gave the credit for this to Gustavus of Sweden.) These were the first carronades. He experimented with guns from 2-pounders to 132-pounders, and it is said he achieved a range of 5,000 yards with the latter. At his own expense (or possibly the expense of the Bank of Scotland), he fitted out a privateer, the *Spitfire* with sixteen 18-pounders, and sent it off to fight the French. There was a bloody battle with a French frigate, the *Surveillante*, which resulted in many dead and wounded, when the *Spitfire* was captured and the *Surveillante* had to run for port with its holds full of water.

As a farmer Miller is credited with the first drill plough in Britain, with a threshing-machine worked by horses, and an iron plough. He fed cattle with steamed potatoes, and dressed his land with burned clay instead of lime. He cultivated fiorin grass and thought this his most important contribution to agriculture, introducing the grass to Scotland after hearing of it from the Rev. Dr. Richardson of Clonfeckle in Ireland.

His experiment at Leith in 1786 with a paddle-wheel and two hulls was not a small affair. He claimed that the paddle-wheel was his own invention, and he later patented it. The ship had five masts (one writer has said that 'a plurality of masts was a favourite idea of his'), and he mounted carronades on the double vessel. When the government showed no interest in his unusual boat, he presented the vessel to Gustavus III of Sweden, who acknowledged it with the gift of a gold box, in which was a packet of seeds which Miller planted, to produce what were reputedly the first Swedish turnips, or swedes, in Britain.

About this time James Taylor was employed by Miller as tutor to his sons. Like Allan Ramsay, Taylor had been born in the village of Leadhills, and had attended university in Edinburgh where, presumably, he met Miller. It is probable that Taylor was present at the Leith experiments. He is said to have suggested the use of steam to drive the paddle-wheel, and Miller is reputed to have resisted at first, but later consented to finance the experiment. At any rate, there was subsequently contention as to who invented the steamship, and if rival claims cannot be decided in favour of one person more than another, there is no doubt that Miller, Taylor, and Symington were the triple parents. Bell came later to develop it. As Cullen had said: 'It is always by the successive labours of several that an art is brought to perfection . . . and all claim the honour of the invention.'

Symington was a young engineer, who had made a small reputation as an improver of the steam-engine. He had devised a new construction, without an air pump. He was employed at Leadhills, where it seems that Taylor came across him. He was introduced to Miller, who engaged him to fit an engine to one of his own paddle-boats. The first trials were in October 1788, on the loch at Dalswinton. They were successful, and the double-boat moved at about five miles an hour. (The engine is to be found in the Kensington Patent Museum.) The following year a larger vessel was fitted with a double engine, with cylinders eighteen inches in diameter, made at Carron foundry. This was sailed successfully on the Forth and Clyde canal, at seven miles an hour, to the great interest of Lord Cullen who wrote about the event in the newspapers.

Miller then seems to have lost interest in the matter. He dropped out of the affair, and Taylor had not enough money to continue. Symington, however – the only one of the three who was an engineer – waited until 1801 when, with Lord Dundas as his patron, he was able to make another experimental ship, in which both hull and engine were to his own design. This was the *Charlotte Dundas*, the true prototype of the steamship. Lord Dundas was on board when the *Charlotte Dundas* hauled two loaded barges, each of seventy tons, at six miles an hour for nineteen miles on the canal. The destination was Port Dundas. In his account of the voyage, Symington noted that his ship moved against a breeze strong enough to prevent any other vessel in the canal sailing to windward.

A proposal to substitute steamboats for drag horses on the canal was not entertained by the owners of the waterway, who claimed (as the citizens of Venice do to this day) that the wash of the vessels would destroy the embankments. After the successful trial the Admiralty was still uninterested, but the Duke of Bridgewater ordered eight boats, with the intention of using them on his canals in Lancashire. His death put a stop to the project. An attempt was made to secure Symington a pension, but the government refused and he eventually died in poverty.

It was not yet time to launch a steam vessel on water less predictable than a canal, and the *Charlotte Dundas* lay for many years in a creek near Bainsford drawbridge, where in later years it was inspected by Fulton and Bell. Fulton's father had gone from Ayrshire to America. Fulton, a visitor to the land of his ancestors, took the idea of a steamship to America and built the *Clermont*, which operated on the Hudson in 1807.

Henry Bell, who was eventually successful in putting a steamship to sea, had been working on the same lines as Symington. He came to Glasgow in 1790 with experience as millwright, shipwright, and engineer. He had begun life as a stone-mason, and had served under Rennie in London. In 1800, before the historic journey of the *Charlotte Dundas*, he had built an engine into a small boat on the Clyde, and written to the Admiralty about 'the practicability and great utility of applying steam to the propelling of vessels against winds and tides'. Like Miller, he discovered the Admiralty was loyal to the wind.

He was provost of Helensburgh in 1811 when he arranged for the construction of the *Comet*. It was built by John Wood at Port Glasgow, and the engines were made by David Napier. It was forty-two feet long and had a three-horse-power engine. It plied between Glasgow and Helensburgh, and once made a voyage up the west coast to Oban.

During the next ten years forty-eight steamers, increasing in size and power, were built on the Clyde, including the *Marjory*, built by Denny, the first steamship to operate on the Thames. The *Britannic* (109 tons) was built in 1815. Steamship building also began in Dundee. The development of iron hulled ships followed, again on the Clyde. (The further development of steamships is outside the scope of this book, but it is worth noting that the Clyde pioneered many major advances in steam navigation, from building the original *Comet* to devising the stabilisers fitted to the *Queen Elizabeth* and the *Queen Mary*, both products of Clyde yards.)

David Napier was one of the important figures in the advance of steam navigation. He had great confidence in steam:

'Seeing that steam navigation was likely to succeed, I erected new works at Camlachie, for the purpose of making steam-engines, where the engines were made for the *Dumbarton Castle*, the first steamer that went up Loch Fyne, and for the *Britannic*, the first that went to Campbeltown. Although these vessels did not venture outside the Cumbraes in stormy weather, they suggested the idea to a Company in Dublin of having steamers between Holyhead and Howth.'

It seemed at first that steamships might not stand the trials of the open sea. The Dublin company built two vessels at Greenock and put in engines made by Cook. It was hopeless. 'The idea of making machinery of any kind that would withstand the shock of a heavy sea in a gale of wind was put down as an impossibility.'

Napier believed that steamships could be built not only for fair-weather sailing in an estuary.

'Whether it was from pique at not having been employed to make the engines of these vessels, or from a conviction that the ocean could be safely navigated by steam, I cannot now say, but I commenced, I think about the year 1818, to build a steamer on my account for that purpose called the *Rob Roy*. I recollect the day before starting on the first trip from Glasgow to Dublin, Mr. Charles McIntosh, the celebrated chemist and inventor of waterproof cloth, saying we should all be drowned. Nevertheless we did start, and although we encountered a gale from the south-west, performed the voyage out and home successfully. I afterwards placed the *Rob Roy* on the station between Glasgow and Belfast, and commenced to build others to run between Greenock and Liverpool and Holyhead and Howth.'

David Napier left his firm in 1836 and was succeeded by his cousin Robert, who introduced many improvements in engine design. In 1839 a firm of Glasgow agents received a letter: 'I shall require one or two steam-boats of 300 horsepower and about 800 tons. I am told that Messrs. Wood and Napier are highly respectable builders, and likely to fulfil any engagement that they may enter into: will you be so good as to ask them the probable sum for which they would engage to furnish me with these boats in all respects ready for sea in twelve months.' The letter was from Samuel Cunard, of Halifax, Nova Scotia, where his loyalist family had moved from America after the Declaration of Independence. Napier advised larger ships, and it was necessary to form a new company, with greater capital than Cunard had intended. Napier persuaded Glasgow merchants to subscribe, and the British and North American Royal Mail Steam-packet Company was formed, to be known later as the Cunard Line.

By now many others were interested. Marc Isambard Brunel was an engineer from Normandy who played a major part in the construction of the Battersea Tunnel, London, and was interested in steam navigation. Abroad he had built the Battery at New York.

His son, Isambard Kingdom Brunel, was an engineer of bridges, railways, docks and ships. He built the first vessels to make regular steam voyages across the Atlantic. Using skills and engines developed on the Clyde he built the largest vessels of his day, the most famous being the *Great Eastern*.

26

THE IMPROVERS

The hungry years.   Introducing the potato.   The
English example.   Plough and fallow.   Millions of
trees.   The publishing pioneers.   *The Gentleman
Farmer*.   The Devil's wind.   A threshing machine and a
plough.   Bigger beats and better sheep.   Seed for
sowing.   The trek from the land.

TRAVELLERS' ACCOUNTS of the Scottish countryside, at the beginning
of the eighteenth century, describe a bleak and desolate landscape, a treeless
waste of moors and hills, where the art of husbandry was very primitive indeed.

Agriculture was at subsistence level, and frequently failed to achieve even
that. In the previous century a succession of crop failures ended in the seven
hungry years known as King William's Years. It was famine and poverty that
made inevitable the 1707 Union (accentuated by the failure of the Darien
Scheme, itself an attempt to undo the economic mischief caused by the English
Navigation Act.)

Fletcher of Saltoun, a republican strongly opposed to the Union, pointed
out that of Scotland's population of 1,110,000 one in every five or six lived in
appalling misery and destitution. It was reckoned that two out of three people
died in childhood.

It took many decades for agriculture to revive. For two hundred years –
ever since the overwhelming defeat at Flodden in 1513 – Scottish husbandry
had in fact deteriorated. Even when the country began to prosper again there
were occasional crop failures that caused immense misery.

Three main factors put Scottish agriculture into better heart for the
immense improvements that eventually became possible. One was the
abolition of hereditary jurisdictions following the '45. This more or less
banished feudalism and brought about a general betterment of social
conditions. It permitted an altered system of land tenure to develop larger and
more compact holdings.

Secondly, the potato, almost unknown at the start of the century and even
then regarded suspiciously as a useless exotic tuber, had by the end of the
century become part of the staple diet of men and beasts. This was especially
true of the more distant and agriculturally primitive parts of the country. In the
Hebrides the potato was not introduced until 1743 when the inhabitants,
though forced to grow it by their chiefs, refused to eat what they grew. But fifty

years later the potato comprised four-fifths of the Hebridean diet and contributed towards a phase of over-population which, in turn, contributed towards emigration. The turnip too played an important role as a new provider of nourishment for man and beast. It was introduced in the first half of the century but was not grown widely until later.

The last factor was the use of lime to sweeten sour land, and this became possible in the later part of the century through the development of roads and the acceptance of wheeled transport. One of the earliest carts astonished the people of the west around 1723 when it was seen carrying coal from East Kilbride to Cambuslang. Many of these carts were no more than tumbrils, but by the end of the century the wheelwright, the carter, and the navvy had made the country mobile, at least in the important central regions.

Early in the century such advances as were contemplated were usually a straightforward copying of the more progressive English methods. The Duchess of Gordon – daughter of an English duke – is said to have imported English ploughs, with English ploughmen to use them. Hutton the geologist was another who brought techniques from foreign countries and developed them on his own Border estate. Yet at the end of the century, even after Small had invented his new horse plough, progress was so piecemeal that in Aberdeenshire, the Duke of Gordon's country, some land was still being ploughed with twelve oxen. Very much depended on the attitude of mind of the particular landowner. One man might pioneer improvements; his neighbour would have none of them.

Around 1690 John Walker of East Lothian is reputed to have been the first man to practise 'fallowing' – which meant no more than ploughing land hitherto unploughed and then leaving it for a period before sowing. He was the first, in consequence, to grow a good crop of wheat on ground that had been neglected as only good enough for sparse grazing.

As far back as 1695 the wasteful runrig system had been tackled in legislation by the Scots Parliament. Under this system – the traditional method by which arable land was worked by the local community – a number of narrow strips of land were allocated to individual peasants. The strips worked by any one peasant were not side by side but could be scattered over the whole parcel of land. Strips were allocated according to the importance of the families in the community and might change hands every few years. The untilled ground between the strips was wasted. The whole process was so uneconomic that it totally prevented the efficient use of land.

It was not till mid-century, however, that runrig began to be substantially replaced in the Lowlands by separate holdings. Runrig lasted longer in the north. Its abolition meant the development of large farms and the emergence of the professional farmer, intent on doing far more than scratch a living. One inevitable result of the growth of modern farming – and one that still operates in the Scottish countryside – was depopulation. At the beginning of the century there were many peasants bending their backs in primitive toil: a few generations later there were far fewer workers, but much more productive work.

A vast amount of upland territory – land that was not considered rich enough for cultivation – was held as common ground. Burghs and villages all had their acres, sometimes of huge extent, which were used for common grazing. This ground was held by very ancient usage, and in different parts of Scotland was a heritage of Celtic, Saxon and Norse custom. It began to be divided up under various Acts of Parliament.

The enclosing of land, the building up of large farms and estates, was ostensibly for the good of agriculture. Indeed it was an essential preliminary to better husbandry. What actually happened of course was that small farms and villages vanished completely. Rural distress caused large shifts in the population and sent thousands across the Atlantic to seek their fortune in the Americas. The large landowners also took the opportunity to increase their private estates.

Accompanying these changes there arose amongst the city intellectuals an interest in the better use of land. The defeat of the Stuarts made its own contribution. Some of the gentlemen who found it prudent to go abroad (and so escape the inconvenience of being disembowelled alive) eventually returned to Scotland in later and safer days. They brought with them a knowledge of foreign farming, together with a taste for vegetables still unknown in Scotland.

A start was made by progressive landowners in transforming the physical appearance of the country. They planted trees by the million, and the bare, naked look began to be clothed.

Edinburgh inevitably became the intellectual centre of the new farming. In 1723 the Society of Improvers of Knowledge of Agriculture was founded in the capital by one marquis, four earls, three lords, and others. The first president, Thomas Hope, who had travelled in England and Europe, took the marshy land to the south of Edinburgh, drained it, and turned it into a recreational park that remains a feature of modern Edinburgh, known as 'The Meadows'.

The society produced an amount of serious writing, in simple language, showing how improvements could be effected – the fallowing of ground, the raising of grass seed, the development of flax growing and linen manufacture, ploughing and manuring, the use of clover. A description was published of dairy farming in England, dealing in detail on methods of management and the profits obtained.

The importance of fallow was blazoned abroad. One writer, William Mackintosh, was a political prisoner in Edinburgh Castle. He spent his days encouraging his free countrymen to improve their ways and prophesied that Scottish agriculture could be as considerable as in any other European country. In many ways he underestimated his countrymen.

The Lord Provost of Edinburgh, Patrick Lindesay, published a book in 1733 which included a section on agriculture, as well as an examination of the poor, the police, trade, manufactures, and fisheries.

In 1741 Alexander Blackwell produced a book dealing with improving 'cold, wet, and barren land'. Blackwell had been a pupil of Boorhaave. He went to Sweden with a proposal to drain marshes but happened to fall foul of the law and was beheaded.

A country schoolmaster (James Hamilton of East Calder) translated Virgil's *Pastorals* into English and then added to the text a further sixty pages dealing with the theory of husbandry. He, too, wanted to see the management of the countryside brought up to English standards.

In 1755 the Edinburgh Society for Encouraging Arts, Sciences, Manufacturers, and Agriculture offered a gold medal for a study of agriculture. This was won by Francis Home, a doctor of medicine, who had been a student at Leyden and a military surgeon in Flanders. Science began to look seriously at the land. Home studied the chemistry of growth, the importance of atmosphere, disease, types of soil, and so on.

In 1757 Sir Archibald Grant of Monymusk published the first of a number of pamphlets on agriculture, based on his vast knowledge of practical estate management. He said that 'the greater part of farmers must be in as pinched and miserable a way as the fields, which they labour.'

Principal Leechman of Glasgow University farmed in Lanarkshire. One of his professors attended to his estates near Loch Lomond. Ministers of religion, in a less passionately theological age, gave their attention to terrestrial as well as to heavenly pastures. Dickson and Wilkie were two divines who carried on agricultural work.

In Aberdeenshire, around 1760, six professors were amongst the members of a farming club that existed to examine the backwardness of current practice. It was in that same county, where progress and backwardness existed side by side, that Grant of Monymusk made his immense progress. He took the estate over from his father in 1717 when he was a young Edinburgh advocate. He spent some years in London as a Member of Parliament while a friend, Archibald Jaffray, began the long process of draining, enclosing and tree-planting that eventually made Monymusk a model estate.

An English farmer, Thomas Winter, settled at Monymusk where he and Jaffray laboured for years. They had their own tree nursery. Around the main house a wasteland was slowly transformed. A million trees were planted on one portion of the estate – beech, firs, alders, oaks, and elms. Fields were carved out of rough land, enclosed by stone dykes and sheltered by tree belts.

Fifteen years of progress had been achieved before Grant returned. By then turnips, clover, rye-grass, potatoes, and peas were being grown. From then on work was driven forward over the whole estate. The land was surveyed, mapped, and planned for enclosing. And the rental value to the tenants grew five times.

Meanwhile the community was learning about the rotation of crops – many of which had been unknown not long before. Those who accepted the new farming had the chance to prosper. Those who were dour and recalcitrant – 'Whit was guid eneuch for ma faither is guid eneuch for me' – were required 'to flit and remove themselves'. Progress was beneficial but not always kindly.

The 1760s saw this change of emphasis throughout Scotland. The years of basic exhortation and teaching were passing. Action had to follow and a more willing audience was required to accept instruction. Even so, in 1785 a Scottish writer, David Young, pointed out that 'at present Scotland is a century behind England in points of improvement, liberal sentiments and the arts.'

One of the best-known practical theorists of the time was Henry Home, Lord Kames. With the authority of the bench and with considerable knowledge of landowning he published *The Gentleman Farmer* in 1776. It was a thorough examination of the scene, and showed how much had already been accomplished. At the beginning of the century fresh meat was a rarity and stalled cattle were so weak in springtime – if they had survived the winter – that they had to be carried bodily to the fields. Kames wrote that 'we now have fresh meat in plenty all the year round.'

The agricultural revolution was in full swing, but it was a hard task to persuade the innately conservative country people to adopt new ways. Another writer complained of 'country people's bigottedness to old customs'. Yet the advances were being made, mainly on the animal and vegetable side of farming. Meanwhile a few people were considering the role that machinery might play on the farm.

Corn was threshed by hand, using flails, and winnowing was done either by letting the wind blow through an open-ended barn, or by taking the corn to an exposed and windy site. Either way, the wind blew away the chaff. 'The shilling law' was the name frequently given to the outdoor place where the winnowing was done. 'Shilling' is grain which has been freed of husk. 'Law' is a small round hill, e.g., Berwick Law. The labour and wastage in this tedious occupation – often conducted by women who acted as beasts of burden – was made even more inefficient by the poorness of the crops.

James Meikle, who lived at Saltoun in East Lothian, visited Holland and brought back fanners which could be used to winnow corn indoors, without benefit of natural wind. This was early in the century, about 1710. It was too early. Though the Dutch device gave independence of wind and weather, Meikle was accused of 'making the devil's wind and taking the power out of the hands of the almighty.'

Many years later fanners were accepted. Andrew Rodger came across an old Dutch fanner in a Leith granary and from it constructed the first winnowing machine. Soon he was supplying farmers throughout Scotland, at £3 a machine, and he started to trade with England.

James Meikle also developed the processing of barley in a mill, and built such a mill at Saltoun, where it was in use for many years before being accepted elsewhere. The idea for the mill was another fruit of his visit to Holland, where he had gone at the instigation of Fletcher of Saltoun, the republican, who had himself been there and been so impressed that he sent his employee Meikle to apply his knowledge of mechanics to Dutch methods.

But even within this progressive group there was reaction. Fletcher's brother's wife took over the running of the mill. She sat in the mill office all day taking orders, but kept out everyone who might discover how the mill operated. The monopoly was profitable and to be protected.

James Meikle's son Andrew inherited his father's inventive skill. He was the master under whom John Rennie, the engineer and builder, served his apprenticeship. One of Andrew's inventions concerned the windmill, then being developed as a source of power. This may have been a second-generation benefit from the trip to Holland. Until mid-century the windmill head was turned into the wind manually, by the use of a long pole. As well as being cumbersome and awkward it meant that in a variable wind someone had to give constant attention to the apparatus.

In 1750 Meikle devised the fantail gear, a small auxiliary windmill mounted at right angles to the sails. This kept the head into the wind. Twenty years later he improved the device by making it spill excess wind automatically.

In 1776 he experimented with a threshing machine and it took him eleven years to bring it into use. He worked on ideas that had been developed by others – Menzies in 1743, Stirling in 1758 – and some years later north of England farmers, Elderton near Alnwick, Smart of Wark, and Oxley at Flodden, had all experimented with threshing machines.

Meikle brought the work to success. This machine separated grain that lay in the straw, it threshed and it winnowed. It could be operated by horses or by waterpower, and if need be by manpower on the treadmill principle. Its output was twenty to forty bushels an hour, and unskilled labour could be used to feed the machine and take away grain, straw and chaff. The cost was about £80 to purchase, or £10 a year for wear and tear, together with interest to the local bank on the capital sum. Meikle's machine became quickly popular in all corn-growing districts, from Berwick to the Moray Firth. He patented it in 1788.

Thus the farmer became liberated, in part, from wind and weather. Backbreaking work was taken over by the horse and by the windmill. In his barn at night, using candles, the farmer could work long after sunset.

The very basic matter of ploughing had not advanced in Scotland for hundreds of years. In large tracts of the Highlands and Islands the preparation of soil was done by the handplough or *caschrom*, little more than a crooked spade. The plough used in southern parts, drawn by horse or oxen, was a descendant of the great Belgic wooden plough which had been unchanged for seven hundred years.

A vast concourse of animals and people was required to progress the cumbersome plough through the ground. Six, eight, or more oxen and horses were yoked by ropes of hide or hair, or even (in the more primitive parts) by twisted birch twigs.

The reins were held by a gadsman who stood in front of the animals, facing them, and encouraging them to move by striking the beasts on the face. Another person walked in advance of the cavalcade to remove large stones. A third walked beside the plough to guide it along the furrow. A fourth followed with a spade to break up the divots. About half an acre a day was the work accomplished.

There had been attempts in England to improve the plough, but Scotland was unimpressed. Then about 1730 the Earl of Stair introduced a Dutch plough. Lady Stewart of Coltness is also credited with a lighter plough – the Rutherglen plough. The Scots remained unimpressed.

John Small, a native of Berwickshire who had worked for a time in England, returned in 1764 and set up as an agricultural implement maker at Blackadder Mount in his home county. Using soft-wood models he analysed the forces met in ploughing, and in this way discovered what shapes were most fit for the job. He then constructed his two-horse swing plough.

Not even rural prejudice could deny Small's plough an immediate success. In Clackmannanshire in 1791 every one of forty competitors in a ploughing competition used a Small's plough. Two years later it was demonstrated to George III at Windsor, and the monarch was so delighted that he kept the plough, though he rewarded the ploughman, a man named Virtue.

Small improved his invention when he had the Carron Iron Works cast some of the parts. He opened a workshop in Leith Walk, Edinburgh, and made farm implements and machinery. He improved the horse-drawn cart and published a book *Ploughs and Wheeled Carriages*. He built the tools that agriculture needed – rollers, harrows, winnowing machines, ploughs, and carts. But he died at fifty-two, without much money. He had been too enthusiastic about his work to look after his own interests. Sir John Sinclair wrote: 'Small had such a propensity to be useful that he laid personal interest too much aside – a man possessed of more public zeal and of a greater turn for mechanical invention has rarely appeared in any age or country.'

Meanwhile leather replaced twisted hair or heather in harness, and most people stopped the practice of harnessing implements directly to the horse's tail.

The next step was to mechanise the cutting of corn. Both the Highland Society and the Dalkeith Farming Society encouraged the development of a reaping machine. Again the moment had to await the man. Patrick Bell, a divinity student, invented a reaper after seeing a pair of hedge shears on his father's farm. The first trial was in a barn, cutting oats that had been artificially planted in soil. The trial was successful. Bell feared ridicule if his field trial was a failure, so he went out after dark with his brother to test the machine. It did not work and they found a minor fault. When this was corrected all was well. Public trials were held in 1828. The reaping machine was accepted in principle, but it was slow to be adopted in practice. Four years later only ten were working.

Meantime some had been sent abroad, and descriptions of the machine were published in journals. J. A. Symon writes: 'What part, if any, Bell's reaper played in the success of the Cyrus McCormick American machine will never be known. All that we know is that three years later McCormick produced a machine embodying some of Bell's principles.' McCormick's machine was indeed an improvement. It abandoned the scissor action that Bell had used, and cut the grain with a straight blade. American enterprise fostered the making of reapers; in Scotland Bell's was never really adopted.

Other aspects of farming that were developed in Scotland with some foresight included the improvement of seed. Patrick Shirref, working in the Lothians, bred from selected plants and developed a wheat and an oat which were grown in the country for nearly a century.

This development was possible because most single plants breed true. One method of selecting seed corn was to fling corn into the wind. The heaviest grains travelled farthest and these were selected as seed. Shirref developed more sophisticated methods, and from his chosen seed he grew carefully nursed crops over a number of years, breeding true all the time, until there was sufficient quantity for full-scale farming.

It was perhaps in the beef trade that Scotland was significantly successful. As a young man of twenty, Hugh Watson set up as a farmer on the borders of the counties of Perth and Angus. His father gave him six cows and a bull. At Brechin he bought ten heifers and another bull. From these he founded his herd, and from 1810 onwards he exhibited at shows. His success grew only locally at first, but in time he joined the Highland Society and carried everything before him, and went on to Smithfield.

In 1829 at Perth the show included Aberdeen-Angus bulls and cows for the first time: every exhibit came from Watson's herd. Some of his beasts are enshrined in farming lore. One year he sent to Smithfield a vast black polled ox that weighed over 130 stones, yet had a foreleg as fine as a roe-deer. It was outstanding for the quality of its meat and it was immortalised on a medal specially struck to mark its success. Another beast, an Aberdeen-Angus cow, was entered as No. 1 in the handbook of the breed.

Watson was one of many stock and sheep farmers who vastly improved the quality of beasts. The Scotch Shorthorn was created by Amos Cruickshank, a Quaker and bachelor in Aberdeenshire. He built up the largest shorthorn herd in Britain. He bred a beast called Champion of England, and from it, by close inbreeding, he produced an animal that was in great demand in the Americas. The shorthorn populated the prairies. The breed had early maturity, plenty of flesh, and a strong constitution. It was a far cry from the sickly and feeble beasts, so weak that they had to be manhandled to the fields.

While improvements in machinery and techniques transformed the ways in which farmers went about their work, the main change during the eighteenth century was in the way of life of those who lived in the countryside.

In mid-century even a well-doing small farmer lived in primitive quarters, slept on straw in a bare room, travelled to market on foot, and ate out of a bowl on his knee. The farmer and his family lived in the same dwelling-house as his servants. By the end of the century he slept on a feather mattress in a bedroom with curtains, and sat down at table to a properly laid meal, and he dined on meat instead of cereals.

That could be the transformation from father to son. By 1830 the next generation, assuming a prosperous farm in one of the better agricultural districts, enjoyed the solidity and gentility of early nineteenth-century luxury.

The farmhouse was now a stone mansion, set apart from the farm buildings.

A socially ambitious wife had a piano in her living room, and the room – perhaps with finely plastered cornice and freize – was hung with good wallpaper. Trees graced the driveway. The servants lived in improved but separate quarters of their own, but in many farms all still ate together.

This way of life, securely established for the abler farmers, was to change little during the remainder of the nineteenth-century, except when it was sweetened by modern plumbing and eventually lit by electricity. The basic transformation from primitive squalor to relative ease had been accomplished in three generations.

The farm workers were vastly fewer in number and they shared to some extent in the social improvements, though not by any means on the same scale as their masters. They were still ill-paid, though wages steadily advanced. During the Napoleonic Wars wages nearly doubled, and might reach as much as £3 to £5 per year. A shepherd might be paid mainly in sheep. It was the perquisites that really mattered and provided the greater part of whatever standard of living was achieved. Housing improved, but the finest reward a farm worker could have was a good master.

The grieve, the hind, the herd – and their wives – were people of importance if working for a sound farmer. Potatoes, cows, sheep, flax, pigs, hens, coal where it was available, a house, a garden, were part of the bargain that the master struck with his workers. But only the larger farms required this semi-permanent staff – the hiring or rehiring was carried out at regular intervals. It was said that a farm worker's highest ambition was to own 'a good wife, a good cow, and a good razor'. But he often did rather better.

Though in terms of cash the English farm worker was better paid at the beginning of the nineteenth century, the Scottish farm worker was better off. He might eat with the farmer. His housing had improved beyond the dreams of his father. He was used to eating oats instead of wheat so that the war fluctuations of flour prices affected him less. His material perquisites were greater since he was 'thirled to the soil' by a tradition that often offered more than a mere wage. That his money was frequently paid half-yearly made him, with frugal and thrifty habits, anxious to find a place of safe deposit. 'These are some of the factors which explain why in Scotland savings banks made their first appearance in the country parishes, whereas in England the movement started mainly in the towns.'

Meantime an easier relationship developed between town and country. Market towns and county towns, hitherto of little consequence, grew in size and importance. And in the larger towns there was astonishing luxury for those who could afford it. The following items could be bought in the shops of Perth before the end of the eighteenth century: Persian dentifrice, Asiatic hair balm, Genoa capers, Gorgona anchovies. The names were probably more descriptive than geographically correct.

'In nothing,' wrote the author of the *Survey of Midlothian in 1793*, 'is there a more striking contrast than this, that every article of family maintenance which was formerly maintained at home is now purchased in the market or in the shop. Not only the different articles of clothing, but bread, beer, and butcher's meat are all had from the town.'

The basic three-layer structure of society remained unchanged, whatever changes and minor luxuries had appeared. The landowner, the tenant farmer, and the farm worker, were socially distinct. Though the Lothians and Berwickshire took the lead in the advance of farming, other regions developed in their own individual way within the overall pattern. Galloway and the south-west, Ayrshire, the Mearns and Aberdeenshire, the small rich territory of Moray, the sparser land of eastern Ross and Caithness, all 'pursued an individual development that often carried with it traditions of great historical depth.'

It was this depth that gave cohesion to the many disparate elements of land improvement, that integrated it with the cities, the growing market towns, and the proliferating new industries. It was also the historical depth that, in serious measure, stultified the whole process from a full flowering. There was talent and ambition based on the virtues that had been imprinted on the puritan forefathers – hard work, temperance, and thrift. But there was no method of dealing with the problems that these virtues brought about. Vast numbers of people left the countryside to find their fortunes elsewhere. The benefits of industry, commerce, and agriculture could not be transmitted to the very people who were bringing about the vast changes. This was not, of course, a problem unique to Scotland.

A Border shepherd, with a fair amount of education in him and profound skill in his trade, knew that his best hope for prospering in his own parish was to find a post with a reasonable master. But there was little chance of improving his prospects in a structured rural society that did not allow for mobility between one rank and another. Ambition or simple dissatisfaction with his lot might send him across the seas to new lands where his work and skill brought more immediate rewards.

The Highlands had the special problem of the Clearances, when landowners evicted entire populations to turn the ground over to sheep. Large-scale sheep farming began within a few years of Culloden. Villages were set on fire and razed to the ground by factors acting for the proprietors. Thousands upon thousands of people went abroad, especially to North America, and the conditions in which they went were often barbarous in the extreme. Many a 'coffin ship' failed to make its landfall. But amidst the heartbreak and inhumanity many thousands emigrated entirely voluntarily, as they still do.

Around the entire Scottish coast ships left for the far parts of the world carrying what has always been Scotland's major export – people. Meantime those who stayed at home, in city or country, merged slowly into the new pattern of Victorian Britain, where England was known as England, and Scotland was known as North Britain.

Though the occasional farmer's wife with her piano might no longer deign to work in her husband's dairy, the older ways of life were still literally round the corner. Adjacent to the flourishing and fertile fields of the new farming in

East Lothian there was the mining community at Tranent where the miners – men, women, and children – lived as a race apart, in squalor and degradation. Such is human pride that the miners scorned the tillers of the soil as stupid peasants, an attitude that persists to this day in some areas.

By the middle of the nineteenth century the agricultural transformation had proceeded so far that Scottish methods had become the envy of other countries. The wheel had turned full circle.

27

THE POLITICAL AWAKENING

No politics. The Northern Secretary. Mrs.
Calderwood's comments. Kilted soldiers. Lord Chief
Baron Dundas. Bute and Sir Archy MacSarcasm.
Geese and Swans. Professor John Miller. The
Origin of Rank. The Friends of the People. Adult
suffrage. Shoes for the French soldiers. Social
conditions. The Sedition Trials. Transportation of
Muir. John Stuart Mill.

FROM THE UNION OF PARLIAMENTS in 1707 until the French
Revolution in 1789 there was a quiescence and acquiescence in Scottish
politics. It can be argued that the lack of political activity enabled the country's
energies to be turned to other pursuits, to the growth of commerce, and to the
fruitful ferment in the world of science.

Though there was little political distraction on the surface, a great deal was
happening beneath the surface: the entire climate of opinion was changing,
blown on by the winds of Europe and America, and ventilated by the
universities. But until the very end of the century this change of opinion
produced no mass movement to disturb the apathetic tenor of political life.

The stolid city-state of Edinburgh–Glasgow had no sense of uncertainty,
even when the American War of Independence whittled at the tap-roots of
Glasgow's prosperity and infuriated many of its inhabitants. Scotland, still
feudal at the beginning of the century, was stiffly middle-class at the end of it.

There were, naturally, occasional incidents. The Porteous Riot had a strong
political flavour. In the previous decade the Glasgow mob had risen in protest
against Walpole's malt duty, and Edinburgh brewers went so far as to refuse to
brew. The Stuart revolutions of '15 and '45 were dynastic rather than political,
and by the time the faded praises of Prince Charlie were being sung by ladies in
Edinburgh drawing-rooms, there was no such thing as 'Scottish politics'.

Indeed, independent Scottish politics ended in 1714 when the motion in the
House of Lords to repeal the Union was defeated. Instead there was a total
control of the country from the south, through a succession of Scottish
Secretaries and Managers.

Scottish representation in the House of Commons was by forty-five
Members of Parliament, elected by about 2,500 voters out of a population of
around one million. Especially in the burghs, where the town councils returned

the members, the election of Members of Parliament was as exactly controlled as was the bestowal of authority to elect. The voters in the shires (qualifying to vote by the possession of land worth £400 per year) were no less open to manipulation. In 1788 a list was compiled to indicate the political persuasion of every shire voter.

From the Union until the year of Culloden, when George routed his rival for kingship, there were occasional appointments of a Scottish Secretary. For the remainder of the century, the affairs of Scotland were handled by the Northern Secretary until 1782, and then by the Home Secretary, when the office of Northern Secretary was abolished and Home and Foreign Secretaries created.

The Lord Advocate, the crown's chief law officer in the north, played the role of under-secretary, sometimes acting in conjunction with a Manager employed by the government to ensure that no unsuitable person was returned to parliament. The Manager and the Lord Advocate were endowed with vast powers of patronage. By their manipulation Scotland was completely controlled throughout its heyday of achievement. The arrangement was in accord with Scottish political indifference. The yoke was not heavy, and the acceptance of it showed unconcern with active British politics. Joseph Black believed that no more admirable system could exist: it left him in peace.

A Scotswoman, Mrs. Calderwood of Polton, passing through London about mid-century, made some interesting comments:

'We used to laugh at the English for being so soon afraid when there was any danger in state affairs, but now I do excuse them. For we, at a distance, think the wisdom of our governors will prevent all these things; but those who know and see our ministers every day see there is no wisdom in them, and that they are a parcel of old, ignorant, senseless bodies, who mind nothing but eating and drinking, and rolling about in Hyde Park, and know no more of the country, or the situation of it, nor of the numbers, strength and circumstances of it, than they never had been in it: or how should they, when London, and twenty miles round it, is the extent ever they saw of it?'

During the second half of the century, the Highlander was slowly accepted back into society. His civilisation having been destroyed by the king, he was allowed to wear the king's uniform and act as a soldier. The Black Watch was the first purely Highland regiment to be raised. Between 1746 and 1782 the non-military Celt was not allowed to wear his own tartan garb. When the ban was withdrawn the civilian Highlander refused to go back to his kilt, an attitude he has retained to this day, when the kilt is favoured more by English lairds and American tourists than by the Highland Scots themselves.

The Highland soldier, naturally, proved an excellent ally of the royal house that had defeated him, and as memories faded with the passing of generations the northern regiments became an essential part of the British Army. It was possibly James Macpherson, the Highland schoolmaster, who made the Gaelic retort to all this. With his pen he wielded more Gaelic influence over England

and Europe than his clansmen had ever done with their broadswords.

Meanwhile the depopulation of the Highlands had begun, the diaspora of the clans that sent tens of thousands to the New World, where they promptly exercised an authoritative influence on the constitution and culture of the emerging republic of the United States. Even Flora Macdonald, Prince Charlie's heroine, was in America at the Cross Creek rising.

Political apathy within Scotland itself ended with the French Revolution. From the time of the Union until the Revolution – eighty-two years – the Scots had provided only three British cabinet ministers. In the years between the Revolution and the Reform Act – forty-three years – they provided ten.

There was wisdom in London leaving Scotland to be managed by approved Scots. Scotland was left in quietness, and London was untroubled by Scottish politics, though plagued by Scotsmen. For almost a hundred years Scotland was never without a Dundas of Arniston in office, and for most of that period a Dundas was in absolute authority. Four generations of Dundases acted as Judge, Solicitor-General, Lord Advocate, and President of the Supreme Court of Scotland. Even during the brief period 1726–37, when they were not in office, Robert Dundas (who later became the first President of the Supreme Court) was leader in London of the independent Whigs opposing Walpole.

The most powerful of the Dundases, the second President Dundas, was known as the dictator of Scotland. His official title was no less mighty – Lord Chief Baron Dundas. These men were authoritative and absolute in their duties. Their influence in London was considerable. They bestowed office and power to their friends, who were friends of the government. In general they kept Scotland at peace with itself. Their fingers were in every Scottish pie, and their informers, both official and unofficial, were legion. They were, in the days when it was necessary, rigidly anti-Stuart. A report dated 1754 from the Governor of Fort William to Lord Advocate Dundas is interesting for its manner and matter: 'At present the country is pretty quiet, and no manner of theft among these wild Tartars; and, with very little pains, I am confident that in a short time there will not be an outlaw left in this neighbourhood. Glengarry has behaved, among his clan, since his father's death, with the utmost arrogance, insolence, and pride. . . .'

Dundas hid a vast appetite for intrigue and ambition under an amiable cheerfulness. Horace Walpole said he was 'the rankest of all Scotsmen'. His character was forceful enough for him never to minimise or disguise his Scottishness in speech or manner. He was coarse, convivial, and powerful, a shameless schemer, and of considerable ability. He was a zealous friend of Pitt until Pitt fell from power. He was rapacious and inconsistent, but a great hero to his fellow Scots who were in his pocket, and his effigy still stands proudly on top of one of the highest columns in twentieth-century Edinburgh.

During the 1760s Scotland provided one of the most detested statesmen ever to hold high office in London. This was Lord Bute, who first obtained preferment by chance under George II, and under George III (whom he trained in kingship), he became Prime Minister. Bute was hated both for his politics and his Scottishness. Because he was Scottish, and in London, and in power, he was undoubtedly a difficult man even to the Scots. Carlyle mentions the 'insatiable vanity' of Bute which nothing could allay but Home's incessant flattery, which being ardent and sincere and blind and incessant like that of a passionate lover, pleased Bute's jealous and supercilious mind. Carlyle, a striving model of fairness, describes Bute as a 'very worthy and virtuous man – a man of taste, and a good belles-lettres scholar'. It would be difficult to find a more inept description of a major political figure. Bute was hated as the instrument of George's political change from Whiggery to Toryism. Accounts of the relationship between him and the Princess of Wales made salacious tongues wag with stories that still titillate historians.

Many Scots, of course, of whom Bute was the mightiest, had gone to London for fame and fortune. In general they were disliked. In the play *Love à la Mode*, Sir Archy MacSarcasm embodied the Scot as seen through popular Cockney eyes. Macklin's *Man of the World* had been originally titled *True-Born Scotsman*. Horace Walpole said of its character Sir Pertinax MacSycophant that he resembled twenty thousand Scotsmen, and there was little other merit in the play.

The treatment of the Scots in London brought about a strong reaction in the north, sometimes touched with a vainglorious bumptiousness in which every Scottish goose was presented as a native swan far superior to the English breed. It was this feeling that boosted Home's *Douglas* to Shakespearian heights, and gave the poor author (a pleasant, somewhat fawning, but kindly man) a very inflated idea of his place in literature. 'Whaur's yer Willy Shakespeare noo?' cried a gallery wag.

It was the same compensating nationalism in the north that took James Macpherson at his face value. It was, partly, resentment at Macpherson being Scottish that produced the southern antipathy to the Ossian poems. Macpherson was extolled in Scotland for the wrong reasons, and opposed in the south for quite other wrong reasons. Even when there was small merit in a work, as in the *Epigoniad* of Wilkie (the St. Andrews professor who befriended Robert Fergusson), the paeans of Scottish praise survive as fascinating comments of the Scots keeping their end up.

Meanwhile, behind the strong political governing of Scotland, men like Hutcheson and Adam Smith were examining the moral foundations of government and the various principles of social life. Smith's main work was, of course, much more concerned with the broadest analysis of society than with the purely economic aspects of it.

Just as Scotland had the skill, the coal, and the protected seaways necessary for the development of steamships, so it had the changing society required as basic material for the sociologist and the student of politics (as opposed to the active politician) – and also for the philosopher commentator.

In the north of Scotland there was the disintegration of a tribal society; in the midlands of Scotland there was the establishment of a mechanised civilisation. These two processes, a breaking down and a building up, were happening at the same time during the century, in a small country, and under the surveillance of those who cared to study them.

Adam Smith was one. John Miller, professor of law at Glasgow was another. These two men could trace the development of their country from the critical period of the Treaty of Union. The immediate results had been disastrous, with an increase of taxation and a disruption of industry owing to free trade between Scotland and England. Many industries had been killed, with the important exception of linen, which was able to develop because England believed that it did not threaten its own great cotton industry. The export of wool was forbidden. But the Union opened Scottish trade to the colonies, and Glasgow grew rich on tobacco, and at the same time absorbed many of the displaced Highlanders. English manufactured goods were paid for by Scottish agricultural produce, bringing development of farming techniques.

In the Highlands the clan system was destroyed. Chiefs were displaced or turned into landowners. Non-Highland landowners appeared. The Clearances began, and Highland labour, turned out of its own country, went overseas or to central Scotland to create the new 'free labourer' or navvy required by emerging industrialism. All this changed the face of Scotland during the century, and brought about a new economic and social pattern. Added to these changes was the intellectual renaissance itself.

This was the country in which Smith and Millar grew up and which first moved their thoughts. It was an age which prompted Scotsmen to a study of history. David Hume was a historian far longer than he was a philosopher. Adam Ferguson investigated the history of civil society in its widest aspects. He is regarded by some as the first sociologist. William Robertson, principal of Edinburgh University, was another historian. Adam Smith was the first theoretical sociological historian.

Adam Ferguson's *Essay on the History of Civil Society* (1767) influenced his own later countryman John Stuart Mill, as well as Karl Marx. It is not unimportant that he was born (in 1724) and brought up in Gaelic-speaking Perthshire. He went to St. Andrews University and then studied divinity at Edinburgh, became a chaplain in the Black Watch and was at Fontenoy. He succeeded Hume as librarian of the Advocates' Library. His *Essay* is almost a prophetic analysis of the inequalities and cruelties of the industrial state where both the haves and the have-nots are cogs in a machine that destroys man as a social being.

The importance of John Millar is his role as the first man to link the practical and theoretical aspects of sociology and history. His insight into what makes society tick was not paralleled in its totality until Marx wrote in the following century. Millar was a unique man. A century later his views, as Marx's showed, might have been so corrupted by political emotion that their lucidity would have vanished in partisanship. A century earlier he would not have had the intellectual climate in which to work. He is a giant among political thinkers, of far greater importance (but sadly of much less influence) than Karl

Marx.

His ideas, which he delivered to middle-class Glasgow audiences, later became weapons in the struggle of the working-class for their emancipation. It is therefore difficult to see him in his intellectual isolation, an inviolate man, seeking the truth for its own sake.

The aim of Smith, Robertson, Ferguson, and Miller was to produce a science of history. This was the scientific point of view, developed in Edinburgh and Glasgow, projected on to the human scene. They wished to observe the development of societies, to trace a pattern of regularities and differences, to compare one society with another. They did it as their colleagues compared one chemical with another. But they did it also as their other colleagues compared one set of values with another.

Robertson studied modes of subsistence, law, and polity. Smith showed how property and civil government depend on one another. Millar's first book, *Origin of the Distinction of Ranks*, studied the relationships of power and authority within society – husband and wife, father and child, master and servant, king and subject. He supported the Americans in their independence, though Glasgow, where he lived and worked, was opposed to American independence because of the tobacco trade. He was an anti-slave man, both abroad and at home in the coal mines. He was a defender of the French Revolution and a member of the Society of the Friends of the People. He was an anti-militarist and wrote for anti-war movements.

None of this was easy for a professor attempting to be independent and as secluded in his 'laboratory' as were his scientific colleagues. It was very difficult in the 1790s when the political quiescence ended in Scotland and modern politics emerged, fully fledged. But the very nature of Millar's studies of man involved him in mankind. His son was exiled. His finest pupil, Muir, was transported. His other pupils were warned against attending his lectures; but such was his attraction that students came to him from Scotland, from England, and from the Continent. He had a considerable effect on the whole climate of radical opinion as it was then developing.

Millar's work had been made possible by the rapidity of economic change that he had witnessed, and by the facility Scotland offered for observing contrasts – the dying Highlands, the moribund feudalism, the emerging technocracy and capitalism. He could study the overthrow of one kind of society in France and the successful emergence of another. He knew what was happening in America, both to the growing American civilisation and to the superseded Red Indian civilisation. He was aware of the situation in India, imperially, financially, politically, and culturally, both as it affected the Indians and as it affected the British.

Millar was the first political sociologist and Adam Smith was the first economic sociologist. Though one is 'accepted' and classically immortal and the other is almost forgotten, they were equal in their ability and accomplishment. Why should Scotland have produced them in the most mature period of its brief renaissance?

The question must be begged, but it suggests the very many influences that produced the renaissance itself – the reformation and the respect for speculation that it encouraged, and the integrity of the intellect. It suggests the heritage of John Knox's educational policy and the subsequent emergence of the scientific attitude through Pitcairn and his colleagues and successors. It suggests, also, the totality of interest which informed the outstanding Scots of the period, where nothing of significance was to be ignored because it was outside the field of the specialist. Like Cullen, Hume, Smith, and Hutton, Millar was an analyser and a synthesiser. He broke down problems to build up explanations on a scale and magnitude that were possible only by his heritage of total curiosity and detached examination of evidence. And like Burns he loved liberty.

Efforts at representational reform spread from England to Scotland, where the need was no less urgent but where the confusion of public life was static rather than active. Earlier attempts at reform, which were part of the political struggle for power, had been more or less defeated. In the early 1780s there was a genuine effort to put the election of magistrates, town councillors, and Members of Parliament on a 'proper liberal and constitutional footing', but this was thwarted by the failure of Pitt's Reform Bill of 1784. There was much need of such reform in Scotland, especially perhaps with internal matters such as the election of town councils. Since 1469, an Act had allowed outgoing town councils to choose the new council. This meant that local government could perpetuate itself without challenge. The financial jobbery of the councillors was often protected by their town's royal charter.

Such stirrings for reform as existed were effectively stopped by the establishment after the French Revolution. But agitation quickly moved from the skirmishing for power of Tories and Whigs. The new political forces in Europe found quick support in the north, where premonitions of democracy and popular ideas about the Rights of Man found a soil particularly suited to their rapid development. The pupils of Millar were not backward in translating theory into action.

Social and industrial conditions were such that the loose-knit historic 'mobs' of Edinburgh and Glasgow were transformed into political instruments of power and authority, requiring the sternest measures of repression. The progress of the French Revolution appeared to emphasise the forebodings of Burke. Britain began to gird itself for war. The Highlands were called upon to provide soldiers to save those who had destroyed the Highlands. Five Highland regiments were added to the line in the 1790s, and later twenty-four additional battalions were raised for service at home – the Highlander being in the role of a Home Guard to protect his fellow Britons against the French, who a generation before had failed to protect the Highlander against his fellow Britons.

Meanwhile Fox's followers, though without his sanction, formed the 'Friends of the People' to pursue reform without bloodshed, and though this organisation was not avowedly in favour of the Revolution, its political ambitions were such that it could easily be classified as subversive. A more extreme organisation, the London Corresponding Club, was organised in 1791 by the Scot, Thomas Hardy from Falkirk. It aimed to attract working-class members, and based its outlook on Thomas Paine. In 1792 it sent a deputation to France to congratulate the Jacobins as 'brothers and fellow-citizens of the world'.

Two years before, Professor Millar had attended a dinner in Scotland at which the toasts were 'The Rights of Man', 'The Standing Army of France', and 'The Abolition of the Slave Trade'.

In 1792 a proclamation against seditious writing resulted in a sell-out of Paine's book *The Rights of Man* in Scotland. There were demonstrations against the government and against Dundas. Riots in Edinburgh lasted three days. The first Society of Friends of the People in Scotland was established in Edinburgh in July, and by the end of the year there were branches elsewhere in Scotland. The Glasgow branch had a subscription of 3d., showing an attempt to build up working-class membership. Dundas began to get 'confidential letters' about these new and spreading activities. The general convention in Edinburgh, in December 1792, was attended by 160 delegates from eighty societies, and included the government agent 'Spy', whose reports are amongst the most interesting documents of the period.

At the convention a split between moderates and extremists became obvious. Thomas Muir wanted to read the United Irishmen's address, but it lay on the table. Lord Daer and Colonel Dalrymple were offended by some comments 'bordering on treason'. Muir advocated a vote for men over the age of twenty-one. Moderate resolutions on parliamentary reform were passed, amendments being defeated. At the end of the proceedings, one Fowler rose to swear the 'French oath' to live free or die, but this was deleted from the minutes.

The authorities were afraid, far more so than were their predecessors who had seen Prince Charlie at the gates of Edinburgh. Mere shopkeepers and weavers were taking part in political life. Arrests were made, and the following month the sedition trials opened. But supporters of reform came from all classes, and Lord Sempill, of an ancient Scottish family and an officer in the Foot Guards, offered a thousand pairs of shoes weekly for six weeks to the French 'soldiers of liberty'. Dundas was demolished in effigy, and assassination was attempted. The law called upon the soldiery. The societies forswore riot and sedition, but they were heartened when men such as a Colonel Macleod swore to defend their liberties with his sword. The *Scots Magazine* was able to comment that the 'keeness of political enquiry, which for a long time seemed to be confined to England, has now reached this northern clime.'

To the political ferment was added extreme social discontent. There was, it should be recalled, bonded slavery in the coalmines. Punishment was still drastic. Some forty years before a woman had been whipped through the streets of Edinburgh and then banished, for stealing hens. In 1763 there had been one brothel in Edinburgh; twenty years later there were twenty, and hundreds of prostitutes. 'What would you have us do?' one said reasonably.

'We cannot starve!' Strikes were frequent and were broken by penury. In 1776 woollen workers in Edinburgh could earn a shilling a day 'if they chose to exert themselves'. Cotton mills and handloom weavers all over Scotland obtained cheap child labour from the Poor Law authorities. In 1792 there was distress to the point of famine in different parts of Scotland. Trees of liberty were planted, and cries of 'No King' were heard at public meetings.

The sedition trials opened with three young printers being sentenced to several months' imprisonment for having proposed a seditious toast. Captain Johnston, owner of the *Edinburgh Gazette*, followed them to gaol, accused of having printed an untrue account of the printers' trial.

Then Thomas Muir, an advocate, was arrested, and at his first hearing he refused to answer questions and was liberated on bail. He went to France, ostensibly to intercede for Louis XVI, and was declared an outlaw. On his return he was rearrested, and in late summer he appeared before Lord Braxfield and a packed jury on charges of sedition. Dundas was the *éminence grise*. The prosecution failed to prove its charge, but Muir's ability and intellect made him a symbol of the Friends of the People. The jury found him guilty in spite of the evidence, and Braxfield sentenced him to fourteen years' transportation. But the jury was startled by the severity of the sentence and, too late, decided to petition in Muir's favour. This came to nothing, as the members of the jury had to go into hiding to escape reprisals.

Muir had an extraordinary career subsequently. The ship in which he was prisoner in transport to the antipodes was engaged by the new navy of the American Republic, and he was wounded in an international engagement staged by America for his rescue. He subsequently went to France.

The first effect of the trials was not the intimidation of the reforming societies but a new zest for further action. Another convention followed, attended by representatives of the London Corresponding Society and the London Constitutional Society. This British convention, held in Edinburgh, aroused an incidental enthusiasm because of the manner in which it united elements of the two nations in a common cause.

There were further trials and further transportation sentences. These measures, and many other trials, succeeded in repressing for some years the activist side of reform. Dundas nominally achieved some success, but the immediate and confused reaction to the French Revolution began to reassemble itself in a more purposive way so that, many years later in the following century, Lord Cockburn was able to comment approvingly: 'Everything, not this or that thing, but literally everything, was soaked in this one event.'

Such was the swift change of political outlook that in 1844 a monument in Edinburgh was erected as a memorial to Muir and others. The tall pointed column was built in the Calton Burial Ground next to the round tower above the grave of David Hume. Both these edifices are seen daily by the passer-by who may not be aware of their significance. The Muir memorial is inscribed:

'To the memory of
Thomas Muir
Thomas Fyshe Palmer
William Skirving
Maurice Margarot
and Joseph Gerrald

Erected by
The Friends of parliamentary reform in England and
Scotland 1844.

'I have devoted myself to the cause of the people, it
is a good cause – it shall ultimately prevail – it shall
finally triumph." Speech of Thomas Muir in the
Court of Justiciary 30th Aug. 1793.'

And James Mill, son of a shoemaker at Montrose, was preparing his *History of India*. His son, John Stuart Mill (so named after his father's early patron in the north), was to write amongst many other things his essay *On Liberty*, in which he said that 'If all mankind minus one were of one opinion, and only one person were of the contrary opinion, mankind would be no more justified in silencing that one person than he, if he had the power, would be justified in silencing mankind.' This was the ideal if tolerance extended to a degree that mankind was unable to accept. It was the nineteenth-century expression of liberal thought, influenced and moulded by the history of reform throughout the world, yet in line of descent from those Scots who, in one way or another, were fascinated and sometimes obsessed by the idea of freedom – Hutcheson, Hume, Adam Smith, John Miller, Adam Ferguson, Robert Burns, James Boswell, Thomas Campbell, and Thomas Muir. Freedom to worship God, a principle fought for bloodily in the previous century, produced its vital offspring – the desire for an individual's personal freedom in society. The Calvinists had built better than they knew.

28

A LAST WORD ON WORDS

'The bad harsh speech.'   Tri-lingual Scots.   Boswell
bows to Arthur's Seat.   Guns from Carron.   'Pleasures
of Hope.'   The new century.   A drift south.   John
Leyden, Orientalist..   *The Edinburgh Review.*   Susan
Ferrier.   *Confessions of a Justified Sinner.*   The curtain
falls.

THERE WAS WRITING, an immense amount of it. Whereas at the beginning of the century there had been hardly a trickle (Pitcairn's *Assembly* and little else) there was now a flood that grew vastly until one man – Walter Scott – wrote more from his own pen than had previously been written by entire generations.

Gavin Douglas (1474–1522) had long ago apologised for using the 'bad harsh speech' of Scots. His was a polite disclaimer, such as any gentleman of the time might have made about his own language, and his comparison was with the languages of the classics not with English. But the remark was a strange prophecy of what was to follow.

The separate Scottish way of life, apparently defeated in 1707, helped to resurrect itself by partly espousing the southern English culture. With notable exceptions, the English language became for most the preferred medium of expression in writing. Hume and others expunged Scotticisms in order to write with greater percipience on the themes and ideas that were common to Europe. They did not anglicise their language to become better Britons but to become better Europeans, yet they were living in a time of linguistic change and they had perforce to accept it.

Throughout the century the link with Leyden was strong. The Jacobite movement, both before and after defeat, was international though its influence dwindled when 'the cause' was lost. Hume himself was more at home in Paris than in London. Black was partly derived from France. Hutton and others travelled extensively in Europe as part of their preparation for their work. Adam and Mylne were inspired by what they found in Italy. There was also a multitude of Scots performing roles throughout the world – high-ranking soldiers in foreign armies, explorers, travellers, emigrants, and settlers.

In Europe such Scotsmen continued the role that their country had played in earlier more independent centuries. It was the Scottish–European tradition that produced the 'group of philosophers, critics, and historians whose work made eighteenth-century Scotland famous throughout the world', as Professor David Daiches has described it. It was not until the following century, about 1830, that Scotland degenerated into provincialism and regionalism and consented to the appelation of North Britain.

Why did the critics and historians not accept the Scots language, which they all spoke, as sufficient for their literary works? The answer is very simple. By doing what they did they were not breaking with tradition but were following it. They lived when a progression from Scots to English was affecting all educated men, and was percolating downwards in society. It was not a new phenomenon. In the sixteenth century the language of the court had been Scots with a gloss of French, but southern influences at the court were not unimportant. From the time of Malcolm, English princesses who became Scottish queens brought English ways and manners. In the sixteenth century the pace quickened. John Knox, a man of vast influence in that period, had a very anglicised speech. The Bible, in English, was distributed in Scotland. Then the court went south with James VI, the national centre of authority.

By that time the Scots tongue was strongly beset by the sister tongue. Calvin's works were available only in English. As Janet Templeton says: 'The Scots were hearing English in church and reading it in their homes – their children learned to read with an English Bible. English words were not foreign any more.'

Writers and printers began the deliberate alteration of textual Scots into English to cater for larger audiences. It was a cultural process that could not be stopped. A more extensive use of English words and phrases, to supplant their Scottish equivalents, continued throughout the seventeenth century, though the full canon of Scots appears to have remained as the spoken tongue.

Literary devices began to differentiate between the various versions of Scots/English. In *The Assembly* the nobility speak an affected English, the social parvenus speak a striving kind of English laden with Scotticisms, whereas the 'ordinary folk' speak ordinary unaffected Scots. (This device was to be used by Sir Walter Scot more than a century later, and again by Lewis Grassic Gibbon this century.)

The court had been away from Scotland for a century when the Union brought about the disappearance of the remaining central body of authority and communication. With neither court nor parliament Scottish society had no model on which to base its speech. The anglicising process continued. In the cultural poverty of the post-Union years many of the remaining leaders of Scottish society began the deliberate aping of London and its manners, including its way of speech, and they thus reinforced the process that was undermining the Scots tongue. What had been an alien influence was accepted as a directive.

Though most of the eighteenth-century intellectuals in Scotland thought that their native tongue was unsuited for scholarly discourse, they all spoke it and understood it. But they wrote their works in English. So it goes on to this day. Most Scots retain a residue of their own tongue.

In London itself the Scots tongue was laughed at. Janet Templeton writes:
'This was the final demoralisation for a great many Scots. They really felt
themselves to be uncouth. So now we find an active, unconcealed opposition
among Scotsmen to the use of the Scottish features in their language; a
movement to weed out Scotticisms.'

It is not in the least strange that there should have been reaction to this
process. While the philosophers, historians, and writers were expunging
Scotticisms, and comparing their ability in this task with their friends, the
writing of poetry in the Scots language reached a new apogee. Fergusson had
been a precursor of Burns and both wrote eighteenth-century Scots, one east
lowland and the other west lowland. Even then the language was no longer as
rich as it had been two centuries earlier, but nevertheless it was a language very
distinct from English.

Burns's place in the latter half of the century is exceptional. He did not live
long but he left bulk, essential for a reputation. Fergusson lived a very brief life
and left no bulk at all. They were both masters of their craft and to compare
them is invidious. Burns's place on Parnassus is assured. The manner in which
he was lionised in his day, and the idolatry that has subsequently smothered
him, have nothing to do with the merits of his writing. Had he been a little
better, or a little worse, he would still be the folk-poet hero. Like Johnson's
dog, it was not so much that he did it well, but that he did it at all. As it
happened, he did it very well. Only genius could have countermanded the
cultural tide that was sweeping the country. Priorities were not sorted out until
later. In 1796 Burns died in obscure poverty while James 'Ossian' Macpherson
was given a sumptuous burial in Westminster Abbey.

All Scots at that time who were familiar with English were bi-lingual, and
many were tri-lingual. Most of them were very conscious of their separate
Scottish tradition, background, and history. From this they obtained an
identity that was not swallowed up by Englishry. And the Scots language,
though foundering as a national language of total communication, was still a
vivid and highly wrought instrument. The tri-lingual Scots knew Gaelic as a
native tongue and were efficient in handling their three languages. James
Macpherson and Adam Ferguson are two examples of Scots who had three
native languages, irrespective of what foreign tongues they also spoke.

There were of course many Gaelic speakers who had no Scots or English,
and vice versa. In the lifetime of Burns there were more Gaelic-speaking than
Scots-speaking Scots, quite apart from English speakers. And it is of more than
passing interest that the century produced a number of great Gaelic poets, an
efflorescence of language both before and after Culloden that again testifies to
the creative spirit producing great works when under vast pressures, one of
which was the attempted destruction of the Highland and Celtic way of life.

Amongst the lighter works of the period was the considerable output of
Lowland songs, or words for songs, providing a corpus of works written for
music that is essentially Scottish. Many have survived as the only remembered
works of their authors.

It was natural that a man like Burns should be both lionised and patronised. (Robert Fergusson had avoided this by ignoring the *literati* of Edinburgh, who also ignored him, but as an educated townsman Fergusson could easily move amongst them.) For a time Burns was trapped in the tide of adulation and he was sensible enough not to tolerate it for too long. During his visit to the Borders in 1787 he was sometimes put on show like a strange animal. ('Gawd mun, a plooman poet – they'll sune be haein kye that sing.')

There was a visit to Wells House near Bonchester. One Gilbert Elliott seems to have organised the occasion. George Tancred tells the story:-

'Mr. Elliott had known and was a great admirer of James Thomson, and cherished as a sacred memorial the armchair in which the poet of The Seasons sat when composing the *Castle of Indolence*, and he determined it should be occupied by Robert Burns on the occasion of his visit. This chair was made of beechwood with a high back, and one of the arms was charred by a candle falling against it when Thomson was absorbed in one of his profound meditations. Gilbert had several people staying at Wells, who were impatient to behold the ploughman poet. At last he arrived, and his host received him most graciously. He then asked Burns to sit in Thomson's chair, and declared that since it came into his possession, never before had a guest worthy to occupy the seat ever crossed his threshold, and a great deal more to the same effect. This compliment was awkwardly and even somewhat ungraciously received by Burns. In fact Elliott said so much about Thomson that Burns felt that he played second fiddle to the author of *The Seasons*, and it was some time before he would sit down in the chair. The young people present were much amused at the confused manner of the poet, and suppressed laughter was heard.'

Burns must have come across a lot of suppressed laughter when he was patronised by a 'society' that was quickly heading for cultural obscurity.

Burns shared an Ayrshire birth with James Boswell who had been born some nineteen years earlier (1740). Both were mocked in their day, and both survived the mockery, Boswell less well than Burns. Though Boswell for a time thought that London was the centre of all good things, it was to Scotland he brought Samuel Johnson to perambulate through the Highlands and islands. The first meeting with Johnson, when Boswell was twenty-two, is one of the most waspish on record. The mediary was Davies, a bookseller in Covent Garden. Boswell asked him not to mention where he came from. When Johnson arrived Davies introduced Boswell formally. Then came a pause of expectant mischief before Davies completed the introduction: 'From Scotland.'

Boswell excused himself: 'Mr. Johnson, I do indeed come from Scotland, but I cannot help it.'

'That, sir, I find, is what a very great many of your countrymen cannot help.'

Boswell followed the introduction by calling at Johnson's dwelling where he paid proper attention to Hodge the cat, Barber the black servant, and was courteous to blind Mrs. Williams the poetess, who handed him tea after inserting her finger to test the depth of liquid in the cup.

Boswell had attended Adam Smith's lectures, and in Edinburgh he made friends with Henry Dundas who was to become the dictator of Scotland, and with William Temple who was to become the recipient of Boswell's most confiding letters.

There is something of the ridiculous, of the poseur, about Boswell that has always prevented a full appreciation of his work. The manner has seemed bigger than the man. Boswell's own description of his departure for London in 1762 suggests something more than amiable eccentricity.

> 'I made the chaise stop at the foot of the Canongate; asked pardon
> of Mr. Stewart [his travelling companion] for a minute; walked to the
> Abbey of Holyroodhouse, went round the Piazzas, bowed thrice: once
> to the Palace itself, once to the crown of Scotland above the gate in
> front, and once to the venerable old Chapel. I next stood in the court
> before the Palace, and bowed thrice to Arthur Seat, that lofty romantic
> mountain on which I have so often strayed in my youth, indulged
> meditation and felt the raptures of a soul filled with ideas of the
> magnificence of GOD and his creation. . . .'

Dance's portrait of Boswell in the National Portrait Gallery, London, does not bear out the numerous malicious descriptions of Boswell's appearance circulated by fellow Scots and others who may have been jealous of his rake's progress. The periwigged head is neither dashing nor weak; there is a heavy solidity to it and though the second instalment of chin is obviously flaccid, the lips are firm, the single eye that shows in profile is searching and direct. On balance the appearance is on the side of purposeful and intent determination, and not by any means a propitiating weakness.

The blind poet, Blacklock, was one of the inner circle of Edinburgh philosophers, divines, savants, writers, and speculators. Dr. Robertson, the Duchess of Gordon, Adam Ferguson, Lord Monboddo, as well as Hume, Home, and MacKenzie, joined him at breakfast or supper. Gray Graham describes the domestication of the muses. 'The boarders handed scones and cookies to the company, and listened eagerly as great men and bright women discussed and jested, making the little room noisy with their talk and merry with their laughter.' Having weaned itself from claret and mutton the Scottish scene was succumbing to tea and scones.

It was Blacklock who persuaded Robert Burns to give up his idea of emigrating to the West Indies. This happened when Burns's luggage was already despatched to the port of Greenock and the poet was on the point of following it. Blacklock suggested that Burns should come to Edinburgh. The capital would fire him with encouragement. Blacklock's authority put an end to emigration.

The century progressed. The world was changing, becoming larger, more exciting, showing greater promise of happiness. The brotherhood of man was the dream of a few.

Outstanding among those writers who fed their imagination with the spirit of the age was Thomas Campbell (1777–1844) who was born in Glasgow, the son of a merchant. His parents were attentive to intellectual matters – the fruit of Wodrow's teaching, perhaps – and a family friend was Thomas Reid, author of *Enquiry into the Human Mind upon the Principles of Common Sense*, the able response to Hume. Campbell's drum rolls from Upper Bavaria in 1800 still resound in British classrooms. Generation after generation of children plod through the declamatory iambics of *Hohenlinden*, *Ye Mariners of England*, *Battle of the Baltic*:

> 'Britannia needs no bulwarks,
> No towers along the steep,
> Her march is o'er the ocean wave,
> Her home is on the deep.'

It was not Campbell's fault that he was a vehicle for the shabbier virtues of militarism. Nor is it correct to excuse his best-known poems because they were written as patriotic hackwork. There is no doubt he genuinely felt the emotion of his martial poems; that is to say no more than he was of his age, that he saw tyranny stalking Europe and British bayonets stalking tyranny.

Though he was Scottish, and his entire outlook was conditioned by his Scottish upbringing, Campbell was not a Scottish poet. He was British, consciously so. The Napoleonic Wars achieved what all else had failed to do. Scotland and England felt more at one than they had ever done before, or since. Campbell was a spokesman for Britain.

That this Scotsman is remembered for his more meretricious poems is unfortunate. He was a man of strange greatness, a greatness far more significant than any of his poetry. Saintsbury said that 'his depth is altogether out of proportion to his width', which is a manner of saying that Campbell the man was far more penetrative than Campbell the poet. Even today he is remembered more vividly in Poland than in his own country. During the last war many Polish exiles in Scotland, civilians and military, were deeply aware that they were in the land that had produced Campbell.

The man is in the poetry. The first part of 'Pleasures of Hope', the poem which gave him national renown at the age of twenty-two, is in an intense and unsophisticated way a mirror to the emergency of liberty. A few of Campbell's phrases have achieved individual immortality – ''Tis distance lends enchantment to the view' and 'Virtue triumphs o'er remembered woe'.

One passage of this poem found a remarkable echo nearly a century and a half later.:

> 'Who, sternly marking on his native soil
> The blood, the tears, the anguish, and the toil,
> Shall bid each righteous heart exult to see
> Peace to the slave, and vengeance on the free!'

In Edinburgh the scene was being set for a final efflorescence of talent. The sporadic individuals in writing had engendered, if not a movement, a great deal of literary activity. The philosophers and historians moved into criticism and journalism. Politics was important. There had been attempts to condense and codify what was known. The *Encyclopaedia Britannica* had made its first appearance in Edinburgh in 1768. The town was rich with magazines and journals.

At the end of the century the political awakening brought the polemical clash of Tories and Whigs. The new atmosphere of Edinburgh – an expanded graceful city – encouraged new attitudes and a new style of living. Robert Fergusson had known only the old Edinburgh of tenements and alleys. Burns knew an Edinburgh that was pushing southwards as well as occupying the New Town. On the occasion when the young Walter Scott was present at a reception for Burns, the event took place at Joseph Black's house, then a mansion in the southern countryside, now an unregarded property surrounded by undistinguished buildings. (By chance, the soiree bracketed the whole period under consideration in this book. Black, who discovered latent heat, had been a pupil of Cullen, who had been a pupil of Munro (primus), who had studied under Boerhaave, who had been taught by Pitcairn. Scott – who was no scientist – was to carry the literary side of the culture to its temporary termination around 1830).

It was the rise of the middle class, with its Calvinist values (as well as increased taxation) that put an end to the conviviality of the claret-shop and ale-house of old Edinburgh. The 'howffs' never tried to move into the New Town. They dwindled away *in situ* as the old town was abandoned to the poor. The intense interacting business and social life of all classes in the old town came to an end. And the most productive phase of Scotland's history came to an end with it.

It was the New Town rather than the old that Walter Scott, Susan Ferrier, John Gibson Lockhart, and others regarded as home. There they lived and worked when they were not in the country. And it was to the New Town that visitors arrived – James Hogg, John Leyden, John Galt.

The new century opened with zest and great activity, especially in the capital city. Scotland had won a reputation for substantial achievement in most spheres of human activity. It had many new and beautiful buildings, including a whole new town that was still expanding. How different it was from the dreary sullen days of a century before.

In 1802 Walter Scott, aged thirty-one, published his first edition of *Minstrelsy of the Scottish Border* in two volumes. The *Edinburgh Magazine* amalgamated with the *Scots Magazine*, and the *Edinburgh Review* was founded as a Whig journal. It was the year of the birth of Hugh Millar at Cromarty, a man who was largely self-taught and was to achieve eminence as a writer and geologist.

But already there was premonitions of the cultural collapse that would take place in little more than a quarter of a century. Many of the ablest young men of the time went south or overseas. Writing later in the century about those early years, Cockburn said:

'Edinburgh had never contained such a concentration of young men as now inspired it, of whose presence the *Edinburgh Review* was only one of the results. They formed a band of friends all attached to each other, all full of hope and ambition and gaiety, and all strengthened in their mutual connection by politics. It was a most enlightened brotherhood. But about the end of 1802 it began to be thinned by emigration and this process went on till 1806. Within two years (1802–1803) Sydney Smith, Francis Horner, Thomas Campbell, John Allen, and John Leyden, all fell off.'

But many were left. To the natural vivacity of the city was added the increasing tension of the Franco–British situation. Volunteer regiments were raised throughout the country, ready for immediate mobilisation if invasion took place. The Borders mobilised once when a beacon was mistakenly lit at Hume Castle. Martello towers were built.

John Leyden, mentioned by Cockburn, was one of the most kenspeckle and able scholars of his day. Born at Denholm near Hawick, educated at nearby Kirkton School, he was a student at Edinburgh University at the age of fifteen in 1790. He was a friend of Scott in Scott's early days when he was busy with his ballad collecting. (Scott in his cups was described by Robert Shortreed, who accompanied him in ballad-collecting expeditions to remote Border glens: 'He looked excessively heavy and stupid when he was *fou*, but he was never out o' gude-humour.')

Leyden was one of the last to exercise his talents right across the spectrum of scholarly interests – a polymath. He became writer, poet, ordained preacher, doctor, and linguist. He contributed ballads to the third volume of Scott's *Ministrelsy*. He had helped Scott with material for the early volumes, and there is a story that he and Scott, in Edinburgh one evening, were unable to complete the fragment of a ballad. Leyden set off for the Borders. Two days later he returned, having covered about one hundred miles on foot to recover the missing portion orally from an old lady.

'While Mr. Scott was sitting with some company after dinner, a sound was heard at a distance like that of the whistling of a tempest through the torn rigging of the vessel that scuds before it. The sounds increased as they approached more near, and Leyden burst into the room, chanting the desiderated ballad with the most enthusiastic gesture, and all the energy of the saw-tones of his voice.'

His voice and his manner were both awkward. His ability was not. In 1802, under Constable the publisher, he managed the merged publications of the *Edinburgh Magazine* and the old *Scots Magazine*. Leyden was then busy with his poem *Scenes of Infancy*. No church had been obtained for him and he was anxious to travel, to pursue his linguistic studies abroad, and perhaps secure sufficient fortune to relieve himself of the near penury he had always lived in.

Representations were made to William Dundas, who rapidly produced a

job, but it was that of a surgeon's assistant. Leyden was no doctor, but, assisted
by the surgeon John Bell, he rapidly became one and acquired his M.D. after
some months of intensive study.

In April 1803 he sailed from Britain aboard the *Hugh Inglis*, a companion
being Robert, brother of Sydney Smith. He was determined to be a 'furious
orientalist'. He became a professor at Bengal college, then judge of the twenty-
four pergunnahs of Calcutta. In August 1811, when he was proficient in many
Oriental languages, he accompanied an expedition to Java. His task was to
investigate 'the manners, language, and literature of the tribes'. He survived
only a short time, dying of fever before the end of the month, a day before the
battle which resulted in Java being occupied by the British.

Amongst those who started the *Edinburgh Review* was Francis Jeffrey who
soon became its influential editor, a position he held for twenty-seven years,
demitting office only when he became Dean of the Faculty of Advocates in
1829. Through this considerable time he had doubled literature with the law.
In 1830 he became Lord Advocate, and as such was deeply involved in the
Scottish Reform Bill of 1832.

Another founder was Lord Brougham who eventually pursued an English
career to become Lord Chancellor in 1830. Sydney Smith, the English
clergyman and wit then living in Edinburgh, was another founder (he edited
the first issue), as was Francis Horner who also undertook a parliamentary
career in London, to die relatively young.

This extensive flow of able men to the south was a new thing, and a result of
recent history. Magnus Magnusson sums it up well. 'The long Napoleonic
Wars, during which the Scots had fought side by side with the English and
learned to hate their traditional allies the French, had drawn the two parts of
Britain together. The constant threat of invasion by a common enemy had
given them their first sense of unified nationhood.' Campbell was far from
being alone in flying the Union Jack.

The effect of the *Review* was dramatic throughout Britain. It gave an outlet
for theories, feelings, and attitudes that was otherwise unprovided for. It
introduced a new kind of independent argumentative and critical journalism
and writing, totally unsubservient to the publishing houses who supported
other news sheets and filled them with puffery. The first issues of the *Review*
were produced almost in secret, with the contributors going singly and in
stealth to the printing-shop to examine the proof sheets of each other's
contributions. Success came soon, anonymity was cast off, contributors were
paid (a matter the editor insisted on, whether they needed the money or not),
and Jeffrey himself obtained a salary of £300 a year, more than he could then
make at the bar. (There had been an earlier *Edinburgh Review* in the middle of
the eighteenth century; David Hume was associated with it but it had a short
life.)

By 1809 it was necessary to produce a Tory counterblast. This was the
Quarterly, supported by the arch-Tory, Walter Scott. It was not until 1817 that
Blackwood's Magazine emerged partly in reply to the birth of the liberal

Scotsman newspaper. William Blackwood was a bookseller turned publisher. His colleagues and contributors included Professor John Wilson ('Christopher North'), the flamboyant professor of Moral Philosophy whose activities have been described by Hugh MacDiarmid, not without reason, as 'arrant humbug'. But *Blackwood's*, whatever its Tory politics, was soon a vehicle for some of the most important writing of the period. Its contributors, as well as John Wilson himself (as 'Christopher North' he was responsible for the *Noctes Ambrosianae*), included John Galt, many of whose works first appeared in *Blackwood's*; D. A. Moir ('Delta'), a doctor, most famous for *The Life of Mansie Waugh*; James Hogg ('The Ettrick Shepherd'); Susan Ferrier, the novelist of manners; Michael Scott, author of the highly successful *Tom Cringle's Log*; and John Gibson Lockhart, Scott's son-in-law and biographer.

Susan Ferrier was born in 1782 and died, half blind, at the age of seventy-two. She was an Edinburgh person entirely of her day and age. If only because of that she should be better remembered. But there is more than that. Her three novels – *Marriage* (1818), *The Inheritance* (1824), and *Destiny* (1831) – have the sharp bite, the unsentimental clarity, of a brilliant social observer. There was caricature, but superimposed on objectivity. Her biographer Sir George Douglas says with justice that *Marriage* 'deserves to rank with the masterpieces of British fiction'. Highly prized in her day by the two opposites – Scott and Jeffrey – she was something unusual, the extroverted Scottish writer. She merits at least the place that her countryman Smollett has achieved.

That she wrote of the aristocratic and genteel life of her day (what English lady writers this brings to mind!) is of special interest since her talent broke new ground. In many ways she was more readable than some of her eminent contemporaries. A much slighter figure than others in terms of output, though not in contemporary acceptance, probably only three acknowledged masters of the time were her superiors – Scott, Hogg, and Galt.

Of Scott little need be said here. An antiquarian-historian-novelist-poet, he presided over his age with greater authority than an old-time monarch.

Galt as a young man travelled in the Levant, seeking health, but also looking for business opportunities. A companion on the voyage to Malta and Sicily, before both went further east independently, was Byron. Galt's multitudinous works were written in the midst of a busy life. But his temperament was to be unsuccessful and he complained that, in spite of his endeavours for the Canada Company, which had been founded at his own suggestion, he reaped only 'troubles and mortification'. But *The Ayrshire Legatees, Annals of the Parish, The Provost*, and *Sir Andrew Wylie*, place him as a writer in the forefront of his time.

James Hogg is probably the most difficult to assess, and it is only now, with the rediscovery of two of his works, that he can be seen as the *éminence grise* of his day. He participated in Christopher North's frivolous *Noctes Ambrosianae*. He wrote ballads for Scott's *Ministrelsy* because he was dissatisfied with some of the 'new' ballads that Scott published. He was the author of *The Brownie of Bodsbeck, The Queen's Wake*, and that extraordinary poem of faery, *Bonny*

Kilmenny. He included witches amongst his forebears and his grandfather had held converse with Border fairies.

His *Private Confessions of a Justified Sinner* is the essence of the dualism of the Scottish character – the Caledonian antisyzygy, or union of opposites. Like Burns, Hogg was born of the soil. Moreover he came from a part of Scotland that had been in the forefront in developing the theory of the elect. Some generations before, Thomas Boston had been a minister in Ettrick where he wrote his *Fourfold State* and rewrote *The Marrow of Divinity*. And here was the Ettrick Shepherd, guarding the frightful flock. The devil was there of course, and Calvin, and the teaching that an 'elect and justified' person can commit no sin, even if it is murdering his brother for transcendental glory. It is a theme found to a lesser degree in Byron, whose diablerie is the clash of right and wrong, of vice and virtue. (Byron wrote: 'I am half a Scot by birth, and bred a whole one.') It emerges again in Stevenson's *Dr. Jekyll and Mr. Hyde*. It is a consistent part of the Scottish Calvinist character. But nowhere, outside the pulpits, has it been more fearsomely portrayed than in Hogg's *Confessions*. Naturally, when the truth was shown, it was misunderstood and the book ignored. Hogg's other major work is *The Three Perils of Man*. This was the genius who had to write a dignified but begging letter to obtain the tenancy of a farm in the Borders that he might work and look after his aged parents.

As far as literature was concerned, the end of the era came strangely quickly. There had been a partial physical migration, as though the houses and boulevards of the New Town were less congenial than the closes and lands of the old town. Scott went to the Borders to build his architectural phantasmagoria at Abbotsford. Galt, when he settled for a while, came not to Edinburgh but to Musselburgh. Jeffrey, made rich by his writing and his legal practice, bought and embellished Craigcrook Castle, a few miles out of Edinburgh on the slopes of Corstorphine Hill. There the *literati* met. 'No unofficial house has had a greater influence on literary or political opinion', said Cockburn.

To the south there was the Tytler house at Woodhouselea. Tytler was one of a family of Scottish lawmen, a writer himself. He entertained the 'most distinguished in Edinburgh for their manners, their talents, and their accomplishments.' Amongst those who were guests there – in what was intended to be a model community, advanced in hygiene, housing, and planning – were Henry Mackenzie, John Gregory, Dugald Stewart, John Playfair, Sydney Smith, Francis Jeffrey, Walter Scott, John Leyden, and Adam Ferguson.

There was an exodus of talent from the capital city. At any rate, when that generation died there was little left. In *Literature and Oatmeal*, William Plomer puts it succinctly: 'With the deaths of Scott, Hogg, Galt, and Wilson, Scots literature fell at once from a national to a provincial level.' The magazines ceased to be vehicles for new and important work, because there was none to write it. Most of them too fell by various waysides. The vivid, intense, and productive literary scene simply came to an end, like a clock stopping. It was finished in Scotland. The Anglo–Scots wrote elsewhere. There was to be nothing more of importance until Robert Louis Stevenson began to write in the 1880s, half a century later.

Thus there came to an end the Golden Age, or the Enlightenment, the Scottish contribution to what in its full European context is called the Age of Reason. It had distinguished Scotland for more than a century, from the early stirrings of Pitcairn and Ramsay.

On the technical side it would continue into the future; inheritors and developers of the Scottish tradition included Kelvin and Clerk Maxwell. As late as this century the work done by Black and others in the study of heat would provide a background of knowledge which brought Whittle to Scotland when he was investigating the technology behind the jet engine.

For reasons of space many aspects of the Enlightenment have not been dealt with. There was a distinct Scottish tradition in the visual arts, best known through the Naysmiths, Raeburn, and Tassie the medallionist. The Scots made vast advances in the development of banking.

There is perhaps room for a total examination of the influence of and the impact made by this small country. Separate studies have already been made of the Scot overseas, the emigrant Scot, the military Scot. It can be justly claimed that the multitudinous Scottish accomplishments of the eighteenth century are still sending their ripples over the contemporary world. The accomplishments were vast, the influences enormous.

In *Edinburgh in the Age of Reason* Douglas Young has written:

'By the middle of the eighteenth century Edinburgh had become the winter-quarters of the wealthier Scots landowners, who mingled there with their cousins, the lawyers and medical men and ministers of religion, many of whom had taken courses in Dutch universities. In the Old Town, along the ridge from Edinburgh Castle to the Palace of Holyroodhouse, they lived cheek by jowl in the tall blocks of houses, running up to sixteen storeys, with the judges and baronets and dowager countesses on the middle floors, and the lower ranks below or above. In this setting, a unique cross-fertilization constantly took place; *ideas* – as well as *manners* – were pooled in Edinburgh, and from there spread to every parish in the country.'

And in the same work Lord Cameron has written:

'The half century that followed the last Rising for the Stuart cause saw the most brilliant flowering of the Scottish genius in Letters, Philosophy, Law, and in the practical arts of the architect and engineer. And yet all this sprang from a country divided in itself, where the ancient antipathy between Saxon and Gael, Highlander and Lowlander remained unhealed – and the embers of civil war still glowed red and resentful. . . . It was upon such a country with such continuing divisions but with such promise and presage of material improvement and prosperity that the impact of the Enlightenment fell and sparked off such a chain reaction of brilliance as Scotland never knew before – or indeed since.'

REFERENCES
WORKS FREQUENTLY REFERRED TO

Alexander Carlyle, *Autobiography* – ACA.
Gray Graham, *Social Life of Scotland in the Eighteenth Century* – SLS.
Gray Graham, *Scottish Men of Letters of the Eighteenth Century* – SML.
Sir John Clerk, *Memoirs, 1676–1755*, ed. John M. Gray – JCM.
Edward Burt, *Letters from a Gentleman in the North of Scotland* (1754) – EBL.
Lord Kames, *The Gentleman Farmer* – KGF.
Archibald and Nan Clow, *The Chemical Revolution* – CCR.

CHAPTER 1
Letter dated 6th February 1700 from Duncan Forbes of Culloden to his brother Colonel Forbes.
Daniel Defoe, *Tour through the Whole Island of Great Britain* (1724–27).
Joseph Taylor, *A Journey to Edenborough in Scotland* (first published in 1903).

CHAPTER 2
Rev. Thomas Boston, *Human Nature in its Fourfold State*.
Introduction to *The Household Book of Lady Grizel Baillie*.
John Struthers, *History of Scotland*. There are various versions of Belhaven's speech. The quotations in this chapter are from Struthers.
The City of Edinburgh (H.M.S.O., 1951).

CHAPTER 3
Lord Cockburn, *Letters to His Gardener*, ed. Scott-Moncrieff.
SLS.
SML.
George Chalmers, Life of Ruddiman.

CHAPTER 4
David Daiches, *Robert Burns*. Quoted with the author's permission.
SML.

CHAPTER 5
Bishop Burnet, *History of His Own Times*.
Henry S. Wellcome, in the foreword to the second edition of John D. Comrie's *History of Scottish Medicine*.
The Works of Dr. Archibald Pitcairn, done from the Latin Original (London 1715).
Archibald Pitcairn, M.D., *The Assembly, or Scotch Reformation* (edition printed in Edinburgh, 1817).

CHAPTER 6
> Robert Wodrow, *Analecta.*
> George Saintsbury, *Short History of English Literature.*

CHAPTER 7
> SML.
> T. F. Henderson, *Scottish Vernacular Literature.*
> David Masson, *Edinburgh Sketches and Memories.*

CHAPTER 8
> *News Letters of 1715–16.*

CHAPTER 9
> SLS.
> ACA.
> John McKerrow, *History of the Secession Church.*
> David Hume, *On the Parties of Great Britain.*

CHAPTER 10
> General Wade, *Report on the Highlands, 1724* (included in *Historical Papers Relating to the Jacobite Period*, New Spalding Club, 1895).
> EBL.
> Cosmo Innes, *Scottish Legal Antiquities.*
> JCM.
> KGF.
> ACA.
> Grant, *Old Edinburgh.*
> *Scottish Historical* Review, No. 110, 'Jacobite Rumours', p. 164
> *History of the Scottish Highlands*, ed. J. S. Keltie.

CHAPTER 11
> A. T. Pledge, *Science Since 1500* (H.M.S.O., 1939).
> ACA.
> *The Diary of Sylas Neville*, ed. B. Cozens-Hardy. A picture of the life of the Edinburgh medical student of the 1770s is contained in the diary of Sylas Neville, a man who was something of a mystery, had certainly a brilliant scholastic mind, and appeared to enjoy being a hypocritical rip.

CHAPTER 12
> A. Duncan, *Memorial of the Faculty of Physicians and Surgeons of Glasgow.*
> Sir William Ramsay, *The Life and Letters of Joseph Black.*
> A. Bower, *History of the University of Edinburgh.*
> Lord Cockburn, *Memorials of His Time.*
> Professor John Read, University of St. Andrews, broadcast talk, B.B.C. (Scottish Home Service), 1st February 1951.
> Joseph Black, *Lectures on the Elements of Chemistry*, ed. John Robison.
> Andrew Kent, *An Eighteenth Century Lectureship.*

CHAPTER 13
> *Transactions of the Royal Society of Edinburgh*, Vol. V (1805).
> *The Diary of Sylass Neville.*
> Professor T. C. Phemister, University of Aberdeen, broadcast talk, B.B.C.
>> (Scottish Home Service), 18th January 1951.
> D'Arcy Wentworth Thompson, 'The History of Science in Scotland', included
>> in *Scotland and Its People*, ed. J. N. Wright and N. S. Snodgrass (1942).

CHAPTER 14
> George Williamson, *Memorials of James Watt.*
> T. H. Marshall, *James Watt.*
> James Patrick Muirhead, *The Origin and Progress of the Mechanical Inventions of
>> James Watt.*
> M. Araga, *Elogue Historique de James Watt.*
> Professor Read, B.B.C. (Scottish Home Service) broadcast.

CHAPTER 15
> SML.
> Ronald L. Meek, 'Adam Smith's Glasgow Lectures', article in *Scottish Journal.*
> V. A. Demant, *Religion and the Decline of Capitalism* (The Holland Lectures for
>> 1949).
> A. Wolfe, *History of Science, Technology and Philosophy, 18th Century.*

CHAPTER 16
> Bertrand Russell, *Human Knowledge.*
> David Hume, *Treatise*, Book I, Part II.

CHAPTER 17
> David Hume, *Treatise*, Book I, Part IV.
> A. Wolfe, *History of Science, Technology and Philosophy.*

CHAPTER 18
> George Chalmers, *Life of Ruddiman.*
> Thomas Sommers, Burgess and Freeman of Edinburgh and His Majesty's
>> Glazier for Scotland, *The Life of Robert Fergusson, The Scottish Poet.*
> *The Works of Robert Fergusson*, ed. A. B. Grossart.
> A. B. Grossart, *Robert Fergusson* (Famous Scots series).
> *Robert Fergusson, 1750–74*, ed. Sydney Goodsir Smith

CHAPTER 19
> St. Beuve, *Causeries de Lundi.*
> ACA.
> SML.

CHAPTER 20
> Ebenezer Henderson, *Life of James Ferguson, F.R.S.*
> Hector Macpherson, *The Intellectual Development of Scotland.*
> *Scotland and Its People*, ed. J. N. Wright and N. S. Snodgrass (essay by Pro-
>> fessor D'Arcy Thompson on Thomas Henderson).

CHAPTER 21
    CCR.
    T. Craig Brown, *The History of Selkirkshire*, Vol. 1.
    Herbert Butterfield, *The Origins of Modern Science*.
    J. T. Merz, *European Thought in the Nineteenth Century*.

CHAPTER 22
    Thomas Pennant, *A Tour in Scotland and Voyage to the Hebrides*.
    Henry Hamilton, *The Industrial Revolution in Scotland*.
    James Mackinnon, *The Social and Industrial History of Scotland*.
    CCR.

CHAPTER 23
    James Lees-Milne, *The Age of Adam*.
    J. G. Dunbar, *The Historic Architecture of Scotland*.
    A. J. Youngson, *The Making of Classical Edinburgh*.

CHAPTER 24
    A. E. Richardson, *Robert Mylne*.
    Agnes Muir Mackenzie, *Scotland in Modern Times*.

CHAPTER 25
    David Napier, *Autobiography*.
    Henry Hamilton, *The Industrial Revolution in Scotland*.

CHAPTER 26
    J. E. Handley, *Scottish Farming in the Eighteenth Century*.
    William Mackintosh, *An Essay on Ways and Means of Inclosing, Fallowing,
        Planting &c. in Scotland; and that in Sixteen years at farthest*.
    David Young, *National Improvements upon Agriculture, in Twenty-seven essays*.
    KGF.
    'A True Scotsman', *The Laird and the Farmer*.
    J. A. Symon, *Scottish Farming Past and Present*.
    H. Oliver Home, *A History of Savings Banks*.
    Laurence J. Saunders, *Scottish Democracy, 1815–1840*.

CHAPTER 27
    Mrs. Calderwood of Polton, *Letters and Journals*.
    Arniston Memoirs, ed. W. T. Ormond.
    L. B. Namier, *Avenues of History* (brief and illuminating examination of Lord
        Bute).
    Adam Ferguson, *An Essay on the History of Civil Society*, ed. Duncan Forbes.
    T. Johnston, *History of the Working Classes in Scotland*.

CHAPTER 28
    Janet N. Templeton, paper in *Lowland Scots, Occasional Papers No. 2*
        (Association for Scottish Literary Studies).
    George Tancred, *Rulewater and Its People*.
    Henry Mackenzie, *Life of Blacklock*.
    Henry Mackenzie, *Life of John Home*.

SML.
Kurt Wittig, *The Scottish Literary Tradition.*
Marie W. Stuart, *Old Edinburgh Taverns.*
Lord Cockburn, *Memorials of His Time.*
Magnus Magnusson, *The Clacken and the Slate.*
Sir George Douglas, *The 'Blackwood' Group.*
David Craig, *Scottish Literature and the Scottish People, 1680–1830.*
Edinburgh in the Age of Reason.

SELECTED CHRONOLOGY

1550   b. John Napier. Logarithmic tables. d. 1614.

1611   b. (Sir) John Urquhart. Translator of *Rabelais*. d. 1660.

1615   (circa) b. Mary MacLeod. Gaelic poetess. d. 1705.

1624   (circa) b. John MacDonald (Iain Lom). Gaelic poet. d. 1710.

1626   b. George Dalgarno. Educ. of deaf and dumb. d. 1687.

1630   b. (Sir) William Bruce. Architect – restored Holyroodhouse, built Kinross House, Harden House, part Hopetoun House, etc.

1635   Three-day post: Edinburgh–London.

1638   b. James Gregory. Inventor of reflecting telescope. d. 1675.

1641   b. (Sir) Robert Sibbald. Physician and naturalist. d. 1722.

1652   b. Archibald Pitcairn. Doctor and teacher. d. 1713.

1635   Pub. of part 1 Urquhart's *Rabelais*.
       b. Andrew Fletcher of Saltoun. Anti-Unionist. d. 1716.

1660   d. Sir Thomas Urquhart.

1661   James Gregory invented principle reflecting telescope.

1662   George Sinclair pub. *Short History of Coal*.

1663   James Gregory pub. *Optica Promota*.

1665   b. (Lady) Grizel Baillie. Poetess and writer. d. 1727.

1668   b. William Paterson. Financier. Bank founder. d. 1719.
       b. Hermann Boerhaave. Clinical teacher at Leyden. d. 1738.

1669   Twice-weekly post: Edinburgh–Aberdeen.
       Once-weekly post: Edinburgh–Inverness.

1670   (circa) Sibbald's 'physic garden' laid out in Edinburgh.

1671   b. Rob Roy Macgregor. Freebooter. d. 1734.

1673   b. (Field-Marshal) George Wade. Red-coat military commander in Highlands. d. 1748.

1674   b. James Gibbs. Arch. – Radcliffe Camera, St. Martin's in the Fields, St. Mary's in the
        Strand, etc. d. 1754.
        b. Thomas Ruddiman. Writer and publisher. d. 1757.

1675   b. Earl of Mar (Bobbing John). Statesman. d. 1732.

1676   b. (Sir) John Clerk of Penicuik. Landowner, improver and politician (succeeded
        similarly named father in 1722). d. 1755.

1677   b. Thomas Boston. Minister and writer. d. 1732.

1679   b. John Cockburn of Ormiston. Land improver. d. 1758.
        b. Robert Wodrow. Religious historian. d. 1734.

1681   Foundation Royal College of Physicians, Edin.
        Incorp. of Edinburgh Merchant Company.

1682   b. William Aikman. Painter. d. 1731.

1684   (circa) b. John Smibbert. Painter. d. 1751.

1685   Argyll beheaded, Edinburgh.
        b. Forbes of Culloden. Statesman. d. 1747.

1686   b. Allan Ramsay. Poet. d. 1758.

1688   b. William of Orange.

1691   William Paterson proposed founding Bank of England.

1692   Massacre of Glencoe.

1693   Pub. of Part II Urquhart's *Rabelais*.

1694   Bank of England founded.

1695   Bank of Scotland founded.
        Post office est. by parliament.
        b. John Glas. Founder of Glassite religious sect. d. 1773.

1696   Education Act (schools to be estab. all parishes) (cf. 1803).
        b. Henry Home (Lord Kames). Lawyer, writer and agriculturalist. d. 1782.
        b. Marshal Keith. Soldier. d. 1758.

1697   b. Alexander Munro ('primus'). Anatomist. d. 1767.
        b. William Smellie. Obstetrician. d. 1763.

1698   First Darien expedition.
        Sibbald's Edinburgh *Pharmacopoeia* completed.
        b. Colin MacLaurin. Mathematician. d. 1746.

1699   Pitcairn brings Ruddiman to Edin.
b. Robert Blair. Minister-poet.

1700   Pop. Scotland (est.) less than 1,000,000.
Pop. Glasgow (est.) 12,000.
(circa) b. Alexander MacDonald (Alasdair MacMhaistir Alasdair). Gaelic poet. d. 1770.
b. James Thomson. Poet. d. 1748.

1701   Convicted thieves made 'perpetual servants' or slaves with metal collars.

1702   Act of Settlement.
Only one witch hanged in Edinburgh.
David Gregory pub. *Elements of Physical and Geometrical Astronomy.*

1703   Pub. of *Spiritual-Merchant* (in which Christ is likened to a warehouse keeper).

1704   Act of Security.

1705   Joseph Taylor, traveller from London and diarist, arrives in Edinburgh.
Courant starts pub.

1706   James Watson pub. collection of traditional verse (also 1709, 1711).

1707   Final article of Treaty of Union passed (January).
Union had effect (1st May).
Savings Bank started at West Calder, Midlothian.

1708   d. David Gregory. b. 1661.

1709   Famine.
b. James Brown. Traveller in Persia. d. 1788.

1710   Savings Bank started at Ruthwell, Dumfriesshire.
(circa) James Meikle introd. agricultural 'fanners' from Holland.
b. William Cullen. Doctor. d. 1790.
b. James Fergusson. Astronomer. d. 1776.

1711   b. David Hume. Philosopher. d. 1776.

1712   Re-introduction of lay patronage.

1713   Edin. Town Council appointed first prof. of chemistry to the Town's College
        (university).
b. James (Athenian) Stuart. Architect.
b. Allan Ramsay, jnr. Painter. d. 1784.
d. Archibald Pitcairn. b. 1652.

1714   Death of Queen Anne. George I on throne.
Cockburn of Ormiston succeeded to estates and started improvements.
Ruddiman pub. *Latin Rudiments.*
Motion before House of Lords to repeal Union.

1715   Bobbing John raised standard for James VIII (Old Pretender), at Braes of Mar.
Battle of Sheriffmuir.

1716   Old Pretender fled Scotland.

1717   Grant of Moneymusk succeeded to estates and started improvements.

1718   Merchants of Glasgow possessed one ship.
         Re-pub. *Marrow of Modern Divinity* (by Hogg).
         b. William Hunter. Physician. d. 1783.

1719   Publication of *Hardyknute*.
         Battle of Glenshiel.
         Railway with wooden rails – 'trams' – built at Port Seton for coal haulage.
         d. William Paterson. b. 1658.

1720   (circa) Start of Scottish kelp manufacture.
         Adam Petrie pub. *Rules of Good Deportment*.
         Thomas Boston pub. *Fourfold State of Man*.
         b. Prince Charles Edward Stuart, at Rome (31 Dec.), son of James VIII and
               Clementina Sobieski, the Young Pretender.

1721   b. Thomas Blackwood. Blind poet. d. 1791.
         b. Tobias Smollett. Novelist. d. 1771.
         b. William Robertson. Historian. d. 1793.

1722   b. Alexander 'Jupiter' Carlyle. Minister-diarist. d. 1800.
         d. Robert Sibbald. b. 1641.

1723   Merchant bank of John Coutts & Co. found. Edinburgh.
         Found. of Soc. of Improvers in Knowledge of Agriculture.
         b. Adam Ferguson. Writer on state of society. d. 1816.

1724   Pub. of Ramsay's *Tea-Table Misc.*
         Pub. of Ramsay's *Eevergreen* (includ. Hardyknute).
         General Wade appointed c-in-c Scotland.
         Cockburn of Ormiston experiments with potatoes.
         b. Duncan MacIntyre (Donnachadh Bàn nan Òran). Gaelic poet. d. 1812.

1725   Pub. Ramsay's *Gentle Shepherd*.
         Disarming Act.
         Forbes of Culloden becomes Lord Advocate.
         Wade started building 250 miles of roads and 42 bridges in Highlands (completed
               1738), built barracks Forge George, Fort Augustus, strengthened Fort William
               and Ruthven.
         Pub. of Francis Hutcheson's *Inquiry into the Originals of Our Ideas of Beauty and
               Virtue*.

1726   Re-publication of *Marrow* (by Boston).
         Monro (primus) pub. *The Anatomy of the Human Bones and Nerves*.
         b. James Hutton. Discoverer of geology. d. 1797.
         b. (General) William Roy. Surveyor. d. 1790.
         b. (Sir) Eyre Coote. Soldier in India. d. 1783.
         b. (Sir) Hector Munro. Soldier in India. d. 1805.

1727   d. Janet Horne burned as witch (reputed last in Scotland).
         Found. of Royal Bank of Scotland.

Creation of Board of Trustees for Manufacturers, Fisheries and Improvements in Scotland.
Death of George I. George II succeeds.
b. Neil Gow. Violinist, fiddler and composer. d. 1809.
d. Lady Elizabeth Wardlaw.
d. Lady Grizel Baillie. b. 1665.

1728 b. Robert Adam. Architect. d. 1792 (with James – Sion House, Luton Park, Admiralty Gateway, Register House Edinburgh, The Adelphi, Charlotte Sq. Edinburgh, etc.)
b. Joseph Black. Chemist. d. 1799. Discoverer latent heat, CO_2.
b. John Hunter. Anatomist and surgeon. d. 1793.

1729 Textile printing introduced to Scotland.
Invergarry iron smelting furnace started working.

1730 Francis Hutcheson, aged 36, succeeded Gersholm Carmichael, chair of philosophy, Glasgow.
Ruddiman app. Keeper of Advocates' Library.
b. James Bruce. Explorer in Africa. d. 1794.

1731 Forerunner of Royal Society of Edinburgh inaugurated (Monro primus secretary).
b. Thomas Coutts. Banker. d. 1822.
b. Patrick Miller of Dalswinton – worked with James Taylor, Wm. Symington in dev. of paddle-wheel and steam propulsion of vessels. d. 1815.
d. William Aikman. b. 1681.

1732 Michael Menzies of Edinburgh made primitive threshing machine.
d. Thomas Boston. b. 1677.
d. Earl of Mar. b. 1675.

1733 A theatre established in Edinburgh.
b. Alexander Monro (secundus). Anatomist. d. 1817.

1734 Prince Charles Edward, aged 14, had first experience of active service in war (Gaeta).
b. Ralph Abercrombie. Soldier. d. 1801.
b. Robert Mylne. Architect and builder (Greenwich Hospital, Inverary Castle and town, Blackfriars Bridge, Rochester Cathedral, etc.). d. 1811.
d. Rob Roy MacGregor. b. 1671.
d. Robert Wodrow. b. 1679.

1735 Glasgow merchants had 15 ships.
Small scale cultivation of potatoes.
Death penalty ended for witchcraft.
b. John Millar. Professor of law, Glasgow, and writer on society. d. 1801.
b. James Tassie. Miniaturist. d. 1794.

1736 Porteous Riot.
b. Alexander Dalrymple. Hydrographer. d. 1808.
b. Alexander Runciman. Painter.
b. James Watt. Inventor and engineer. d. 1819.

1737 Edinburgh's theatre closed under Walpole administration.
Forbes of Culloden became Lord President, Court of Session.
Disruption in Church of Scotland – formation of original church of secession.

1738   b. James Macpherson. Translator of Ossian. d. 1796. d. Hermann Boerhaave. b. 1668.

1739   Small scale cultivation of turnips.
Formation of Black Watch regiment under General Wade.
Edinburgh's first professor of midwifery app.
David Hume pub. *Treatise of Human Nature*.
b. John Robison. Mechanical scientist and prof. natural philosophy. d. 1805.

1740   Harlem Dye Co. est. Glasgow.
Wade demitted military appointment in Scotland.
b. James Boswell. Writer and diarist. d. 1795.
b. Charles Cameron. Architect.

1741   David Hume pub. *Essays Moral and Political*.
Alasdair MacMhaistir Alasdair (Alexander MacDonald) pub. Gaelic–English
      vocabulary.
Robert Foulis app. official printer to Univ. of Glasgow.

1742   b. John Kay. Caricaturist. d. 1830.
b. Henry Dundas Melville, 1st Viscount – 'manager for Scotland' – controlled elections.
      d. 1811.

1743   Adam Smith at Balliol, Oxford.

1744   Cullen moved to Glasgow to set up medical school.
Pub. of original and short-lived *Edinburgh Review*.

1745   12 July – Prince Charles sailed for Scotland.
19 August – standard raised at Glenfinnan.
17 September – Edinburgh occupied.
21 September – battle of Prestonpans won against General Cope.
6 December – army reached Derby, retreat started.
Forbes of Culloden used his authority strenuously against the rising clans.
b. William Creech. Bookseller. d. 1815.
b. Henry Mackenzie. Author. d. 1831.

1746   17 January – Prince Charles Edward won battle of Falkirk: Duncan MacIntyre on
      Campbells' side.
16 April – Prince Charles defeated at Culloden by Cumberland.
British Linen Company incorporated.
Highland dress forbidden.
Office of Secretary for Scotland abolished.
d. Colin Maclaurin. b. 1698.

1747   b. Paul Jones. American naval commander. d. 1792.
d. Forbes of Culloden. b. 1685.
Duncan MacIntyre settled in Edinburgh, joined city guard.

1748   Duncan MacIntyre pub. first ed. of his Gaelic poems.
David Hume pub. *Human Understanding*.
Abolition of heritable jurisdictions.
Tobias Smollet pub. *Roderick Random*.
b. Archibald Cochrane, 7th Earl of Dundonald, technologist. d. 1831.
d. William Adam (father of Adam brothers).

d. James Thomson. b. 1700.
d. Field-Marshall Wade. b. 1673.

1749   Founding of Aberdeen Banking Company.
        Sulphuric acid produced at Prestonpans.
        b. Benjamin Bell. Surgeon and medical writer. d. 1806.

1750   Founding of first Glasgow bank (the Ship Bank).
        Turnpike act.
        Invention of swing plough.
        Andrew Meikle devised fan-tail gear for windmills.
        b. Robert Fergusson. Poet. d. 1774.

1751   Adam Smith to Glasgow chair of logic.
        (circa) Joseph Black discovered 'fixed air' – CO_2. (Thesis in 1754).
        David Hume pub. *Enquiry concerning the Principles of Morals.*
        Chambers pub. *Cyclopaedia.*
        Bute became Lord of the Bedchamber to Prince of Wales.
        d. John Smibbert. Artist. b. 1684.
        Lord Kames pub. *Essays on the Principles of Morality and Natural Religion.*
        Alasdair MacMhaistir Alasdair (Alexander MacDonald) pub.
        Ais-eiridh na Sean Chanain Albannaich (Revival of the Old Scottish Tongue).

1752   David Hume app. keeper of Advocates' Library and sec. of Royal Society of
                Edinburgh, resigning latter almost immed.
        Window glass first manufac. in Scotland.
        Plans drawn up for 'New Town' of Edinburgh.

1753   Adam Smith starts lectures on Justice, Police, Revenue, Arms.
        James Hutton travels in Holland, Belgium and France (1753–54).
        William Robertson began *History of Scotland.* (Pub. London 1759).
        b. James Taylor. Inventor paddle-wheel and collaborator with Miller and Symington in
                creating steam-propelled vessel. d. 1825.

1754   David Hume pub. first vol. *History of England.*
        Robert Adam left Scotland for Italy.
        Robert Mylne also to Italy.
        d. James Gibbs. b. 1674.

1755   Adam Smith to chair of moral philosophy, Glasgow.
        First Scottish census by Alexander Webster – pop. 1,265,380.
        b. (Sir) Alexander Mackenzie. Canadian explorer. d. 1818.
        d. Sir John Clerk of Penicuik. b. 1676.

1756   Robert and Andrew Foulis pub. famous edition of *Homer* (1756–58).
        Francis Home pub. *Experiments on Bleaching.*
        b. (circa) John Macadam. Civil engineer and surfacer of roads. d. 1836.
        b. (Sir) Henry Raeburn. Painter. d. 1823.

1757   Monro (secundus) discovered lymphatics.
        David Hume resigned app. Advocates' Library.
        b. Thomas Telford. Civil engineer (Menai Suspension Bridge, Gotha canal in Sweden,
                chief engineer Caledonian canal, Dean Bridge, Edinburgh, etc.). d. 1834.

b. Robert Willan. First dermatologist. d. 1812.
d. Thomas Ruddiman. b. 1674.

1758   Robert Adam returned from Italy.
b. Alexander Naysmith. Painter. d. 1840.
d. Cockburn of Ormiston. b. 1679.
d. Marshal Keith. b. 1696.
d. Allan Ramsay, snr. b. 1686.

1759   Adam Smith pub. *Theory of Moral Sentiments.*
Robert Mylne returned from Italy, started Blackfriars Bridge, London.
Carron Iron Co. founded.
The year of the famous supper attended by Benjamin Franklin, Hume, Cullen, Adam
        Smith, 'Jupiter' Carlyle.
b. Robert Burns. Poet. d. 1795.
b. William Roxburgh. Botanist. d. 1815.

1760   Boswell's first visit to London.
First molten iron tapped at Carron (1st Jan.).
Robert Mylne became engineer and architect to City of London.
        d. George II. Succeeded by George III.

1761   b. (Sir) John Moore. Soldier. d. 1808.
b. John Rennie. Civil engineer. d. 1821.

1762   Black discovered latent heat.
Bute became prime minister.
William Robertson became principal, Edinburgh University.
Boswell first met Johnson.
Thomas Reid pub. *Enquiry into the Human Mind.*
James Macpherson pub. *Fingal* by Ossian.
Smollett pub. weekly paper *The Briton* (29 May).
Wilkie replied with *North Briton.*
Lord Kames pub. *Elements of Criticism.*
b. Joanna Baillie. Writer. d. 1851.
b. John Bell. Surgeon, anatomist, writer and illustrator. d. 1820.
b. James Horsburgh. Hydrographer. d. 1836.

1763   Bute 'retired'.
One brothel in Edinburgh.
Small made his first iron plough.
The Briton ceased pub.
James Craig pub. his plans for a New Town of Edinburgh.
Robert Adam pub. *Ruins of the Emperor Diocletian's Palace at Spalato.*
James Macpherson pub. *Temora* by Ossian.
b. William Symington. Collaborator in creating ship propelled by steam-engine.
d. William Smellie. b. 1697.

1764   Thomas Reid app. chair of moral philosophy, Edinburgh.
William Hunter app. professor of anatomy to Royal Academy, London, and physician
        extraordinary to Queen Charlotte.
Adam Smith in France (1764–66).

1765   Boswell to Corsica.
        Bute's influence finally ended.
        Promissory notes for less than £1 forbidden.
        d. James III and VIII, the Old Pretender.

1766   Black suggested experiments with hydrogen filled balloons or bladders (cf. 1785).
        Attempt to make alum in Scotland.
        Adam Ferguson pub. *Essays on Civil Society*.
        Adam Smith returned to Kirkcaldy, worked on *Wealth of Nations* for next ten years.
        (circa) b. William Nicoll. Inventor of polarizing prism. d. 1851.

1767   Allan Ramsay, jnr. app. court portrait painter.
        David Hume app. under-secretary of state, Home Dept., London (till 1769).
        James Craig laid foundation stone of 'New Town'.
        b. Henry Bell. Developer of steam navigation. d. 1830.
        d. Alexander Monro (primus). b. 1697.

1768   Benjamin Franklin received freedom of the city of Edinburgh.
        Boswell pub. *Journal of a Tour to Corsica*.
        A theatre opened again in Edinburgh under Lord Chamberlain's 'patent'.
        Collapse, through neglect, of roof of Holyrood Chapel, Edinburgh.
        Construction started on Forth and Clyde canal.
        Pub. started of *Ruddiman's Weekly Magazine*, or *Edinburgh Amusement*.
        b. David Hamilton. Architect (Glasgow Exchange, Hamilton Palace, Toward Castle,
            Lennox Castle, etc.). d. 1843.

1769   James Watt invented separate condenser for steam engine, and so made steam power
            practical.
        William Robertson pub. *The History of the Reign of Charles V*.

1770   Deepening of River Clyde begun to improve navigation.
        Alexander Monro (secundus) pub. *Treatise on the Lymphatics*.
        b. James Hogg. Poet and writer. d. 1835. (Hogg himself gave birth as 1772.)

1771   Macintosh produced cudbear, a purple dyestuff, at Glasgow.
        Alkali man. est. by Keir at Tipton, England.
        Henry Mackenzie pub. *The Man of Feeling*.
        Robert Fergusson started contributing to *Ruddiman's Magazine*.
        William Smellie started pub. of first ed. *Encyclopedia Britannica*, Edinburgh.
        b. Mungo Park. African explorer. d. 1806.
        b. (Sir) Walter Scott. Poet and novelist. d. 1832.
        d. Tobias Smollett; year of pub. of his *Humphrey Clinker*. b. 1721.

1772   Collapse of the Bank of Ayr.
        Robert Fergusson began writing his Scots Poems.
        Charles Cameron, architect, pub. *The Baths of the Romans*.
        b. Robert Stevenson. Civil engineer (built 23 lighthouses, inc. Bell Rock, Inchkeith,
            Sumburgh, Cape Wrath, Barra Head, etc.
        Son, Alan, built 10 lighthouses, inc. Skerryvore. Other sons, David and Thomas, also
            involved in lighthouse service.
        Thomas, father of Robert Louis Stevenson.) d. 1850

1773   Boswell and Johnson – visit to Edinburgh and tour of Scotland and Western Isles,
            producing J's *Journey to the Western Isles* and B's *Tour to the Hebrides*.
        Coke ovens at Carron.
        b. Robert Brown. Botanist. d. 1858.

b. Francis Jeffrey. Lawyer and editor. d. 1850.
b. James Mill. Writer. d. 1836.
b. Alexander Monro (tertius). Anatomist. d. 1859.
d. John Glas. b. 1695.

1774   Watt made first efficient steam engine.
        William Hunter pub. *Anatomical Description of Human Gravid Uterus.*
        Cullen laid foundation stone of Physicians' Hall, George Street, Edinburgh. (Later
                head office of Commercial Bank, now incorporated in Royal Bank).
        b. Charles Bell (brother of John). Anatomist and physiologist.
        d. 1842.
        b. Robert Tannahill. Poet. d. 1810.
        d. Robert Fergusson. b. 1750.

1775   American war of independence started.
        Smelting furnace opened at Furnace, Argyll.
        Abortive act for freeing of Scottish slaves.
        b. Thomas Cochrane (Earl of Dundonald and Baron Cochrane, son of Ninth Earl of
                Dundonald, scientific investigator), naval commander, liberator of Chile, etc.
                d. 1860.
        b. John Leyden. Doctor and oriental linguist. d. 1811.

1776   Collapse of Glasgow tobacco trade.
        Adam Smith pub. *Wealth of Nations.*
        Robert Adam designed auditoreum Drury Lane Theatre.
        James Anderson pub. *Practical Treatise on Chimneys.*
        Woollen workers in Edinburgh earned 1/- per day.
        John Hunter app. surgeon extraordinary to the king.
        Andrew Meikle began experiments with threshing machine (patent 1788).
        Lord Kames pub. *Gentleman Farmer.*
        b. William Blackwood. Publisher. d. 1834.
        b. Archibald Constable. Publisher. d. 1826.
        d. David Hume. b. 1711.

1777   William Robertson pub. *History of America.*
        b. Thomas Campbell. Poet. d. 1844.
        b. (Rear-Admiral Sir) John Ross. Arctic explorer. d. 1856.

1778   Incorporation of Barber-Surgeons became Royal College of Surgeons of Edinburgh.
        Adam Smith app. a commissioner of customs for Scotland.
        b. Francis Horner. Whig politician. d. 1817.
        b. (Rev.) John Thomson. Artist. d. 1840.

1779   Charles Cameron goes to Russia, summoned by Catherine the Great.
        b. John Galt. Novelist. d. 1839.

1780   b. (Sir) Archibald Galloway. Soldier (General in India), and writer on Mahometan and
                Indian law. d. 1850.

1781   William Hunter app. president, Royal College of Physicians, London.

1782   Wedgwood ordered Watt engines.
        Twenty brothels in Edinburgh.
        Watt invented rotary steam engine.

Food shortage.
b. Susan Ferrier. Novelist. d. 1854.
d. Lord Kames. b. 1696.

1783   Royal Society of Edinburgh founded.
Watt (et al.) discovered chemical composition of water.
Mills at New Lanark employed 'child slaves stunted in growth'.
Famine.
Monro (secundus) pub. *Structure and Function of the Nervous System.*
Complaint of 'licentiousness and ferocity of manners' in Edinburgh.
d. Eyre Coote. b. 1726.
d. William Hunter. b. 1718.

1784   Murdoch made model steam carriage.
b. James Baillie Fraser. Eastern traveller. d. 1856.
d. Allan Ramsay, jnr. b. 1713.

1785   Joseph Hutton delivered paper, *Theory of the Earth.*
Turkey red manufacture est. by Macintosh.
Thomas Bell invented textile cylinder printing.
Monro (secundus) pub. *Structure on Physiology of Fishes.*
Lunardi made balloon ascent in Edinburgh.
b. (Sir) David Wilkie. Artist. d. 1841.
d. Alexander Runciman. b. 1736.

1786   Robert Burns pub. 'Kilmarnock' edition; visited Edinburgh.
Miller experimented with steam paddle-wheel at Leith.
John Hunter pub. *On the Venereal Disease.*
b. Patrick Naysmith. Artist. d. 1831.

1787   Watt and Copland introduced bleaching by chlorine to Scotland.
Adam Smith elected Lord Rector Glasgow Univ.
Robert Burns pub. second edition of poems, ed. Creech; toured Borders, Argyll, central
        Highlands.

1788   Symington and colleagues made trials of paddle-steamship on Dalswinton Loch.
Burns m. Jean Armour.
First mail coach London–Glasgow.
Monro (secundus) pub. *Description of all the Bursae Mucosae of the Human Body.*
b. Hugh Clapperton. African traveller. d. 1827.
b. (Capt.) Basil Hall. Naval traveller and writer on Far East, North America, etc.
        d. 1844.
d. James Brown. b. 1709.
d. 'Bonnie Prince Charlie', the young pretender. b. 1720.

1789   Paddle-steamship sailed on Forth and Clyde canal.
Robert Burns app. to excise duties, also farmed Ellisland.
b. William Burn. Architect (in Edinburgh – Nelson Column, St. John's Church,
        Edinburgh Academy, Melville Monument, John Watson's Hospital, Music Hall,
        etc., also many country houses). d. 1870.
b. W. H. Playfair. Architect. d. 1857.

1790   Five Highland regiments added to the line.
Forth and Clyde canal completed.

2655 parliamentary votes in the Scottish counties, of which 1318 were fictitious.
(circa) Lord Dundonald introduced phosphatic fertilisers.
d. William Cullen. b. 1710.
d. General Sir William Roy. b. 1726.

1791   London Corresponding Club organised.
Burns resigned lease of Ellisland, went to Dumfries.
Sir John Sinclair prepared *Statistical Account of Scotland* (1791–98: pub. 1799).
William Robertson pub. *Historical Disquisition concerning the Knowledge which the
        Ancients had of India.*
1,508 deaths recorded in parish of Glasgow, of which 63% were children under 10,
        46% children under 2.
b. (Col.) Daniel Mackinnon. Soldier, defender of Hougoumont. d. 1826.

1792   Convention of the Society of the Friends of the People.
'Rights of Man' sells out in Scotland.
Average wage in cotton mills – 1/- per day.
Corn – 43/- per quarter.
Charles Bell started pub. *System of Dissections* (1792–1803).
Murdoch lit his Cornish home with gas.
Dugald Stewart pub. vol. 1 *Philosophy of the Human Mind.*
b. (Sir) Thomas Livingstone Mitchell, Australian explorer. d. 1855.
b. James B. Neilson. Inventor of 'Hot blast'. d. 1865.
d. Robert Adam. b. 1728.
d. Paul Jones. b. 1747.

1793   Political trials, Thomas Muir, advocate sentenced to 14 years transportation for
        sedition.
John Bell pub. vol. 1 *The Anatomy of the Human Body.*
        (vol. 2, 1797, vol. 3, 1802)
Macintosh manufactured aluminium acetate.
b. John Gibson Lockhart. Writer and biographer. d. 1854.
d. John Hunter. b. 1728.
d. William Robertson. b. 1721.

1794   Political trials, hanging of Robert Watt, transportations.

1795   One eighth of population of Edinburgh on 'charity'.
d. James Boswell. b. 1740.

1796   Famine.
Corn – 75/- per quarter.
Lead carbonate patent – Lord Dundonald.
d. David Allan. b. 1744.
d. Robert Burns. b. 1759.
d. James (Ossian) Macpherson. b. 1738.

1797   Spread of Society of United Scotsmen.
Chemical works of St. Rollox opened Glasgow.
Monro (secundus) pub. *The Brain, the Eye and the Ear.*
d. James Hutton. b. 1726.

1798   Bleach liquor patented by Tennant of St. Rollox.
Average wage Kirkcaldy linen workers – £7 per year.

1799   Tennant manufactured bleaching powder.
Serfdom in mines abolished by law (cf. 1775).
Robert Owen took over New Lanark mills.
Thomas Campbell pub. *Pleasures of Hope.*
Famine.
d. Joseph Black. b. 1728.
d. James Tassie. b. 1735.

1800   Meal riots – famine.
Charlotte Square, Edinburgh – Robert Adam's masterpiece – postumously completed.
David Mushet discovered black band ironstone.

1801   Population of Scotland – 1,608,420 – 1st government census.
Charlotte Dundas, first real prototype steamship, sailed successfully.
Charles Bell pub. *Engravings of the Arteries, of the Nerves, and of the Brain.* (1801–2).
d. Sir Ralph Abercrombie. b. 1734.
d. John Millar. b. 1735.

1802   Factory gas lighting est. by Boulton and Watt.
Walter Scott pub. *Ministrelsy of the Scottish Border* (2 vols).
Health and Morals of Apprentices Act.
Edinburgh Magazine amalgamated with *Scots Magazine.*
Edinburgh Review founded.

1803   Education Act (schools in every parish).

1804   b. William Gregory. Prof. of chemistry. d. 1858.

1805   Walter Scott pub. *The Lay of the Last Minstrel.*
d. Alexander (Jupiter) Carlyle. b. 1722.
d. Hector Munro. b. 1726.
d. Dr. John Robinson. b. 1739.

1806   d. Benjamin Bell. b. 1749.
d. Mungo Park. b. 1771.

1807   Food shortage.
Robert Tannahill pub. *Poems and Songs.*

1808   d. Alexander Dalrymple. b. 1736.
d. Sir John Moore. b. 1761.

1809   *The Quarterly* founded.
d. Neil Gow. b. 1727.

1810   Trade depression.
Found. of Commercial Bank of Scotland.
d. Robert Tannahill. b. 1774.

1811   The Comet sailed between Glasgow and Helensburgh.
Pop. Scotland 1,805,864 (12.3% increase on 1801).
d. Baron Dundas. b. 1742.
d. John Leyden. b. 1775.
d. Robert Mylne. b. 1734.

1812   d. Dundan MacIntyre. b. 1724.
        d. Robert Willan. b. 1757.

1813   James Hogg pub. *The Queen's Wake.*

1814   Walter Scott pub. *Waverley.*

1815   Waterloo.
        The *Britannic* steamship built, 109 tons.
        d. William Creech. b. 1745.
        d. Patrick Miller. b. 1731.
        d. William Roxburgh. b. 1759.

1816   Trade depression.
        d. Adam Ferguson. b. 1723.

1817   Food shortage.
        The Scotsman newspaper founded.
        Blackwood's Magazine appeared.
        d. Alexander Monro (secundus) b. 1733.

1818   Glasgow – 3,000 typhus cases in 8 months.
        Edinburgh – 6,000 typhus cases.
        Susan Ferrier pub. *Marriage.*
        Thomas Telford became founder member of Institute of Civil Engineers.
        d. Sir Alexander Mackenzie. b. 1755.

1819   Trade depression.
        d. James Watt. b. 1736.

1820   d. John Bell. b. 1762.
        d. George III, succeeded by George IV.

1821   John Galt pub. *Annals of the Parish.*
        Pop. Scotland 2,091,521 (15.8% increase on 1811).
        Leonard Horner founded school of arts in Edinburgh for mechanics and tradesmen,
                now Heriot-Watt University.
        d. John Rennie. b. 1761.

1822   Caledonian Canal completed.
        George IV visited Edinburgh.
        Macintosh patented his waterproof.
        John Galt pub. *The Entail* and others.
        d. Thomas Coutts. b. 1731.

1823   Foundation stone laid for new school, The Edinburgh Academy.
        d. Sir Henry Raeburn. b. 1756.

1824   James Hogg pub. *The Private Confessions of a Justified Sinner.*
        Founding of world's first municipal fire brigade, Edinburgh.
        Royal Botanical Gardens move to new site at Inverleith, Edinburgh.
        b. (Lord) William Thomas Kelvin. Physicist. d. 1907.

1825   Trade depression.
Foundation stone laid of new High School, Calton Hill, Edinburgh.
d. James Taylor. b. 1753.

1826   Earl of Haddington prevented from further quarrying of rock from Salisbury Crags, Edinburgh.

1827   Edinburgh Improvement Bill.
Sir Walter Scott admitted authorship of Waverley novels.
d. Hugh Clapperton. b. 1788.

1828   Neilson invented hot-blast.
Public trials of Bell's reaping machine.
James and George (sons of Naysmith the artist) ran a steam coach in Edinburgh.
Burke and Hare murders.
Edinburgh included: 1 royal palace, 1 college, 31 professors, 1 riding school, 1 military academy, 700 teachers, 1 royal exchange, 70 churches, 2 theatres, 13 courts of justice, 400 advocates, 800 writers to the signet (solicitors), 86 accountants, 40 physicians, 70 surgeons, 100 apothecaries, 7 libraries, 42 insurance offices, 11 public hospitals, 60 charitable institutions, 25 literary societies, 80 royal mail and stage coaches, 86 hackney coaches, 400 sedan chair carriers, 80 public houses.

1829   The Rocket – George and Robert Stephenson.
First show appearance of Aberdeen Angus cattle.
Editor of *The Scotsman* and editor of *Caledonian Mercury* fought a pistol duel.
Collapse of Fife Banking Company.

INDEX